MARRIED
—to the—
CHURCH

Raymond Hedin

MARRIED
—to the—
CHURCH

INDIANA UNIVERSITY PRESS
Bloomington & Indianapolis

The paper used in this publication meets the minimum requirements of
American National Standard for Information Sciences—Permanence of
Paper for Printed Library Materials, ANSI Z39.48-1984.

Manufactured in the United States of America

Library of Congress Cataloging-in-Publication Data
Hedin, Raymond William, date
    Married to the church / Raymond Hedin.
        p.   cm.
    ISBN 0-253-32943-4 (alk. paper)
    1. Catholic Church—United States—Clergy.   2. Seminarians—United
States.   3. Ex-priests, Catholic—United States.   4. St. Francis
Seminary.   I. Title.
BX1912.H43   1995
262'.14273—dc20   95-5918

1 2 3 4 5   00 99 98 97 96 95

Contents

To Ivona, and to the memory of my father

Acknowledgments

$\mathcal{B}$y its very nature, this kind of book could not have been written without the help of many people, and it is my deep pleasure to thank them here.

I am grateful to the Lilly Endowment for granting me a Lilly Open Fellowship for the year 1988–89, the year in which most of the interviews central to this book took place; I especially want to thank Fred Hofheinz of the Lilly Endowment for his time, for his warm response to the manuscript, and for his support throughout. Educational Testing Service and the Indiana University Office of Research and the Graduate School also provided me with essential financial support at early stages of this project.

Rev. Daniel Pakenham, then rector of St. Francis Seminary in Milwaukee, allowed me to live at the seminary for ten days in the fall of 1988; that stay was crucial to my gaining a sense of how the seminary has and has not changed since I was a student. Similarly, Rev. Paul Janette, then supervisor of Weakland Hall, the residence for college seminarians in Milwaukee, allowed me to live there for several extended periods from 1988 through 1990. His personal warmth, his receptivity to this project, and his many conversations about seminary life and the contemporary priesthood helped me immeasurably. The seminarians at both locations were also friendly and informative, as were the lay students at St. Francis.

David Bleich, Patrick Brantlinger, JoAnn Campbell, Mary McGann, and Michael Rosenblum read portions of the manuscript and showed that they are in the right profession as readers of texts. The students in JoAnn Campbell's graduate seminar on writing practices read a chapter of the text and provided perspectives that had not occurred to me and needed to occur to me. Rev. Steven Avella provided essential background information on the history of the seminary and of the Milwaukee Archdiocese.

Robert Orsi of the Indiana University Religious Studies Department and Rev. Richard Ruach read the entire manuscript with great care, both in stages and as a whole; their comments, suggestions, and friendship along the way have been invaluable to me. Don Gray read an early version of the manuscript, helped me to rethink it, and then read the entire revised manuscript with equal perceptiveness. Paul Zietlow and Virginia Martin read the nearly final version; their specific, cautionary comments were as helpful as their overall enthusiasm. And at times when I was not sure any of this made sense, the generous response of Rev. Andrew Greeley to the manuscript and his continued support for the project were central to my survival.

My children, Mark and Paula, have been genuinely understanding about having a little less time with me during the writing of this book; their encouragement kept me going at times when I was starting to wonder. Above all, my wife, Ivona Hedin, has read every sentence more often than she would care to remember, has commented with great insight, and has engaged with me every issue this book has raised; her unstinting contribution to a project that has cost her a good deal is something I plan never to forget.

And of course, my classmates: in the course of the last several years, they have invited me to eat in their rectories and homes; they have given generously of their time and of their stories (sometimes at considerable risk); they have offered invaluable insights into the priesthood, the church, their own lives, and mine. I cannot thank them enough.

Finally, I am grateful to John Gallman, the editor of Indiana University Press, for enthusiastically taking on this book when he might just as well have reminded me that I still owe him another one; to Bob Sloan, my sponsoring editor, for his gentle but pointed suggestions; to Jane Lyle for a superb job of copyediting (thanks to her, I have not referred to the Cuban Missal Crisis); and to my agent, Diane Mancher, for helping me keep the faith.

Introduction

Perhaps no group of men is as surrounded by an aura of mystery as are Catholic priests. All most people know is that priests are—or are supposed to be—celibate, that they do the work of the church, and that they are—or are supposed to be—somehow different from the rest of us. But how different are they? What are their satisfactions, frustrations, and fantasies? Are they, as publicly declared celibates, lonely, and if so, what do they do about it? Has their metaphoric "marriage" to the church undergone any changes in the context of a culture which has tried to redefine marriage in a number of ways? Has their sense of God and of their own spirituality changed in the wake of Vatican II, and within an American culture which offers definitions of its own in these areas? What are their attitudes toward the institutional side of the church, toward the laity they work with, and toward one another? Are they really immune from earthly concerns, or do they too care about money, status, job security, and professional advancement? We know they are priests; in what ways are they men?

For reasons both past and present, I feel peculiarly well suited to answer these questions. I spent nine years studying to be a priest before leaving the seminary in 1966.[1] A class reunion in 1985 led me to see that my classmates had intense, ongoing issues of personal commitment and institutional friction not unlike my own. It also led me to suspect that many of our shared concerns had roots in our seminary past and in the ethos of the priesthood.

So I have spent the last five years interviewing the men I went to school with and trying to make sense of our collective story. I have had extended conversations with all twenty-two of the current priests from our class, ordained in 1969; six of the seven former priests and one in the process of leaving; and a sampling (fifteen) of the more than one hundred men who, like me, left before ordination. Most of them were eager to talk; because we shared a common past and because I told them my own complicated story, they trusted me and opened up in a way they would not have been willing to with an impersonal, detached researcher.

I recorded all of our conversations, except for those which took place in the car or in restaurants; in those cases, I took notes immediately afterward and later checked with my classmates if I was unsure about what I remembered. The conversations lasted from two hours to three hours; in several cases, we talked more than once. The resulting transcripts ran from 40 pages to well over 150, with the total running more than 2,500 pages.

This book interweaves the overall story of our class with a number of individual stories that are suggestive of our class's shared dilemmas and strategies; included among the individual stories is my own, both as representative of those who were not ordained and as a guide through the larger story. The center of the book, however, is its depiction of the priests, since the priesthood was the common ideal that united us once and continues to reverberate even now in those of us who have left either the seminary or the priesthood.

Precisely because this book is personal in nature, and because I did not approach my classmates with an extended series of identical, "objective" questions, I think I minimized the chance of obvious omissions and distortion. I asked each of them for a brief biographical sketch covering the time since they left the seminary, I asked about their memories of the seminary and about how that experience had affected them, and I asked them to describe their present satisfactions and frustrations. Beyond that, I learned quickly that conversations between classmates were more productive than question and answer sessions between interviewer and subject. I discovered that my letting go of the controls allowed my classmates to do the same; it allowed genuine voices to come through, discoveries to be made, surprising issues (such as the priests' deep anxieties and anger over their salary and retirement situation) to emerge. Letting go of the controls during the conversations balanced off my having to reassert them in the writing.

So the core of this book is what my classmates and I found ourselves talking about because the subjects energized at least one of us enough to begin talking. Problems with alcohol do not appear very often here, for instance, because that subject did not originate with me or with most of them. Nor did the current issue of child abuse; it had not surfaced yet at the time of these interviews, and even if it had, it would have been all but impossible for them to admit such behavior with a tape recorder on. For the same reason, I make no attempt to offer authoritative statistics on how many priests have been sexually active. When they chose to discuss those issues, I listened; when they did not choose to do so, I did not press them.

What our free-form conversations lacked in terms of quantitative information, they more than made up for in terms of revealing priorities, issues of intense interest, and even obsessions. In our willingness to follow where our energies led us, our talks were ideal for discovering that there were recurring concerns and overlapping stories not only between two people but, over the long run, within a large pool of conversationalists.

Because my desire to hear my classmates' stories was personal as well as scholarly, I became, I think, a good listener; my lack of detachment, in that sense, helped rather than hindered the process of finding out what my classmates had to say. Ultimately, I was hoping to discover—I think I did discover—our shared concerns and what they might mean for all of us.

In the interest of protecting my classmates' identities—and, in a few cases, their very careers as priests—I have changed their names, the names of the private individuals they refer to, and in some cases the names of the parishes in which they worked; I have not changed the identities of public figures. I have also refrained from highly detailed descriptions of my classmates, although I know that such details would add immediacy; instead, I have tried to individualize them for the most part through gesture, voice, and my own response to them as individuals, as well as through the specifics of their stories.

1

An
Unfinished
Story

$\mathcal{T}$his is my recurring dream: I have decided to leave the seminary, and there is no doubt about my position on this—I want out. But in the dream, it's mid-September or October, another academic year has begun, and I'm still in the seminary. In the dream, I don't know why I'm still there. I'm already married (or divorced and remarried—the dream varies in its currency), already teaching American literature at Indiana University, I have two children—but I'm still in the seminary. I have the anxious sense of another year slipping away. But just as I don't know why I'm still there, I also don't know how to escape. I wake up squirming.

I have been having this dream two or three times a year for the last twenty-seven years, ever since I did, in fact, leave in 1966, after eight years of high school and college at St. Francis Seminary in Milwaukee and a year of theology at Catholic University in Washington. At our twenty-year college reunion in 1985, I recounted that dream as my contribution to an after-dinner session in which each of us stood and shared some memory of seminary life. Most of my classmates told stories of pizzas smuggled into the dorm, low-level food riots, emergency confession lines before morning mass to handle the only late-night sin readily available to us. When my turn came, I said I didn't have a funny story to tell, that in fact, although I was happy to see my classmates and would have come a good deal farther than the 350 miles it took me to do so, I felt uneasy about being back in an institution I no longer belonged to, an institution I had chosen to leave. So my remembrance was not of the seminary in my past but of the seminary as it forcibly occupied a disconcerting chunk of my present. When I finished, seven classmates stood up and said that they had had, and continued to have, essentially the same dream.

When the invitation to the reunion had come, I knew immediately that I would go. I also realized that at any other moment in the previous twenty years, I would not have gone. For me, leaving the seminary had been the first step in a deliberate process of severing myself from nearly everything I could think of that had characterized my life up to that point: the priesthood; the Catholic Church; Glen Ellyn, the conservative western suburb of Chicago where I had been raised; the Midwest; the middle class itself. It all added up, I had thought, to blandness, repression, rigidity, anti-intellectualism, inertia, death. I was going to become a different person, and to define myself by that difference.

So after getting a master's degree in English at the University of Wisconsin, I took a job teaching at Norfolk State, a black college in Virginia. I barely knew any blacks (they had not been welcome in Glen Ellyn; there were none in my seminary class, one in the entire seminary). I once joked to my roommate at Wisconsin that the best way to soften the revelation to my parents that I was dating a Jew would be to tell them first that she was black. It was 1968, and Martin Luther King had just been killed. I accepted the job at Norfolk State for the same reason that I had begun studying literature: not because I had a well-developed sensitivity toward the issues involved, but because I knew I did not. At that point in my life, still numb from years of rationalism both temperamental and instilled, I was nearly incapable of acting instinctively. I had to *decide* to develop what I lacked.

I soon found myself drawn to the instructors I met at Norfolk State and at the other twelve black colleges participating in an experimental program to develop interdisciplinary humanities courses. Those instructors tended to be socially engaged and irreligious, and I found that combination more attractive than what I perceived as the church's—and the seminary's—combination of intense religiosity and social apathy. So after all those years of going to mass every day, I simply stopped. I remember the first holy day I skipped—August 15, 1968, the Feast of the Assumption; the evening mass I had planned to attend conflicted with a date I had already made with my eventual wife, Anne. I decided, without a struggle, that I would rather go to the movie. Except for weddings and funerals, I never went to a church service again until my class re-union. After all those years of daily mass, spiritual reading, and medi-tation, after all the rituals and reinforcement, sloughing off the church seemed surprisingly easy. I remember thinking serenely that the whole experience hadn't really taken hold.

But I realize now that if it had not taken hold, I would not have spent so much energy moving as far away from it as possible; nor would I have had those dreams. In the summer between my two years at Norfolk State, one month after that date with Anne, I became engaged to her during a mescaline trip on Cape Cod. She was an instructor at Bishop College, in the same black college program. She was also an intensely articulate, acidly anti-Catholic ex-Catholic from Boston, a woman one of whose major appeals was that she could not possibly have been spawned, I felt, by my midwestern suburb.

Two weeks after our engagement, Anne and I were married in a Cam-bridge chapel by a priest whose friendship with her mother was stronger than his reservations about validating the union of two ex-Catholics who would acknowledge belief in nothing more specific than the "life force." For the wedding, Anne wore a miniskirt, I wore a turtleneck. We wrote our own ceremony, read e. e. cummings to each other at the altar with a Nina Simone ballad in the background, and later drank our wed-ding toast from a frisbee. I was trying hard to leave my old self behind and to catch up with the 1960s, and I thought I had succeeded.

After one more year at Norfolk State, we sold nearly everything we owned and traveled around Europe for ten months in a decrepit Volks-wagen van. We visited all the mandatory churches; but already I was regarding churches the way I regarded Stonehenge. While we were in Greece, we participated in the census, as everyone does, foreigner or not. A fan of Kurt Vonnegut's *Cat's Cradle* at that time, I put down "Bokonon-ism" as my religion. In 1971, that was the "Greece of the Christian Greeks" run by the colonels; a Greek might have gotten into serious trouble es-pousing a religion whose identifying trait, as I recall, was making love with the soles of one's feet.

We smoked dope when we could get it. I had left the seminary with a crewcut; now my hair was, at last, long enough to outrage my parents—and to get me frisked by airport security. In most ways it was a wonder-ful year, punctuated, however, by intermittent anxiety attacks about what we were going to do when we came back. It had never been easy for me to let go, to let things happen.

During the 1970s I continued to keep my distance from anything that smacked of my religious past. When Anne and I returned from Europe and entered graduate school in American literature at the University of Virginia, we were visited by two of my best friends from the seminary.

They left after two days, convinced, they now tell me (we are friends again), that they did not feel welcome; they were right. When Anne and I were applying for jobs in 1974, I put down on my curriculum vitae that I had attended "St. Francis College" in Milwaukee. It was not until three years after we were both hired by the Indiana University English department that I was willing to start telling friends that St. Francis was a seminary. I remember stammering that out like an adolescent confessing masturbation.

It may be that I would never have been willing to reconnect with my classmates if my post-religious life had not developed complications of its own. Anne and I divorced three years after taking our full-time jobs at Indiana, two years after the birth of our son Mark. Within a year, I was living with Ivona, who had been my student the year before in Poland, where I had gone with Anne to set up an American Studies Center at Warsaw University. Teaching at Norfolk State, traveling in Europe, and returning to graduate school had been exciting but temporary activities—exciting because temporary. Career and fatherhood felt more permanent, more threatening. They were "worldly" responsibilities of the first order, of the very sort I once thought I would be immune from, and I was not ready for them. In Poland, I sought refuge from them.

But instead of refuge, I discovered more complication than I had known possible. In the seminary, I had perched myself above the murky world of ambivalence, uncertainty, and emotional turmoil; and now I crashed into it, hard—or rather, I leaped blithely into it, without any idea that it was there, waiting for my plunge. I discovered, the old-fashioned way, that emotions were not as subsidiary and malleable as my scholastic training had suggested; and I had no idea how to sort them out. Later I would discover that many of my classmates had crashed—fallen, I am tempted to say—in similar fashion.

The end result, though not the end in any real sense, was that Anne and I got divorced, and Ivona came a year later to Bloomington to be with me. Ivona and I were married in 1977, although Anne and I were not really unmarried yet. When I got tenure in 1982 and Anne did not, our relatively workable joint custody arrangement fractured. When the court allowed her to take Mark with her to Chicago—or, in the more personal terms which I could not avoid feeling, when the *judge*, the very embodiment of order with whose predecessors I had been on such good terms in the seminary, preferred her to me—another cornerstone of my old world was shattered. The judge's decision assaulted my conviction, which I had never articulated until events undermined its premises, that good things would come to me and bad things would not because I was who I was: a good man by definition regardless of how I acted, a man once chosen by God and still, somehow, deserving of His favor—of everyone's favor—even if I had turned my back on Him. Later, I would come across this same abiding assumption in my classmates, who, like me, have found it hard to shake.

For five years after Anne moved, we fought, not very gracefully (how could she be saying these things, how could I be saying these things?), until I conceded custody in 1986. That concession was painful, yet putting an end to our all-consuming battles brought a kind of peace. It also allowed other issues, previously unacknowledged, to press forward to the front of the line.

My research on black fiction, for instance, which had been the basis for my tenure, had slowed for reasons not wholly clear to me at the time. What was clear was that, in a research institution, I was flirting with the one unpardonable sin. Divorce, custody fights, lost time with my son, and academic inertia had succeeded in engendering in me a guilt and uneasiness that leaving the church had not. I felt stagnant, adrift. "Midlife crisis," Ivona said, and I scoffed. My problems, I insisted, were unique, not reducible to easy categories. At least negatively, I was still special.

By the time the invitation came to the reunion, my sense of distance from my classmates was less secure than it had been. In the atmosphere of the university, where the life of the mind was genuinely exciting but where salvation was emphatically earthly and individualistic, I had come to miss the sense of community, the sense of shared purpose and inherent, higher meaning I had known with my classmates; I wanted to see if any of that still resided with them.

I also wanted to see if I could do something about the unfinished business my dreams kept suggesting. I had come to realize that many of the traits which I still wrestled with had their origins in my seminary experience: not only my sense of specialness, but my inability to immerse myself in what often struck me, even after all these years, as the "mere" things of this world; my inclination to the rational at the expense of the emotional; my continuing need for institutional support along with a deep distrust of institutions—most notably, my own, the university; my tendency to see teaching as the higher, vocation-driven, and hence justifiable part of my job, and academic writing as the earthly, career part—hence suspect, of no real value. I didn't expect one trip to obliterate a lifetime set of attitudes, but I wanted to see if my classmates had similar issues on their minds.

Still, I went with apprehensions. I wanted to be with my class, wanted to feel that I belonged with them; but I did not want to "belong" again to the seminary, to the institutional church, to my old world. My general uneasiness at being on the seminary grounds (my old turf, the turf of my old self)—an uneasiness, I discovered, shared by several others, including a number of priests—made me wonder whether I could have one kind of belonging without the other. It is a question which has been on my mind throughout the writing of this book. What would reconnection drag with it? How far would I be willing to take it? What would be its price?

To my relief, I did find that I was comfortable with my classmates. I discovered that many of them had come up against complications that made mine pale, and that they were more willing to talk about them than I had expected. They included troubled priests as well as ex-priests, some of whom retained their allegiance to the church while others were bitterly alienated. They included, as I had expected, Catholic laymen deeply involved in church activities. They also included, however, a significant number of unbelievers (a few fiercely so) and of men leading lives that would not have been recognizable to any of us twenty years earlier: a divorced single parent who is a gay rights activist; a classmate who had undergone a sex-change operation ten years ago.

On the first evening of the reunion, hers was the most moving statement of all. She said that on one level she was comfortable with the life she had chosen, but that nonetheless for years she had feared meeting any of her old classmates. She had finally decided to attend the reunion, she said, "to reclaim my past." The warmth of the response she evoked suggested that many of us had faced and were still facing similar problems of reconciling the conflicting impulses of past and present. I came back to Bloomington exhilarated, with some of my cherished sense of uniqueness gone, along with some of my isolation.

But it took a while for me to decide to reconnect more fully. I found myself telling amusing stories about the reunion to my university friends— and then feeling increasingly troubled by their amused response. During the same period, my research finally thudded to a complete halt. I was feeling less and less comfortable with my academic voice and with my outsider status toward black literature. I found that I wanted to write something out of my own experience, something where I could not hide entirely behind my analytic voice. And in relation to my own life, I had plenty to analyze.

Around the same time, I took refuge from my unresolved tensions by moving to the brink of an affair with another woman. Ivona's pain when I told her was intense; it shook my confidence that I knew what I was doing in any basic sense at all. The only thing I was sure of was that my marriage was now at risk along with my career. All this gave urgency to my desire to address my past. Wasn't the study of history supposed to be the only preventive to repeating it?

So I joined a men's therapy group. Therapy was something else I had disdained earlier. My stated position had always been that therapy was a middle-class indulgence for people who enjoyed wallowing in their own importance; beneath that position was the smug assumption that problems were for others, not for someone still residually coated with God's special regard. In the group, however, I discovered further evidence for what the reunion had suggested: that I was not unique, that others had problems similar to mine, and that sharing our problems offered genuine relief, though not ready solutions.

In fact, "solutions" seemed increasingly irrelevant to me, or at least unattainable in the form I had once expected to find them. "Know the truth and the truth shall set you free," I used to think. Taking this biblical notion one step further, my seminary training had implied that knowing the truth would be *enough* to set you free. Whatever the issue, think it out carefully, work out the syllogism; human problems, like philosophy itself, could be solved by reason alone—our highest faculty, after all. Once you *saw* the truth, everything consequent on it, such as the appropriate behavior, would fall into place—perhaps after a bit of resistance—and stay there.

I came to the discomforting realization years ago that I could not blame the seminary for instilling this rationalist bias in me; I had it already. For I entered the seminary not because I was particularly drawn to the life of a priest, about which, like most of my classmates, I knew very little. I entered, I think now, out of a sense of duty based on a buried syllogism. I wanted to do the best thing I could do; the nuns had made it clear that the best thing a young man could do was to become a priest; therefore I wanted to be a priest.

But although the seminary did not create this bias in me, it nurtured it well. And since I left, it has proven, like a lingering virus, hard to shake; it is my version of malaria. "If you talk yourself into thinking your intellect is the only thing that runs your life," one of my classmates said in describing our seminary training, "you are making a big mistake." Knowing that, however, does not automatically eliminate the tendency.

Now, twenty years after leaving the seminary, I would have flashes of insight into my marriage and into the patterns of my behavior. These flashes, however, proved to be just that; they did not imprint themselves once and for all on my emotions and behavior. So in my men's group, out of frustration, I tried another approach: simply telling my story over and over in all its confusion, complete with all my uncertainty—and then listening to the stories, also often repeated, of other men. By giving me a feel for the complicated lives we all were leading, these intertwined stories gave me a perspective I could not get on my own. Such stories became for me what the mass never was: a ritual whose power I could feel, the word made flesh among us.

It was in one of those sessions that I finally realized that I wanted to write this book. I wanted to find out how my classmates were negotiating their relationship to their institution, how their long-term commitments (weren't they "married" to the church, after all?) were wearing with them, how they were doing "in the world" after all these years. I had spent the previous twelve years teaching stories and insisting that they revealed our most basic values and problems. My classmates, I sensed, had important stories waiting to be told, and I wanted to help get them out. Even more, I needed to hear them.

At the point when I began this project in the fall of 1987, with the first of a series of weekend interviewing trips squeezed into the academic year, I had just moved out of the house and was staying with a friend. When I left for Milwaukee, I threw my clothes into the back seat, not knowing where I was going to live or what I was going to do when I returned. I listened to Judy Collins and Jimmy Buffett on the way up— old pathos and slightly more recent—and let myself go, at least for a while. Then, two weeks later, I returned to Bloomington—and to Ivona.

That conjunction of events was no accident: the first set of interviews, my return to my wife, and the slow beginning of our coming to grips with the issues which we had buried for years while focusing first on my tenure and then on the custody fight with Anne. Those brief early trips in 1987 were followed by more extended trips during the 1988/89 year; the repeated process of leaving home, talking with my classmates, and then returning home played a central role in the process by which my life began to come together. My experience confirmed what I had been claiming in the classroom and what I had begun to realize more fully in my men's group: that sharing stories can be intimate, cathartic, moving, thought-provoking, reorienting. Shared stories can go a long way toward changing lives.

Across the board, with a few classmates who stayed only through high school, with more who left after college, and with a surprising number of priests, I discovered that our stories had many of the same central elements. The common point of origin for my class is of course our powerfully formative seminary experience. We are not temperamentally identical, to be sure, and we brought to the seminary a variety of family histories which constitute their own kind of origin. Nonetheless, the years we spent together at the seminary constituted a shared beginning and shaped our sense of where we wanted to go, where we thought we were going. Looking carefully at those years, I discovered, can help to clarify what is still underway here in the middle, both for my classmates and for me.

So in the next chapter, I will try to describe that experience, how we perceived it then and how we regard it now, as we inevitably reshape our sense of the beginning to help us explain our (current, shifting) sense of the middle. I will then go on to suggest in what ways my classmates' stories and mine became interwoven again after twenty years and how, in spite of the separation of years and of the seeming differences in experience, we can legitimately be said to have lived a group story, the story of my class.

One final introductory note: Although I didn't think of it in these terms at the time, I realize now that the death of my father in the summer of 1987 was one of the motivating forces behind this project. My father was a shy, friendly, gentle man who idolized priests. Since late in his teens, when he dropped out of high school to help support his family during the Depression, he had made his living selling Catholic church goods to priests, and fifty years of contact did not diminish his admiration for them. They were his heroes. So when I entered the seminary—influenced by him, I am sure, but not pressured—he was very happy. I would be, he told me a number of times in the next nine years, the only Father Hedin in the Official Catholic Directory. When I decided to leave, he was disappointed, but showed no sign of disapproval.

Over the next twenty years, I mystified and disappointed him a number of times: by leaving the church, by getting divorced, by living with Ivona long before we married. But he never criticized me, never cut me off, and he welcomed Ivona as well; he made it clear that I was his son, no matter what.

Early in my career at Indiana, I would always show him the articles I was publishing; he would look them over and say, with admiration, "Boy, the words, the words!" Years later, I wrote him a letter telling him how much I appreciated his acceptance; but he died of a heart attack before I had a chance to talk to him for the last time, and before I fully realized how much that acceptance had meant to me. Going back to interview my classmates and to try to tell their story is one of the few gestures I can think of, at this point, to use "the words, the words" to honor what my father valued and passed on to me.

2

The
Haven of the
Seminary

An Army of Youth, flying the standards of truth,
Fighting for Christ the Lord.
Heads lifted high, Catholic Action our cry
And the Cross our only sword.

—Hymn sung at nearly every seminary convocation
I can remember

On the day I arrived at St. Francis Seminary for the first time, in the fall of 1957, I was frightened enough to observe it closely. My parents and I pulled in off Kinnickinnic Avenue onto a tree-lined driveway which wound among the main buildings: the residence hall and chapel on the left, the old gymnasium on the right, and beyond it, the classroom building/faculty residence. The football field and track lay directly beyond the residence hall, and behind it the hockey rink. To their left, and curving back around toward the Kinnickinnic Avenue entrance, were softball diamonds, two tennis courts, and a good deal of undefined space for freelance athletics and general roaming.

Inside the walls, the seminary was a series of usable spaces, too unadorned to be charming, too graceful to be merely functional—a place of moderation, an approximation through landscape of the cherished "golden mean" of Thomas Aquinas about which we would hear so much over the years. The chainlink fence surrounding the seminary seemed to set it off from "the world," as we would come to think of it, but without declaring war on it; the commercially friendly neighborhood along Kinnickinnic lay just beyond the gates, with the drugstores, soda fountains, and barbershops we would visit nearly every week on our free afternoons. It was the major seminary, observable behind the minor but cut off from it by a fence of its own, which seemed genuinely remote. With Lake Michigan on the other (east) side, a convent to the north, and open land to the south, the major seminary proclaimed its separateness on every front.

I liked the minor seminary immediately. To be sure, I would soon learn that the brick buildings weren't quite large enough to accommodate us. The residence hall was overcrowded, with seventy students in each of four open dormitories. One faculty member lived in a crudely converted fifteen-by-six storage closet. In the communal washroom, two students were assigned to each sink. The gym was your basic crackerbox, a true antique. It was small, underheated, with minimal seating, all in the balcony; there were only three feet between the out-of-bounds lines and the two side walls. Until a modest renovation had rescued it a few years earlier, its sagging roof had been supported by a pole planted squarely in the center of the court. The varsity basketball team on which I would later play was all but unbeatable at home.

Nonetheless, that first favorable impression would hold, not only for me but for most of my classmates: the seminary looked old and used, and partly for those reasons, alive. Both the minor and the major seminary, in fact, were bursting their limits. Two years earlier, the last (sixth) year of the minor seminary, which traditionally comprised four years of high school and the first two years of college, had been moved to the major because of inadequate space to accommodate its clientele. Meanwhile, the major seminary was undergoing a $3.5 million expansion, turning an old gym into a large, renovated auditorium and adding a new dining hall and a new residence/administration building. In 1955, the combined minor and major seminaries had 691 students, the highest enrollment in their hundred-year history; in that same year, the major seminary presented forty-eight priests for ordination. Neither figure has been matched since. Between 1953 and 1958, the archdiocese of Milwaukee created twenty-five new parishes and upgraded six others from mission status. We had arrived during what turned out to be, in terms of sheer numbers, the peak period for the seminary and for the archdiocese—in many ways, the culminating period of post–World War II growth in American Catholicism itself.[1]

Soon after we entered, we heard that Milwaukee was planning a new, state-of-the-art minor seminary along the lakefront, and we fantasized about the cushy life it promised: double rooms instead of large dormitories, the best high-school library in the city, a real gym with glass backboards and bleachers, etc. In retrospect, I'm glad my class never made it there; by the time the new De Sales Prep opened in 1961, most of us had become enamored of the old minor seminary. For even on the physical level, it offered us what we had come for: a functional traditionalism, rickety but thriving. In good time, we would become drawn to the new; but the fact that the seminary had been around for a while was part of its original, and lasting, appeal.

St. Francis Minor Seminary in 1957 was in more than its statistical prime: it was a nearly perfect embodiment of the ideals of American Catholicism at that time. This fit between the seminary and the Catholicism in which we had been raised helps to explain why we entered, why almost all of us were praised by family and friends for doing so, and why we stayed. It also helps to explain why we tend to be so dissatisfied with our current institutions, whatever they may be. For the minor seminary showed us that a close fit between institution and individual was not just a fantasy; it showed us how good it could feel to be part of an institution which reflected our values within a larger (Catholic) world of belief which reflected them as well. That fit also helps explain, however, why many of us who attended happily then are ambivalent about the experience in retrospect, now that we no longer feel at ease with some of those values or with that world.

In discussing the seminary, nearly all of my classmates talk first about the rules. The rules were never far from our minds while we were in the seminary, and my classmates' instant recall of them now suggests that for most of us, twenty or more years later, the rules still constitute the essence of seminary life. Our memories are not playing us false here; for the rules embodied a way of life: we were told repeatedly that they were, simply, the will of God for us. They revealed the church's sense of how we should live and determined how we actually did live on a daily basis. As an implicit ideal, they gave us something to aspire to; as a code of restrictions, they gave us something to resist and circumvent. A look at the seminary rules offers the best introduction to the complicated issue of what the seminary meant to us then and what it means to us now, what it has done for us and what it has done to us.

The minor seminary rule in 1957 laid out every detail of the day. We rose in silence at 6:30 A.M. and had to be in chapel by 7:00 for prayers and mass; for me, that required literally jumping out of bed as soon as the bell sounded in the dormitory. After breakfast, a normal high-school schedule followed, after which we had two hours of recreation, 5:30 P.M. prayers, dinner, another free hour, chapel, and a ninety-minute study hall until night prayers and bed. Lights went out at 9:30 P.M., seven nights a week; during my minor seminary years, with the exception of an occasional movie or in-house festivity, none of us ever spent a weekend night anywhere but in study hall. Talking was forbidden in the dorms between lights out and chapel in the morning. We had assigned seats in the refectory, in study halls, and in chapel. We could leave campus for five hours on Wednesday, Saturday, and Sunday afternoons, provided we signed out for an acceptable activity. We received a specified number of demerits for violating any of these rules. In theory, too many demerits could mean expulsion, although it rarely did in practice.

Any movie we wanted to attend off campus had to be approved by the disciplinarian, Father Busch, who was nominally second to the rector in authority but unquestionably primary in our consciousness. Father Busch also had the right of approval for any reading matter we brought onto campus. I was put on probation (the worst punishment available short of expulsion; it meant you couldn't leave campus for two weeks) in my senior year for being caught with an unapproved copy of *The Diary of Anne Frank* on my desk (there was an approved copy in the school library). The *Milwaukee Journal* and the *Milwaukee Sentinel* were posted daily on a bulletin board; no other newspaper or magazine was allowed. We had no television and one communal radio in the recreation room. We could check out our private radios on our free afternoons; at all other times, they were kept under lock and key. The church knew the truth; other sources of information were inherently suspect.

These restrictions reflected the church's traditional assumptions that a priest, as Pope Pius XI had put it, is "a man taken from among men"[2]—and the further taken, the better; that spirituality was nurtured by removal from the things of this world rather than by engagement with them. We were to be "in the world but not of the world," mediators between heaven and earth, with a foot in both camps but a clear proclivity toward the higher—more remote—ground.

Accordingly, using the then-standard model of modified monasticism, the seminary did what it could to create a separate world of its own with as little corrupting influence as possible. We entered the seminary at fourteen. We were taught exclusively by men who had embraced precisely the life to which we aspired; the one exception was an elderly, eccentric Catholic bachelor who served, I suspect, to show us what could happen to us if we left. We had very little contact with the nuns who cooked for us and none at all with the workers who hovered over the grounds. From their number, I cannot conjure up a single face, except for one of the groundskeepers at the major seminary. He was slightly retarded—at least, that was how we thought of him—and we would amuse ourselves by circling slowly to his left, which inevitably drove him into an evasive circle of his own. I remember his face only because it was necessary to look him in the eye to set off his little dance.

During the minor seminary years, most of us lived on campus and went home only for monthly weekends, major holidays, and summers, during which time we were expected to act like embryonic celibates rather than adolescents. The minor seminary did allow commuting students, but we residents considered them second-class citizens, "day dogs" in our jargon; the more they brushed up against "the world," the less pure we assumed them to be.

The seminary disengaged us as much as possible from family, from financial responsibilities, from awareness of social issues. We did not have to cook, wash clothes, or make money. Our sole duties were to study, pray, and keep the rules—and thus, by these self-oriented, asocial activities, become holy. We were so protected that many of us barely experienced adolescence at all—at the time. One classmate, now a therapist, is fond of saying that he entered the seminary in 1957 at age thirteen and left eight years later at age thirteen. His story is more the rule than the exception. During a period when the beat generation was raising its voice and hitting the road, a period when, according to the standard sociology of the era, even outwardly placid, middle-class youth were often lonely, alienated, and rebellious, my classmates and I lived in an environment successfully designed to keep us inexperienced and—its synonym at the time—pure.

The ideal of protected innocence presented some problems, however. We were expected to enter the seminary as boys and to come out twelve years later as priests; no one thought much about the need to become men along the way. "Growth" was not the operative term in that period; we were to be "trained." The *Catholic Encyclopedia* of our day had the tone right: "To teach candidates for the priesthood what a priest ought to know and to make them what a priest ought to be is the purpose of seminary education."[3] To that end, taking courses and obeying the rules were enough, the one endeavor as passive as the other. The ideas that learning was active, that certain developmental struggles might be necessary to maturation, that "priesthood" was not a state to be conferred by ceremony but the culmination of considerable intellectual, psychological, and emotional processes, did not register.

The seminary did everything it could to ignore emotions in the seeming hope that these messy forces would simply go away. One of the primary goals of the rule was, as the seminary self-study of 1962 would reaffirm, "to assist the students in the development of . . . emotional control" (p. 12). Emotional expression was a loss of control; it implicitly broke the rules. This was true even in chapel; students who responded with evident intensity to the liturgy were regarded by the rest of us as weird. Other than sports, which took on great importance, we had no sanctioned outlet for adolescent energy.

By extension, sexuality was an unfortunate encumbrance, an ineradicable problem that could never be licked, so to speak, but could be held in check through the help of grace, a kind of spiritual steroid always available to help us transcend our natural limits. One of our professors compared orgasm (not that the subject came up often) to a sneeze: both activities were suspect because for a moment you lost control.

If heterosexuality was dangerous, the seminary authorities were so terrified of homosexuality that they were afraid to name it; their incessant warnings never became clear enough for us to know what we were being warned against. I was not alone in my class in going through high school and college without knowing why "particular friendships," the subject of many a cautionary sermon, were dangerous; what other kind, I wondered, were there? In the absence of distinctions, closeness of any kind became suspect. For Charles Olinski, who later became a therapist, the underlying message was that "if you feel good about somebody, there's something wrong." Eliot Grayson, an ex-priest, summarizes the seminary ethos succinctly:

> The direction I got in the seminary was basically to be very suspect about relationships, and go it alone, and maintain a low trust level with people. The only one you could probably trust is God. [We got] a lot of indirect messages that people around us were occasions of sin.

No doubt the celibate model underlay this ethos: save yourself for God. But instead of coming across as a positive ideal with a complicated history of its own, celibacy simply loomed as the unavoidable prerequisite for priesthood, the ultimate rule, the supreme test of self-control. The seminary "trained" us to meet that prerequisite by denigrating the alternatives, including genuine intimacy of any kind.

The Present Tense of Past Selves

My classmates and I give the seminary mixed reviews. With near-unanimity, we look back on its obsessive legalism as "offensive," "unreal," "repressive," "silly," "crazy." (I once asked the rector if it was okay to eat Bacon Thins on Friday, to which he responded, "Yes, it's all right, because they don't have enough bacon to make them meat." The sad thing is that both my question and his answer were straight, without irony.) The seminary's proud resistance to change—"the church moves slowly," we were told repeatedly and with relish—now seems regrettable; it left many of us in a time warp we are still trying to escape.

We (a "we" which emphatically includes the priests in our class) now see the all male, pre-celibate culture of the seminary as unnatural; in the words of Derek Hartman, "It canceled our sexuality." We lament that the seminary instilled in us a distrust of intimacy and a model of extreme emotional control which we see as a parody of a parody, an intense version of a now-discredited 1950s maleness. We resent the fact that, as one classmate says, "they put a fence around the seminary and kept you inside. They controlled all of our information." We now regard the priestly model of being "in the world but not of the world" as excessively protective, retarding, a "total divorce from reality." We ask, with former priest Hans Ziegler, "Why the hell were we sheltered from those responsibilities? Is this really what it is all about?"

Our distaste for these traditional aspects of the seminary is understandable, for we have come to think of ourselves as children of the 1960s, advocates of change instead of stasis, of personal growth rather than external compliance. In consort with our generation at large, we tend to value emotional fulfillment more than self-denial and to prefer "spirit over law," in the terms of Father Brent, who has spent much of his priesthood expressing that preference; only one member of our initial class of 130 would become a lawyer. We feel uncomfortable in institutions, even when we still function within them. The structure of the 1950s seminary is a sour memory for us.

And yet, with a few exceptions, we look back on our experience of the minor seminary very favorably. For if many of us remember the seminary as a place which denigrated intimacy, we also remember it as a supportive community, a "warm space," in the words of Derek Hartman, who left after college and misses such support; he remembers comradeship and trust, being surrounded by "good people" genuinely well-intentioned toward us. He remembers shared, high purpose, the conviction that "we were going someplace" and that we knew how to get there.

Although Scott Lawson became unhappy later in the major seminary and left after graduating from college, his unabated enthusiasm for his minor seminary years captures the contentment many of us felt there:

> I sure was comfortable the first five years of seminary life—I loved it. It was a real happy place. To have people that, because they were sensitive to good and bad, kindness and unkindness, sin or not sin, were more sensitive to making fun of and hurting . . . we were each other's brothers, or we were certainly part of each other's family life. I don't think I would have found that in the regular lifestyle.

To some extent, the discrepancy between our present critiques of the minor seminary and our positive memories of our lives there is more apparent than real. For our sense of community developed at least in part in response to the rigidity of the rules. We united against a common oppressor; in the traditional manner of boarding students, we valued one another precisely because we could not abide the regime. Nor, in our isolation, could we engage with the rest of the world; we had only one another. By contrast, the current college seminary, a dormitory adjacent to Marquette University, has virtually no rules and enjoys considerable engagement with what is no longer thought of as the "outside world."

As far I could tell from my three extended stays there, however, it also enjoys a much less intense sense of community.

It is also true that at the time, our resentment at seminary restriction was alleviated—and our sense of *our* community heightened—by our keen awareness of our less fortunate peer institutions. We knew that the other minor seminaries in Wisconsin had less free time and fewer vacations; we relished their repressions as confirmations of our own relative freedom. We developed our own folklore. At Mundelein, the major seminary for the Chicago archdiocese, so the story went, Jell-O was forbidden: too sensuous when it shook. At an unnamed Canadian seminary somewhere in the Northwest, the students were required to wear robes while showering ("Never look down on the unemployed," we said) and had to use wooden paddles to tuck in their shirts. We had unrestricted access to Jell-O and could shower and dress hands on. Context is everything. We had it good.

The particular ways in which we experienced community had some questionable long-term effects, however; and that awareness mitigates our appreciation of what the seminary provided. We did support one another, for instance—as male adolescents often do: through comradeship, common enterprise, shared fantasies, and a united if low-level subversion of the rules. That support certainly constitutes a form of genuine relationship, perhaps as much as teenagers are likely to seek.

For the most part, however, it involved, like the traditional intimacy of the confessional, a kindness and sensitivity without risk to us. For insofar as close relationships suggest individuals' discussing and negotiating what is most important to each of them and making adjustments to keep together, we did very little of that—partly, no doubt, because we were too young to think about it; partly because, since we were not dating one another, we had a reduced stake in negotiation and compromise; and partly because we learned quickly, as we did in confession, that relationships could be—should be—negotiated through the proper authorities rather than directly with one another: offend your friend or spouse, confess to the priest.

Most important, however, we did not negotiate with one another because we assumed that we were sufficiently alike not to require it. We were all seminarians, after all; we were all heading for the priesthood. Didn't that by definition mean that we all had the same values, that we were the same kind of (good) people? To a considerable extent we were, like soldiers at war, a community held together by a common mythology about our own goodness. It was a mythology not without substance; but precisely because it was so comforting, its immediate effect was to preclude scrutiny.

The priests in our class, for instance, assumed that there would be a "fraternity of priests" awaiting them after ordination, a supportive extension of the seminary community. But after ordination, when serious problems of adjustment began to surface for them as they faced adult responsibilities for the first time, problems begging for expression and understanding, they discovered in their rectory "mates" an older generation of priests who were not very much like them at all and who were often highly unsympathetic to their perspective. And yet, like newly married couples expecting easy and continuing compatibility, they did not expect to have to negotiate in order to get along because they had rarely negotiated earlier. So especially in their early parishes, they rarely worked at the relationship; instead, they moved from rectory to rectory in nostalgic search of an elusive harmony.

Nor are priests alone in this trait: those of us who have in fact married have shown a similar tendency to expect relationships to come effortlessly and to produce great satisfaction. The one acceptable model of intimacy presented to us had been the Beatific Vision, after all, and the image of a perfect lover whose mere presence can produce endless, unmarred bliss is a hard model to follow; the oft-lamented effect of traditional fairy tales on actual relationships pales by comparison. Clashes of values and needs within marriage, the realities of two imperfect people in an inevitably imperfect match, are particularly hard for men who, for years, shared—or assumed they shared—their most central values, without effort, with those around them.

But there is more to our mixed assessment of the seminary than our present sense of its ambiguous effect. For what we now lament about the seminary was, although we don't like to admit it, what attracted us to it in the first place; what we now denigrate satisfied something in us then. This discrepancy is, I suspect, characteristic of many self-defined 1960s people on the downward side of the slope: we do not find it comforting to acknowledge how thoroughly we belonged to a traditional church, how fully we once accepted a worldview we now see as outmoded, how content we felt within it before we converted to change. Nor do we like to admit the extent to which we have not changed. When we remember the minor seminary fondly for our sense of community and high purpose, we are embracing those parts of it which we could comfortably take with us into the 1960s and beyond, things we still value openly. When we disparage the seminary for its legalism and authoritarianism, for its escape from society, for its denial of sexuality and fear of intimate involvements, we are not only trying to distance ourselves from American/Catholic culture of that period; we are trying—hard—to repudiate ourselves at that stage of our lives. While America in the 1950s lived in fear of the Bomb, we lived in fear of our emotions; now that we have rediscovered them, we are chagrined that we once sought shelter.

Many of us, for instance, now complain that the seminary deprived us of our adolescence; we regret having missed not only the freedom but also the uncertainties and anxiety which adolescence entails; such experiences bring growth. But the seminary did not deprive us of our adolescence, although I for one insisted for many years that it had. Rather, we went out of our way to avoid it. At the very least, we colluded with those who protected us from it.

Conventional mythology would have it, for instance, that seminarians come from good Catholic homes and are drawn to the seminary by parental encouragement, the example of admirable priests, and the energetic recruiting of grade-school nuns. Many of my classmates fit that model. So do I, on the face of it: my parents were devoted Catholics who revered priests, and my eighth-grade nun was equal to any Division I basketball coach in the package of (otherworldly) incentives she offered me to sign on.

Many others, however, who felt moved by those factors at the time, now feel that they were fleeing to the haven of the seminary from troubled homes and adolescent turmoil. Eliot Grayson, who now regrets that the seminary inculcated a distrust of genuine intimacy and human connection, feels that he entered the seminary precisely to protect himself from those emotions:

> The seminary was basically an escape from life. I came from an alcoholic family, and they didn't work through any feelings. I think I was scared of going to hell. My sexuality and deeper relationships were the things that led you to hell, so I had to stay away from those. Then going to the seminary, I took the high road away from sex, individual initiative, relationships, intimacy, all the things that were really at the core of my being.

For those who fled to the seminary, the lure was often a sense of approval beyond what a shaky family could provide. Father Jeff, for instance:

> In retrospect, I'm pretty well convinced that I came to the seminary at the age of fourteen because it was a way of getting out of a very painful family situation. The idea of running away from home and striking out for New York or Hollywood didn't occur to me. It didn't seem something I could manage. Going to the seminary seemed to be an all-win kind of thing. I could do something good; I could leave my family and they would be happy and proud of me for leaving. It got me out of an environment which was very sad and not healthy for me. I didn't know that at the time. I thought I was going to go out and conquer the world for God or something.

Charles Olinski now feels that he entered the seminary to run away from a troubled family in an acceptable way—to create, for public display and private satisfaction, an ideal family in his image by the very act of becoming a seminarian:

> At the time I really thought that was a great thing. A noble thing. The right thing for me to do. I wanted to be a priest. Really, when I look back, that was my way of running away from home in a very acceptable way. Not only acceptable but envied. I had a father who was an alcoholic. Because of his drinking there were family crises between him and my mother. I couldn't admit it to anyone because you don't tell people—you're supposed to come from a good family. So in a way I had a little lie, and I lived it to its fullest by saying how I come from such a good family. I'm going to be a priest. And how can I come from a bad family if I'm a priest?

As a counterforce to our adolescent sense of inadequacy, confusion, and turmoil, the seminary in fact offered more than acceptance; it offered the balm of seminarian specialness. In the spiritual sense, of course, specialness was our overt but difficult goal: as Pope Pius XI had written, "To fulfill the duties of Holy Orders, common goodness does not suffice; but excelling goodness is required."[4] Specialness, however, was also, in psychological and social terms, the atmosphere we already walked in, a sense of ourselves we were given without any effort on our part. By simple virtue of entering the seminary, we became kings in our home parishes, princes in our own families. When I returned home for vacations, my grade-school nuns would gather around after mass, laughing at my stories; my parents' friends would congratulate me on my presumed good work. At Christmas and Easter, all the seminarians would march down the aisle before mass, the valiant troops home on leave. In the words of one classmate, we felt "totally reinforced from the outside," and the reinforcement worked its way in.

In that sense, in our otherwise relatively ascetic context, specialness was our licensed narcotic, our prescribed intoxicant. In a Catholic tradition which at that time considered that ordination raised the priest far above the laity—"elevation is separation"[5]—and whose current theology still insists that ordination produces ontological change in the candidate, the seminarian of our day was special by anticipation as well as acclamation. Within the Catholic community, we shared the priest's cultic status—and something of his sexual mystery; I received a good deal of female attention during summer vacations, and I don't think this was solely a result of my personal charm.

We did not consider ourselves hot shots; that crass form of egotism would have violated the humility to which we simultaneously, if paradoxically, strove. But since our own community considered us special, how could we avoid agreeing? After all, we were, as Scott Lawson, now a therapist, said, "a chosen group"; for had not God Himself singled us

out? When we took the Minnesota Multiphasic psychological test in
our senior year in college, Scott was not the only one in the class who
checked "yes" to the question "Are you a special messenger from God?"

We gravitated to what the seminary offered, in short, because we
wanted it. This is true even in regard to the rules. We may have seen
specific rules as ludicrous even then, but overall the "rule" provided a
sense of order and security which we valued for a number of reasons.
For some of us, a life of rule formalized the underlying assumptions of
our traditional homes, or else (much the same thing) they satisfied a personal, temperamental need which we no longer feel, or at least no longer
acknowledge. Even Father Brent, who has come a long way from his initial submissiveness, acknowledges, "I liked the discipline in the sense
that this time was for this, that time was for that. I fit with it because of
the disposition with which I came to it." For others, the rules provided
what was missing at home—in the case of one priest classmate, a form
of order more benign than he suffered from a physically and verbally
abusive father:

> He was a strict tyrant. It was not uncommon for him to lose control of
> his emotions and hit me. He was one of those fathers who had no prob-
> lem giving you a spanking. So when you get to the seminary and had
> all these rules, it was like, "Yeah, well, that's what dad would have
> done." But then you find out that the priests weren't as strict as your
> dad was. So it's a better situation.

Of course the rules precluded dating, partying, and other enticing activities. But even if the rules were irritating, at least they were clear—and
isn't that what the psychologists keep insisting now, that "adolescents
need to know what the rules are"? The rules also protected some appealing freedoms: they mandated three hours of "recreation" a day, for instance, more than my teenage son usually gets. Perhaps most important,
keeping the rules and studying were virtually our only responsibilities.
And very few of us in 1957, at age fourteen, were actively looking for
the kinds of responsibilities and complexities which we now claim to regret having missed; the lure of the seminary was precisely, as one classmate puts it, that it "was like being in camp."

The underside of this carefree life was, as former priest Hans Ziegler
points out, that "it never freed me to make an honest decision." But for
Hans, as for many others, the complaint that we had no obligations then
is coupled with a guilty relish for the easy, burden-free quality of seminary life. After wondering "why the hell we were sheltered," Hans goes
on to say:

> To this day, from a selfish point of view, I don't regret staying at the
> seminary. From a growth point of view, I would have to say that it might
> have been better for me to go home every night and to assume some

of the responsibilities that young people that age assume, like helping around the house, maybe having a paper route. But I'd have to say, in thinking about it in my honest moments with myself, I had it good in those days.

Most of us did feel that we had it good. It is important to remember in general that seminarians, unlike their secular equivalents, at every point have a ready way out: the option of simply returning to the "normal" world and attending school there. To stay in the seminary for any extended period is almost by definition to acknowledge that the seminary is a good fit.

We were, in fact, considered a model class by several faculty members, "the best class I ever had" by one twenty-seven-year veteran; today we retain a strong sense of ourselves as a "unique class" of "good people," "the cream of the crop"—recurrent phrases throughout the interviews. We did not get that reputation by being morose and discontent then. Thinking back on the seminary a number of years ago, I realized that repression does not necessarily make people unhappy at the time; what is repressed is often—by definition, you could say—out of sight. We would feel most of the effects only later.

Furthermore, not only did the rules establish some freedoms for us, they also created a considerable degree of license. For by the implicit logic of the legalism which some of us found all too congenial, if it wasn't against the rules, it was perfectly okay—and happily, the rules didn't cover everything. Especially in the area of sexual fantasy, we took what we were given. The Legion of Decency listings were a case in point. I hated the Legion of Decency—my family had taken its judgments very seriously—for denying me access to erotic movies. But I also came to love the Legion of Decency for what I conveniently took to be its implicit sanction of any erotic excitement I might derive from an "approved" movie. If the move was authorized, so my syllogistic reasoning went, then so too was any response it might evoke in me.

I was aided in this thinking by my unwitting parents, who would occasionally, though very rarely, allow me to go to a "B" movie—i.e., a movie adjudged to be "morally objectionable in part for all." Their theory was that if I shut my eyes during the "objectionable parts," I would stay clean. I seized this opening eagerly. Of course I wouldn't know which parts were objectionable until I had started watching them, at which point, if I was lucky and my reflexes slow (to this day I can still see Samantha Eggar naked on the couch in front of the fireplace in *The Collector*), it might be too late to remove the pernicious images from my fevered brain.

I remember the way this worked in the seminary. On Saturday morning, Father Busch would read off the approved movies available in Milwaukee at the time. But occasionally he would misread or misremember the Legion of Decency listings. As a result, my two best friends and I, steady moviegoers partly for this reason, would find ourselves in a darkened theater a long way from campus in front of what seemed to us a wildly erotic movie—not that it took much to qualify. But Father Busch, the seminary's embodiment of order, had approved the movie; who were we to undercut his claims to moral authority by looking away from what he had sanctioned? When I interviewed these two friends, they had memories as strong as mine, thirty-five years after the fact, of *No Place to Land*, an obscure, low-budget movie in which a beautiful (though slightly seedy) actress rose slowly from her sunbathing position and turned her uncovered breasts toward the camera. None of us could—or needed to—remember anything else about the movie.

The assumption that what the rules did not totally forbid, they implicitly sanctioned created a mindset which has retained its force for many of us long after we recognized its deficiencies. I wish I did not have this memory: "Okay, I had coffee with her and we talked for three hours. Okay, so maybe I love her. But what's the problem? I didn't go to bed with her! I didn't commit adultery!"

Whatever our attitudes were to specific rules, our underlying respect for authority remained strong. This is evident from the fact that most of the class greatly admired Father Busch and saw him in fact as the guiding spirit of the seminary. (I have to separate myself here: Father Busch's affiliation with the rules was too close for my comfort; I respected him, but he was too much like me for me to revere him.) They saw the rules as foolish, but accepted his right to enforce them—hence too the seeds of their later distinctions between law and authority.

Respect for a disciplinarian is less surprising than it might seem. After all, we too aspired to be God's representatives and fully expected to enjoy the status and power that went along with the job—or so we thought at the time. Like the military cadets to whom our faculty so often compared us, we were to follow orders and ask no questions; implicitly, someday others, docile "flock" to our wise "pastor," would defer to us in the same way. The priests who taught us and regulated us already had that authority; to rebel against them would be to reject an image of the priesthood that few if any of us were ready to reject at that time.

And in any case, why rebel against rules which seemed as fixed and permanent as the church itself? We knew the rules were silly, but we did not seriously imagine that they were ever going to change. For we were operating inside a seemingly immutable paradigm; we embraced a way of thinking without knowing that it was only a way of thinking. "We bought into more than a school," Derek Hartman acknowledges; "we bought into a whole system, a whole mode of being. We embraced it without question."

The most positive statements about the seminary come not from priests but from those of us who left the seminary or the priesthood and have not found anywhere else the same sense of purpose, the same sense of inherent meaning, the same degree of community—nor the same sense of protectedness, of immunity, of our own specialness, of escape from responsibility, from emotional complexity and ambiguity, from the tensions of sexuality. No doubt many men end up nostalgic for the period of their relative innocence. But as seminarians, we expected (we were part of a Catholic ethos which led us to expect) that the period of protection would extend indefinitely, that after ordination we would still be "in the world but not of the world," that as God's chosen representatives we would remain permanently special, and that the church would take care of us and buffer us.

Of course, that has proven to be true neither for the priests nor for the rest of us; and coping with that realization is one of the underlying issues of the interviews. Knowing now that immunity is not available, and feeling now that adults should not expect it, we tend to underplay or forget the fact that we wanted it—and still want it. Father Craig's cry of disbelief when he was fired from his seminary teaching position—"They fired *me! Me!*"; Scott Lawson's amazement as well as distress when a former colleague sued him in a highly public fashion for sexual harassment; the pervasive dismay on the part of priest classmates when once-deferential laity criticize them; my own shock that people would actually gossip about *me* after my divorce—are representative. We continue to feel special long after we know our license has expired; we continue to want immunity and to be surprised when it doesn't operate for us. We entered the seminary, in short, partly for reasons we are now uneasy with; and I think we miss it partly for reasons we are similarly uneasy with.

Seminary Timelessness: A Cost/Benefit View

To put some of this in a different context: on the one hand, St. Francis's emphasis on rules placed it squarely in the mainstream of a seminary history reaching back to the Council of Trent's highly specific guidelines for seminary study and behavior, which remained normative for more than four hundred years.[6] More recently, in 1907, Pope Pius X's attack on an independent, critically inclined "modernism" reasserted the idea that obedience and ideological conformity were the preeminent priestly qualities to be instilled by seminaries.[7] Even within seminary circles, St. Francis itself, founded in 1855 by German priests for German

Catholics in America, had an established reputation (especially in its "major" half) as a seminary where the rules were taken with exceptional seriousness, a reputation reinforced by Monsignor Frank Schneider, who served as rector from 1946 to 1965 and who, in the words of Father Robert Massey, archdiocesan historian, "evinced a scrupulous deference to canonical dictates."[8] The seminary we attended, in short, was operating inside a longstanding tradition.

On the other hand, we were told nothing of this history while we were students, lest it become "mere" history to us, one actual course of events among other possibilities, and thus be reduced from absolute to relative status; for us, the contingencies of history were buried under claims of timelessness. By extension, on more substantive issues, when church authorities insisted that the priesthood and celibacy and our Catholicism-as-currently-formulated were forever, we had no idea that they were doing anything other than repeating changeless truths. It did not occur to us then—we were not encouraged to have it occur—that such claims were historically based constructs open to reformulation. To us they weren't based on anything; they simply were, and would continue to be. Both the church and the seminary felt all but eternal to us.

The seeming timelessness of the seminary rule, however, sowed the seeds of a later, more emphatic rejection in a small number of us who took the rules too literally to laugh them off. I was one of them. I obeyed every rule they threw at me, not because I wanted to, but because I took the seminary authorities at their word, that the rule was indeed the will of God for us. I hated having to be silent after lights out, for instance, because most of my classmates quite sensibly ignored the prohibition and surreptitiously went about their business of talking and joking. My obedience made me feel abnormal, odd, and that was the last thing I wanted to be. But since the rule, I believed, was the will of God, I felt I had no choice but to obey it, even if I felt like an idiot in the process.

My resentment toward the rules, even as I clung to them, was never more intense than during a late-night dormitory party, complete with food, drink, and music, in the final semester of our senior year. Everyone in the class took part except me; while my classmates danced up and down the aisles, I lay there in my bed, pretending to sleep through it all: this was against the rules, after all. The fact that I was the only one in the class to escape probation—how could anyone have expected to slip a dormitory-wide party past Father Busch?—was no consolation at all; my refusal to participate highlighted my classmates' guilt, and made me feel even more set off from them.

After I left the seminary and began to question church positions (on sexual behavior and birth control, for instance), I continued to take those positions seriously—which for me meant literally, as fixed absolutes— even as I came to scorn them; so much so that I felt I had to leave an institution which had the temerity to insist on them. I was not alone in this process: a number of us ended up leaving the church because of its rigidity and legalism; we "got back" at the church by turning our particular seminary legacy—our own rigidity, our ultimate fit with the seminary—against it. We might not have reacted so strongly, however, had the seminary itself been more open about its own history, about the mere fact that it had a history, and that what it taught us had a history.

Yet one more discomforting awareness, however: the perceived absence of history had its lure, too. It has now become clear to me (but only because I have done some homework) that the Catholicism we embraced at that time was not as monolithic or unchanging as it seemed to us then, that the "old church" which my classmates and I tend to stereotype was more complex than our construction of it. The liturgical movement, for instance, well underway by the 1950s, was already in the process of altering the relationship between priest and laity in a manner which would reverberate in the more dramatic changes soon to come. Similarly, the Catholic Action Movement, with its emphasis on engagement, was implicitly redefining the relationship between spirituality and the "world" long before Vatican II seized the idea and ran with it.

The ideal of docility was taking its blows as well. The Christian Family Movement, which stressed the need of every Catholic "to observe, to judge, and to act," especially by looking carefully for oneself at the scriptures, was already contributing to a more independent and critically inclined laity—who thus reincarnated from within the very walls much, though certainly not all, of the modernism dreaded by Pius X. And close to home, Monsignor John Tracy Ellis's 1955 address, "American Catholics and the Intellectual Life," set off a debate on the (anti)intellectual tenor of American Catholic education that began to affect seminaries as well as Catholic colleges. It was in the context of this debate that St. Francis Major Seminary produced its first self-study in 1962, the year the Vatican Council opened, to be followed by a post–Vatican II self-study in 1969, the year my classmates were ordained.

Thus what Tod Gitlin points out about American culture in general, that the fifties were "a seedbed as well as a cemetery," that "the surprises of the sixties were planted there,"[9] was true for our small slice of it as well: the 1960s were more continuous with the past than those of us who identify with that decade like to acknowledge. The 1960s-sounding urge to "change the world" drew on many of the same energies that had gone into the seemingly more conservative urge to "save the world"; my classmates' eventual liberalism was not a virgin birth.

And yet, for me, learning now about these incipient changes in the church is like learning about an admirable but secret life once led by a former spouse; where was this knowledge when I would have been more personally invested in discovering it? For my classmates and I sensed little if any of these currents; we were, after all, still isolated, our information was still controlled, and the seminary faculty were still talking an emphatic language of timelessness and tradition. As a result, the minor seminary as we experienced it seemed a bastion of untroubled American Catholicism; we felt it to be one of those rare moments when time does not seem to be at work, when an institution seems consistent with its own ideals and congruent with the needs of its clientele, when the tensions and excitement of change do not seem to be operating because they don't seem necessary. It was because of this fit that the seminary's claims to timelessness had weight with us then; because of it we still feel the seductive pull of timelessness as an undertow to our current, learned preference for change.

In 1961, the year before my class went over to the major seminary for its last three years of college and four years of theology, the Milwaukee archdiocese opened the extravagant new seminary we had been hearing so much about, complete with a gymnasium on which the Milwaukee Bucks now practice because it has the best floor in the city. Twenty years later, the new minor seminary shut down. The archdiocese had radically misread enrollment trends. In conventional terms, vocations began to drop dramatically in the mid-1960s. More likely, from my classmates' current perspective, fewer young men were willing to respond to a definition of vocation which involved entering a self-contained, celibate world at age fourteen; and the church was not willing to welcome the female aspirants to the priesthood who could have kept it going at full strength.

My class would go on to become one of the largest ordination classes in the history of the Milwaukee archdiocese. When one of our former teachers referred to us as "the best class I ever had," he was saying, I think, that as a class we truly fit the old minor seminary and its culture. That seminary is gone now; the diocese razed all but one of the buildings in the 1980s and transformed it back into its original status as Pio Nono High School. Many of us, including the priests, have either rejected or radically redefined the Catholicism we knew there; we consider it a mixed blessing that it suited us at the time. But suit us it did.

The Major Seminary: The Old Church at Its Worst

When we reached the major seminary in 1962, however, we entered a less functional world. Our minor seminary education had been traditional but solid. Its emphasis on Latin and Greek gave it a clear seminary cast; but it also offered a few options along the way, including German and Polish, languages literally "of the people" in Milwaukee. And the faculty, as far as we could tell, believed in what they were doing; most of them taught well and with enthusiasm. In contrast, the major seminary required all of us, regardless of talent or inclination, to major in scholastic philosophy, a field whose only detectable relevance, most of us thought even then, was to prepare us for an equally syllogistic theology.

Although the two priests who constituted our philosophy department were conscientious teachers, the program itself was radically diluted. We did not read any genuine philosophers, even Aquinas, except in occasional excerpts carefully orchestrated to make the right scholastic point. Instead, we studied "manual Thomism," a series of simplified, schematic textbooks written in Latin by a deservedly obscure Canadian Jesuit named Henri Grenier for no discernible reason except so that we would have to translate them. The "green Grenier," so called because of its jacket color, was our official text; most students used the "red Grenier," the illicit pony which was nonetheless available in the bookstore—i.e., an English text ineptly translated from a crude Latin text, one bad joke glossing another.

The scholastic approach to philosophy, enshrined as normative since the Council of Trent, was as hierarchical and removed from reality as the seminary itself: the big truths of the syllogistic premise, we were told, contain at least implicitly all the little truths you can know, all you need to know; so always start from the top down, never from the bottom up. Our philosophy exams were without exception either true-false or, at their most demanding, multiple choice; truth could be complex but never ambiguous.

With only a few exceptions, our other courses were even more openly watered down, because (I remember the rationale well) we weren't going to be scientists or literary critics or anything else anyway; we were going to be priests—a goal whose emphasis on "training" obviated the need for a broad education. Although a few of my classmates still value their exposure to scholastic philosophy for its rigor and logic, the more common response, then as well as now, was that of Father Frank, who currently teaches at the seminary: "Philosophy was ridiculous. How the hell we learned anything, I don't know." In retrospect, my classmates resent not only the lack of options but the attitude behind it, the seminary's seeming indifference to our talents or interests. "I was not challenged," complains Father Tracy, currently a professor of political science at Marquette, "in the areas where my abilities lie." More succinctly, Father Herbert says that he felt "cheated."

Similarly, the heightened rigidity of the major seminary rules seemed to reflect their diminishing sense of inherent authority. At a point where we wanted more freedom and felt that we could handle it, the rules were stricter and more inflexible than they had been in the minor seminary.

They seemed to have lost their moorings in any larger, coherent sense of order; they appeared gratuitous, perverse, counterproductive, self-contradictory—and thus disruptive of true order.

A case could be made that the minor seminary interdiction on dating, for instance, had at least some benefits for boys in their early and mid-teens; in that regard the traditional seminary may have been smarter than the mainstream culture of our day. But as our bodies matured and our sexuality became more insistent, the major seminary simply shrank in fear. It pulled us away from one another by forbidding room visitation—in the manner of traditional coed colleges—and gave us no plausible rationale for the lifetime of celibacy, which, as a result, looked increasingly like a merely arbitrary rule.

At a time when we were starting to develop a taste for more contact with the larger society, the seminary shut us off from it more stringently. Summer vacations remained intact, but otherwise we went home only for two days at Thanksgiving and two days at Christmas. We could have visitors for an afternoon once a year. Except for a frantic fourteen-hour semester break which produced prodigies of concentrated activity—round-trip train rides to Chicago, for instance, along with a movie, lunch, a play, another movie, and dinner—we could never leave campus except to walk along Lake Michigan in the morning, protected by our cassocks. As one faculty member recalls, the primary goal of the major seminary seemed unchanged from what it had been in his day, from what it had been for decades: "to keep us unsullied from the world which could corrupt us. And of course, you were then thrust right out into the world, in the midst of it all. I'm surprised that we're not nuttier than we actually are."

The efforts to set us off from the world felt increasingly like efforts to set us off from normalcy. At a point when our sexual identities, fragile at best at that age, were already under the strain of an anticipated celibacy, we had to wear the cassock at all times except during organized sports; and a black dress by any other name is still a black dress. We even had to wear it during midnight trips to the urinals, to prevent the briefest moment of unmitigated revelation. In warm weather, some of us got an unhallowed thrill from wearing the cassock without pants on underneath; it was an act of private exposure, as if to insist to ourselves that we were still free, still male underneath it all. Those who were caught (the dean of students had a trained eye) were in serious trouble; we were supposed to be celibate to the core.

In that context, the seemingly minor requirement that many of us resented the most was the mandatory wearing, during the winter, of the hated "zimarra." The zimarra was a black version of the long gray coat then worn at West Point and yet another reminder of the seminary's militaristic affinities. It was much heavier than it was warm. But its ma-

jor offense was its attack on our self-image. We were not immune to the
desire to look cool, and we knew that we were thought by outsiders to
be odd anyway; why make it worse? Yet the zimarra, which we univer-
sally considered awkward and ugly, was the garb in which we confronted the world as we took our morning walks along Lake Michigan,
watching the traffic pass us (watching the world go by) on Lake Shore
Drive. We didn't feel like "soldiers of Christ" at those moments; we felt
branded. One of my class's triumphant acts was our gleeful late-night
burning of our zimarras, along with our Latin philosophy texts, in the
seminary woods at the end of our senior year, when the new rector had
indicated that they would no longer be required.

Seminary fear of sexuality by this time had become legend. When
word got out (informers are the bane of revolution) that two classmates
and I were conducting a survey of attitudes on sexuality as part of a sociology course, we were called into the head prefect's office and told that
if we didn't immediately turn in whatever materials we had gathered,
"the rector will hang your asses from the flagpole." The theological tract
on sex, still in Latin—"De Sexto"—was, by explicit seminary guidelines,
not to be taught until the last year of seminary training, when presumably the twenty-six-year-old deacons would be better equipped to handle its inflammatory content. Until shortly before my class entered the
major seminary, the tract had not been studied in the classroom but had
been read in chapel, in front of deacons wearing white surplices and
armed for the occasion, without irony, with lighted candles.

I remember the story, probably apocryphal but so plausible that it had
taken on the force of myth, that a number of older seminarians told
about our archconservative rector, Monsignor Schneider. It seems he had
been looking around for some suitable text on sexuality for his soon-to-
be-ordained deacons now that the reading of a Latin tract no longer
seemed appropriate even to him. In his search, he chanced upon a little
booklet written by a Catholic layman to explain the rudiments of sex to
his six-year-old daughter. Perfect, the rector thought, so he distributed it
to his class, but not before warning them in solemn tones: "For God's
sake, whatever you do, don't let this get into the hands of the underclass-
men." We laughed because it hurt; such stories were our version of the
blues.

The sexually obsessed rule undermined itself by indirectly promoting what it feared the most. That irony was not lost on Father Frank, now
a professor at the seminary and a man who has thought a good deal
about the nature of authority. To Frank, "the whole system was ridiculous":

> You have to go down to the john to talk to people, and yet they were say-
> ing you couldn't go to one another's rooms for fear of homosexuality.

> So you're talking in the john. If you want to set up a situation . . . I mean, what the hell is wrong with these people? The epitome is one night we were standing there, I don't know whether it was junior or senior year in college, and we were having a birthday party in the damn john. We were eating cake and the smells from the urinals were coming out, and I'm thinking, "This is ridiculous."

In short, during the early and mid-1960s, at a time when both secular society and the church were beginning openly to question their own traditions and practices, the major seminary seemed bent on retrenching. "We do things this way," the rector used to say whenever he had a chance, "because that's the way we've always done them." Only two of my classmates, both priests, assert that those years were positive; for the rest of us, they were, in Father Tracy's phrase, "the dark ages," the worst stage of our seminary experience. We had expected to have to "fit" the priesthood; but we were beginning not to like some of the measurements. Years later, we would develop a vocabulary to articulate the centrality of personal growth; without that vocabulary—without even the concept at that time—we merely chafed.

Meanwhile, the faculty themselves began to show signs of discontent—whether at their work or at us, as we began to chafe, it was not always clear. They interacted with us less than the minor seminary faculty had; several of them had undisguised drinking problems, and others complained openly in class that they would rather be doing parish work. They provided us with our first extensive exposure to priests as alienated labor. The concept has stuck; several of the priests in the class now use it to describe themselves.

Eventually, most of us lost respect not only for the rules but for the authority which underlay them. As soon as he arrived at the major seminary, Charles Olinski noticed a culture of cynicism in the older students that jarred with the respect he had brought with him from the minor seminary:

> One of the things that turned me off most about becoming a priest was going to the major seminary. In my naiveté, I expected the guys who were soon to be ordained to have—I don't know what I expected exactly, but what I saw I didn't like. I thought there were a lot of hypocrites. I thought they were playing the system for all it was worth. For some of them it was a damn joke. I was terribly disillusioned.

In the long run, disrespect became more public. I remember, late in my college years, two minor but telling gestures by Father Ledworowski, the dean of students—the major seminary's analogue to Father Busch, but by now an object of scorn rather than reverence. The first occurred when, in response to increased student absences from meals in silent protest against the quality of the food, he stood up at lunch and demanded that the students who were not present come immediately to his office to be punished. We laughed hard, in his face, and the laughter was not kind.

This was not equivalent to torching the administration building, but context, after all, is everything. In a tradition which placed docility second only to purity—virtue defined in both cases as not acting on your own impulses—it was our first communal act of student assertiveness, the first time in my seminary career that I had seen and been part of an act of public contempt for a seminary authority. We revealed openly what we had come to feel privately, that we considered the administration out of touch to the point of being ludicrous. In my memory, that small event signals the beginning of the end of the old-time regime of Monsignor Frank Schneider.

So it was not surprising that later in the year, Father Ledworowski stood up in chapel—again in response to growing discontent, this time at the policy of lights out at 10:00 every night, a rule which held even for the deacons—and announced that a major faculty meeting had taken place, and that after great deliberation the administration had decided to move lights out all the way back to 10:30. He then leaned over the pulpit and solemnly declared that with this single, radical stroke, "the administration has moved fifty years ahead of the student body." His own rhetoric acknowledged the split between administration and students; we were no longer in this together. We were in chapel, however; no one laughed until we got outside.

In short, at a time when authority was beginning to undergo considerable cultural assault, the seminary seemed to be losing its claims to authority with us. Both academically and vocationally, it did not seem to know what it was doing. At the very least, *we* did not know what it was doing, and no one felt moved to explain it to us. If many of us later came to see the church as dysfunctional, our first experience of that dysfunction was here. Like other members of our generation, we were becoming disenchanted with "the system."

The seminary made a few gestures toward change during our college years, but more in form than in substance. Its 1962 self-study is full of homage to the seminary's scholastic traditions: to "the basic Thomistic philosophy of education" (10), to the "scientific and systematic study of Catholic doctrine and morality" (11), to the concept of priest as "general practitioner" (6)—an updated phrase for the traditional notion that the priest is "all things to all men." It also hints, however, that something slightly different might now be necessary, that "the rising level of popular education requires the priest to have a broad level of education so as to be able to meet the laity on their own level and win their acceptance" (8).

In keeping with the study's basic tone of reaffirmation, its most obvious and immediate fruit was not an attempt to change the college curriculum but a successful effort to earn validation from the North Central Accrediting Association for the existing curriculum. I remember that process well: its principal architect was the late Jack Peifer, one of our two philosophy professors, who described (some of) his machinations gleefully to us in class. The upshot of it all was that North Central, without talking to any students, asked for a little tinkering here and there but basically found our Latin texts and syllogistic approach just fine. My classmates and I wondered aloud, but only among ourselves: Who are they fooling? In 1965, my class received newly accredited degrees in scholastic philosophy from St. Francis Seminary.

These superficial changes worked their way down to the scholastic "disputatio" which, since 1930, every graduating class had been obliged to perform. The senior with the best cumulative grades in philosophy would write a lengthy disquisition in Latin on some fine point of Thomistic philosophy, memorize it, and then perform it with great seeming gusto in front of the entire (captive) student body. He would be interrupted intermittently, however, by cries of intellectual outrage from the other top students in the class, who were planted in the audience and who leapt up in turn to dispute his claims—in Latin, of course, and with equal panache. The head man, however, would coolly dismantle their arguments and reassert his primacy—or so the audience would assume from the highly theatrical gestures displayed; no one understood what was being said. I had a perverse fondness for these disputations; they seemed to half-consciously parody the whole obscurantist enterprise we were enmeshed in.

But I have even fonder memories of my own senior year, when I was slated to be the disputator, only to be saved by the administration's decision—not accidentally, in the midst of the accreditation process—to conduct the whole thing in English within an informal talk-show format. Under the new arrangement, I became simply the host, Johnny Carson in a cassock, and the next-ranking student had to write the disputation. The substance had not changed, however. The question under discussion was decided by the philosophy faculty: "Does Thomism have a future?" We didn't have to anguish over the answer; we knew there could be only one.

"From Night to Day"

Toward the end of the 1965 academic year, however, just as the Vatican Council was marking its end with a spate of documents on seminaries and on the nature of the priesthood,[10] Archbishop Cousins dismissed Frank Schneider and installed a new rector, Monsignor William Schuit; from that moment, an institution which had seemed impervious to change began to reform itself dramatically from within. Many in our class did not stay around to see those changes; our college years had been more than enough. But nearly all who lasted through the first year of theology remained through ordination. To Father Tracy, "That was such a dramatic change—just so dramatic. From night to day." For many, the transformation was pivotal: "Had it not changed," says Father Spencer, now happily engaged in parish work, "I don't know if I would have stayed."

The changes over their next four years were various. The ideals of protection against the world began to give way to the notion of engagement. Theology courses incorporated some of the liberal thinking engendered by the Vatican Council. An involved pastoralism began to replace the abstract study of fixed church doctrine; by 1969, the Theology Department had become the "School of Pastoral Ministry." Extensive "field work" in parishes, prisons, and hospitals was introduced to promote the shift. Students still lived on campus, but they were encouraged to attend lectures in Milwaukee and to become more immersed, both on campus and off, in the social issues of the 1960s, most notably in civil rights, where Father James Groppi's marches provided an immediate model.

Students were now allowed to talk in the buildings and to visit one another's rooms; they were encouraged to engage one another as well as the world at large. The dean of students, whose designated role in 1962 had been "to see to it that the rules of the seminary are observed," was now "to see to it that the students are regularly made aware of the spirit behind the Student Handbook, i.e., the responsible use of freedom under authority" (97). To that end, an honor code (an *honor* code?) all but replaced the thick sheaf of rules; the idea, according to the new rector, was to "let the students make their mistakes before ordination instead of afterward."[11] A student council was established in 1965, with two elected representatives from each class. Its most aggressive period, according to Robert Massey, was between 1965 and 1969, my classmates' theology years.

In the past, annual "retreats," consistent with a traditionally self-referential spirituality, had comprised five days of total silence, reflection, and listening to sermons. They now became more psychologically oriented and communal, more like sensitivity sessions, thus providing my classmates with their first (but not last) taste of personalist religion, of spirituality merging with therapy at the same time it was merging with social action. My classmates now had (relatively) new options to replace—or at least to contend with—the seminary's traditional focus on personal, priestly holiness: they could minister by helping people grow or by helping society change.

To Father Tod, all of this constituted a paradigm shift of the first order, from "an institution which was basically a seventeenth-century Prussian military academy to a place which said, 'Hey, look, you guys

are adults, and I expect you to make adult decisions.' " Father Herman,
a traditionalist by his own description, nonetheless, like Tod, gives the
new rector much of the credit for the changed atmosphere:

> I can remember during the Schneider years, there was almost an esprit
> de corps among the oppressed. There were rules and things that were
> strange. But when Bill Schuit took over, you had the feeling that you
> were going to be dealing with a man who would respect you, treat
> you intelligently, expect you to make intelligent decisions, take respon-
> sibility, because that's what you'd be dealing with in life.

The greatest force behind a new, inclusive sense of community, however, was apparently Father Richard Sklba, who was appointed to the
faculty as a scripture scholar in 1965, succeeded Schuit as rector in 1976,
and has been an auxiliary bishop for Milwaukee since 1979. To Mark
Klugman, who later left the priesthood but speaks eloquently of the
Schuit years, Sklba was a "man of the people," the "focus of spiritual
change" who exemplified a new type of interpersonal, communal spirituality which broke down much of the hierarchical distance between
faculty and students. "I'm not going to use the term 'saint,' " Mark says,
"because that's overworked. [But] he is a person through whom God
shines very well." Relatively low-key throughout most of his interview,
Mark became impassioned in describing Sklba's influence:

> At that time, class did not talk to class. Nobody talked to the deacons,
> and nobody talked to the faculty. Ever! If you saw them, you tipped
> your hat and hoped they kept on going. The faculty didn't talk much
> to each other. This man would be seen walking about the campus with
> a fellow faculty member—chatting. A few days later he would be seen
> with a different faculty member—walking around the grounds, chat-
> ting. A month later, three of them would be walking around—chatting.
> Again, he didn't plan this, but he became the focus of it. He got people
> to talk to each other. And he talked to us. We had him in class—nick-
> names, right? The first nickname he got—"honeybear." That was the
> man's nickname. You could talk to him, not just in the classroom, when-
> ever you saw him. I think 80 percent of the guys wanted him for a spiri-
> tual counselor. Then other faculty members occasionally started saying
> hello. It just took shape and it started to spread.

Some of the changes did not come easily, however, either to the faculty
or to the seminarians. As Hans Ziegler suggests, docility had been the
norm for so long that even minor displays of independence felt like—and
were treated as—daring acts of rebellion:

> They were going to expel one of our classmates for asking questions.
> Nobody did that. A professor said something in the seminary, you sat
> there and listened and said, "Well, this must be the way it is. It's going
> to help me. If nothing else, it's going to help me pass the test, which is

going to get me to the next level, so that I can eventually be ordained."
That's the way I thought. Well, this one guy was a rebel. I remember
him asking penetrating questions that the professors couldn't answer.
I remember him getting Father Bertrand so angry that the blood ves-
sels in his neck almost popped out. Those professors were part of the
system.

Yet my classmates worked hard at overcoming their inbred passivity;
several of them became deeply involved in more confrontational expres-
sions of independence. Father Tracy, eventually president of the Student
Council, provides the best extended description of the conflicting vectors
which characterized the seminary in the late 1960s: increased political
involvement and student assertiveness, a divided faculty, and throughout the conflicts, the new rector's support for change:

> Schuit trusted me. I got into some enormous fights with the dead-
> wood faculty when I was president of the student council. I thought I
> had a mandate from the students to make some changes and we went
> after it. I remember, when I was vice-president, I had Nixon and Hum-
> phrey committed to speak at the seminary. '68. The Wisconsin primary,
> a very important primary. Some of the older faculty had an absolute fit
> that Schuit had lost control. The faculty said "No." I called a student
> meeting and got them all revved up and then told Schuit, "We have a
> consensus here. You don't just say 'no' to us."
> That put Schuit in a horrible fire. We said, "We demand to talk to the
> faculty." Schuit told me later that was the first time in the history of that
> institution that anyone would have the balls to go after the faculty and
> demand for them to retract this decision. I recall we got herded in with
> all these people lined up with just hatred in their eyes.
> As it turned out, we couldn't have them in. But we did put on a pro-
> gram and bring in Senator Nelson and a number of those Wisconsin
> types. It was a concession, but some of the faculty hated me from that
> point on. The next year I was elected president and we just kept on. We
> got people doing all sorts of social justice things. Protesting in the semi-
> nary.
> Now if I thought only of my college years, then it becomes very se-
> date, very mellow and repressive in so many ways. That door really
> opened very wide when Schneider was gone and Schuit was in. Schuit
> just gave me an awful lot of room to operate. Our attitude was, we're
> going to be in the parish in a few years. We're going to get involved in
> the kind of things that we think we should be involved in. If you don't
> like us, you can kick us out.

                              *   *   *

Unlike the 1962 self-study, which begins with a confident assertion of
the enduring nature of the priesthood, the 1969 self-study opens with
the acknowledgment that "today there is considerable disagreement

even among theologians as to the function of the priest in contemporary society. His role is not merely that of a social worker, nor is it that of a professional counselor with a full background in guidance and counseling; nor can he be considered as a mere liturgical functionary. . . . The question being raised today is that of the full responsibility of the priest vis-à-vis the Family of God" (2). In short, new questions hung in the air at the very moment of my classmates' ordination: What *is* a priest today, and what is his job?

When St Francis began to reshape its programs during my classmates' final years of training, it did so not only to implement Vatican II directives but also to begin answering these larger questions. At that time, the seminary moved introductory theology courses down into the college program to allow for more specialized postgraduate work leading to accredited graduate degrees in a variety of areas. The goal would no longer be an abstract, scholastic theology—the church's traditional analogue to the academy's "ivory tower" approach, which sets the scholar off from the world with no overt claims on worldly attention or regard—but a practical, pastoral theology engaged with the world (and, not incidentally, worthy of its regard).

This latter impulse, to win respect while winning souls, is revealed in the study's insistence that "the emphasis must be placed on the professional character of ministerial education" (19). Specifically, the self-study compared the new program to the study of law: in both, "the knowledge of the sources is looked upon as a means to an end . . . the focusing of sources into the real-life situations of contemporary ministry" (96). With this stroke, just as many of my classmates would eventually associate themselves more with the laity than with one another, the seminary dissociated itself from other, still-unworldly seminaries—in most of which, the study pointed out, current revisions were still geared toward "various kinds of research-oriented masters' programs" (19)—and linked itself instead with the highly secular profession of law. At one and the same time, the seminary aimed to make itself more theologically current, gave its graduates a leg up on the ladder of job definition, and nudged its once-"elevated" priests into the world and toward its standards.

These attempts to define a new priesthood were highly tentative and raised questions of their own. Once my classmates began to move with enthusiasm toward a world they had once held in contempt, they would face a number of complex issues unknown, at least on this scale, to previous generations of priests. To what extent would their new engagement with the world—and their new desire for its respect—reconstitute them as "of the world" instead of merely in it? Would this shift of focus constitute a shift of allegiance? What effect would it have on their relationship with the laity and with the institutional church? How would a theology of involved pastoral care affect their ability to live a celibate priesthood? And coming out of a seminary which drew them together first against the regime and then in the common cause of liberal change, how would they act—how would they feel—when they were on their own, without communal support?

My classmates were right at the center of what seminary professionals referred to in the 1960s as the "New Breed" of seminarians—restless, assertive, (eventually) questioning.[12] Since ordination, these questions have presented them the more difficult task of becoming a new breed of priests.

A Seven-Year Chasm

In June of 1991, I sat in the Salzmann Library on the major seminary campus and read the seminary self-studies of 1962 and 1969. I am well aware that documents can lie, that "self-studies" are often exercises in self-defense or self-promotion. Yet both documents struck me as true in a basic way: they reflect their very different eras with uncommon accuracy. As a result, they moved me in a way I had not anticipated. The earlier of the two, with its invocation of tradition; with its reaffirmation of scholasticism and seminary rules and its flowery deference to Aquinas as the "Angelic Doctor"; with its confident assumption that the "mind of the Church" was a single, knowable, unchanging, normative entity only notionally distinct from the mind of God, and that the nature of the priesthood flowed clearly and inevitably from it; with its assumption, in fact, that everything a seminarian needed to know could be deduced from that divine/ecclesiastical mind and from the seminary authorities who (somehow) had direct access to it—this document drew me back to its world as soon as I began reading it. Sitting in the library, trying hard to maintain my stance as a researcher, I was *there* again, in the seminary of my memories and my nightmares. It washed over me, all the worst parts of it, along with some of its residual appeal, however retrograde I might judge it—and I began to cry, to the considerable surprise of the research librarian. The two days it took me to read the 1962 self-study were the most difficult research hours I have ever spent.

The 1969, post–Vatican II self-study had an equally strong effect on me for considerably different reasons. In its uncertainty, its acknowledgment of ambiguity, its apparent openness to change; in its attempt to shape working strategies instead of asserting a timeless truth; in its astonishing assertion, utterly unimaginable in my day, that "the priest as teacher must love his world, must live in it, must be extremely sensitive to it, must be able to agonize with it, grow with it" (3); in its more immediate and human voice—especially that—it did not ring true to anything I had experienced in the major seminary or in the church. It did ring true, however, to my classmates' descriptions of the Schuit years and of the sense of possibility it awakened in them. It evoked for me therefore not a world I knew but a world I missed knowing and might have taken to—no doubt would have taken to—had I not missed it.

Reading that document reminded me of a conversation I had had two years earlier with Father Frederick, a priest classmate who had studied philosophy in Europe during the years of the Vatican Council and who had returned there after ordination to earn a doctorate in theology; he now teaches at St. Francis. His description of the excitement he felt at a top-flight European university whose faculty were immersed in the Council; his sense of being on the cutting edge of something worth cutting; his memory of impassioned conversations with sophisticated, informed students from around the world about things that genuinely mattered; his realization that he could never see his old world in quite the same way again—all of this reminded me immediately of my own excitement when, after earning an M.A. from the University of Wisconsin in 1968, I took a job at Norfolk State and drove to Boston in my first car for eight summer weeks of curriculum development with other young instructors from all parts of the country, people who seemed to me to have read everything and wanted to use their knowledge to change the world.

My experience—a genuine awakening, however clichéd the term—was more secular than his and drove me further in that direction, but the energy we felt was similar; nor were our goals as different as I once thought. Talking with him and then realizing how dramatically the seminary had changed after I left did not make me want to return to the church. But together, the two experiences forced me to admit that I might well have had a different story if I had experienced what my classmates experienced, and that even with the differences, there was a common curve to our histories.

The Seminary Imprint

According to Erik Erikson,[13] it is during late adolescence and early adulthood that most young people form the emotional and conceptual grid through which they tend to view the world for the rest of their lives: hence, for instance, the enduring fear of poverty in the Depression-bred generation, the Cold War anxieties of many raised during or immediately after World War II, the career focus of young people who grew up amid the wild economic fluctuations of the 1970s and 1980s. Such a grid,

Erikson suggests, is not deterministic; it can be reshaped. But it is powerful and pervasive; if we are to change, we must confront it, work to
alter it. It is not likely to drop away of its own accord.

I have already suggested some of the ways in which the seminary
shaped my class, without specific focus on any one group. But at this
point it is worth emphasizing the ways in which the seminary has
shaped the outlook of those who stayed the full twelve years and were
ordained. Not having "left" the seminary, the priests in our class tend to
have less charged memories of it than those of us who did; they do not
have a broken connection between then and now to try to fathom. And
yet, precisely because of the continuity of their training with their later
priesthood, it is they who prove to have been shaped by the seminary
most thoroughly; it is they who have the full range of the seminary's
widely—even wildly—differing personalities between 1957 and 1969
imprinted on their memories.

Although there is no doubt that the great majority of them identify
most fully with the transformed seminary of the Schuit years, a few ca-
veats about the extent of its transformation and of its effect on them are
worth acknowledging. Most of my classmates, for instance, embraced
the spirit of liberal change at least in part because new authority figures
such as Sklba and Schuit had emerged to show them the way; in their
evolution toward a more questioning stance, the old habit of docility to
authority played its own ironic role. It is also true that the seminary was
still very much in process when they left it—and so were they; even in
its latter stages the seminary left them with more unfinished business than they would have preferred. Even though psychological and
emotional needs were beginning to be addressed by the time they were
ordained, the overall effect of twelve years of study and training, according to Mark Klugman, was that "you forgot that you still had a little animal running around inside, saying when it lightnings, 'I want to piss on
the rug too.' " And the central issues of celibacy and sexuality remained,
in Father Brent's ironic comment, "a greatly sublimated question."

Their social involvement had its limits as well. My classmates marched
in civil rights demonstrations, and some of them protested against the
Vietnam War—but still within the protection of the automatic draft de-
ferment granted to seminarians. When Bill Schuit drew the line and
threatened to withdraw deferments from those who protested on campus, the protests stopped. Within an institution which still provided
shelter—or imposed it—my classmates were, for the most part, confined
to what Father Herman describes as "watching intently from our seminary perspective those same issues" which dominated the decade.

Further, like some of their secular peers, my classmates seemed to feel
that further institutional change was now inevitable and would come
without resistance—and without much anguish on their part. "The fac-

ulty were not always honest with us about what this institution is about," according to a now-disillusioned Father Herbert. "If they had empowered us to change it right away, in formation, maybe we would have a better church today." And of course my classmates were buffered from the more obvious manifestations of the 1960s; there were no drugs on a seminary campus—not even alcohol in those days—no violent political protests, and certainly no liberated sexuality. The seminary world was small, and the changes it registered were partial.

Yet in context, the transformations in the seminary and in my classmates were dramatic and lasting nonetheless. They entered a seminary in 1957 where stasis was the norm; they were ordained from a seminary in 1969 where change, however partial, had become the norm. In fact, the unfinished quality of their experience was central, for it left them with things to do, with a sense of possibility and mission, with an appetite for more. And in terms of the *taste* of change and a taste *for* change, in the excitement engendered as they watched from within as *their* rigid institution actually began to open up, the twelve-year seminary veterans of 1957–69 experienced a form of institutional transformation that many of their secular equivalents would have envied. It promised to be a pervasive, radical change which would extend beyond its local manifestations to connect with something larger: the post–Vatican II openness which seemed to be altering the Catholic Church around the world almost beyond recognition.

It is important, in reading the chapters that follow, to remember my classmates' initial sense of hope and mission and the energy which their vision sparked in them. They were ordained, as one classmate remembers, into a church "with beautiful sunsets and sunrises, where all things were possible." They flew kites on their final retreat as metaphors for their sense of the future; they were ready to soar. On ordination day, Father Theodore, son of working-class parents for whom the priesthood was a dream, drove up and down the main street of his small home town blowing his horn and watching with glee as his friends and family came out to wave at him. Many of them felt, as Hans Ziegler did as he approached his first parish, that "this is the parish I'm assigned to, and I'm going to save all these people."

They felt that fundamental changes were possible within the church partly because their seminary experience had brought about fundamental changes in them. They had entered the minor seminary with an appreciation for tradition which their later liberalism (or for some, their later disenchantment) has never totally eradicated. They lived at that point under an authority whose legitimacy they respected; they aspired to exercise that authority themselves. But during their college years, they learned firsthand that tradition can harden into rigidity, that authority can degenerate into authoritarian rule. So they knew how it feels to be bound by arbitrary rules which seem to undermine spirituality and growth instead of fostering them. They knew what living under a rigid and autocratic system feels like to subjects who want and need more responsibility than they are granted. They knew, having seen their classmates leave, that not being granted responsibility and respect can lead to total withdrawal.

In short, they knew firsthand what price is exacted of a docile "flock"— the very kind of flock they had once aspired to lead. So it should not be surprising to see that so many of them have come to identify as strongly as they do with the laity rather than with the clergy, with the women in the church rather than with the male hierarchy, with the traditional "subjects" of the church rather than with its ruling authorities. It is not surprising that many of them shy away from exercising authority and that most of those who do have tried hard to redefine it in more egalitarian fashion. This basic shift in their loyalties has stayed with them throughout their priesthood, simultaneously drawing them closer to the church's "subjects" and pulling them farther away from the institutional church, now seen as the "subjugator."

And yet by staying in the seminary through the Schuit regime, they saw the institutional church, in its local manifestation, begin to open up, to break down its own hierarchies, to share authority, to respect its "subjects"; they saw it begin to reflect their own hard-earned values. They saw firsthand what a few good men like Schuit and Sklba could do to implement those values institutionally. Such priests became the underlying models of the *personalized* priesthood my classmates have refashioned for themselves.

With the fervor of converts, they came to think of themselves as standard-bearers of those values. They had entered the seminary as conservative idealists, committed to "saving the world." They were ordained as liberal idealists, convinced that they were part of a 1960s generation of priests unique in their commitment to "change the world." They relish this self-concept; yet it also cuts them off in their own minds both from their traditionalist predecessors, for whom the 1960s were at best an annoyance and at worst a fundamental threat, and from the neoconservative "new clerics" who followed, the Reagan/Bush–era priests whom they regard either as backsliders yearning for the days of automatic deference to priestly authority or as cynical opportunists without genuine idealism.

Father Brent gives voice to a widespread sentiment when he says, "I think we feel a greater sense of freedom, or greater sense of responsibility, to see that some of the creativeness and openness remain [in the church]. I think the groups before don't feel that tension in the same way and the groups after us don't." Father Albert expands on that conviction, coupling an even harsher critique of the younger generation of priests with stronger praise for his own:

> I think we grew up in the 1960s questioning many things, maybe even taught to think independently. I think the me-first generation growing up now is also being reflected in the church. The kind of people we are attracting to the seminary today seem to be coming for what the church can provide for them, a place of sanctuary and safety and security. I think in our era many people were attracted because they saw it as an opportunity to live out a vision, work that idealism into reality. . . . We had the cream of the crop. I don't see that coming up today. We are not attracting that kind of male.

To Father Thurman, now a professor of theology at a different seminary in the area, today's seminarians lack not only idealism but even basic religious conviction and fundamental integrity. His distress with them contrasts sharply with his admiration for his own generation:

> We went to the seminary to become priests. We actually, really meant it. So one of my great crushing blows early in my teaching career was to discover how many students really didn't give a shit whether Jesus was divine or human or both or what. And a second crushing blow came when I discovered that not very many guys really wanted to become holy or to pray. It was something they did in the seminary to get by the system. . . . Half the school finds this all just a big bore or an irritation.

My classmates' disdain for the younger generation is highly charged; it is emblematic, I think, of their anger at the current church, a new church starting to act old again. For if the movement from an unchanging church to a dynamic church was dramatic, so has been their frustration when they discovered that the church did not continue to change quickly or radically or automatically enough to satisfy them, when they discovered that in some ways it was retreating to a pre–Vatican II conservatism. "I'm in the last stages of grieving," laments Father Tod, "over the death of the church I was ordained in."

Marriage and Its Aftermath

Although to this point I have described the seminary as an institution with minor and major halves and various before and after stages, its full impact, especially on those who were ordained, can be seen only by considering the seminary as an anthropomorphic partner with which they developed a complex, changing, and highly personal relationship. This view reflects the deeply felt sense in which we all aimed to be "married to the church" instead of merely its employees; it illuminates the particular way in which my class first internalized and then became troubled by this basic, traditional metaphor of priesthood.

Our minor seminary years constituted, in a sense, a period of early dating and courtship with our future mate, a period to which we brought our youth and eagerness and a consequent willingness to bend to the seminary's wishes in order to please her. At the same time, the seminary showed its best face to us, luring us into a stronger commitment through a genuine initial display of support and warmth, along with a certain degree of flexibility. Of course, even in that period, the seminary had some of the irritating legalistic quirks which would harden later, at the major seminary. The classmates who were less happy at the minor seminary were those who noticed those traits and were bothered by them earlier than the rest of us.

Most of us, however, were still enamored at that time. Only after five years of courtship, after we committed ourselves more fully, did the seminary's less appealing tendencies reveal themselves to be major character flaws. We had gotten ourselves involved with someone rigid and distant and controlling, and by this point we had been in the relationship too long to pass over those qualities lightly. Hence for many of us, the romance ended. We broke off the relationship at its worst. Others stayed with her—they needed her more, they saw analogous rigidity in themselves and so couldn't put all the blame on her—and saw the relationship do what even long-term, stifling marriages can occasionally do: open up and become exploratory and exciting again. And having felt the relationship revive, my classmates were willing to make the final, seemingly lifetime commitment. They became priests; they married the church.

But it did not take long for the church to reveal anew her less attractive side; for Father Alex, for instance, the moment coincided with ordination itself:

> My ordination day was ruined. Monsignor John Francis Murphy, who was on the personnel board, came up to me as we were vesting in the basement of the rectory, and he said to me, "We haven't been able to give everyone a good situation, and yours is not the best." I said, "Where am I going? Who's the pastor?" He wouldn't tell me. Got into the cathedral, I was thinking about this, what a way to ruin . . . All of a sudden, this old, fat, short, bald-headed guy, when they're doing the imposition of the hands, he says, "Hey, you! You're coming with me." "Oh, God," I said, "who is that?" Oh Geez, how about that for a kicker, right?
>
> But I also remember very distinctly walking up, we were high, we had had a real touchy, touchy, feely, feely, sensitive retreat and we were all on a high. It was really wild. I remember walking up the steps from

the basement and we were singing, "Rise and shine, give God your glory, glory" and we were walking over to the cathedral. I was at the tail end. I remember seeing Archbishop Cousins standing at the top of the stairs, laughing to beat the band. That, and "Hey, you! You're coming with me." (*laughs*) Now ain't that a story?

Alex is still a priest, and by his own account, a happy one. But he cannot avoid the tension between the relationship he wants and a partner who still likes to say, peremptorily, "Come with me." My classmates were the first seminarians in the history of St. Francis to fly kites; those kites have now come down to earth. The issue for them now is how to find ways to keep from feeling completely grounded.

It is especially important to understand the extent to which my classmates were demoralized by the election of Pope John Paul II, about whom virtually none of them has anything good to say. Father Herbert remembers calling his best friend as soon as the bad news was announced and saying, "Have you heard? They elected the Polack! There go all of my hopes for the church!" Both of them laughed, desperately, for five minutes. John Paul II's attempt to move the church back to an earlier, more conservative and hierarchical model has had severe and direct impact on them; they see in his handiwork the institutional church's abandonment of the agenda of liberal change which made the priesthood so appealing to them at the point of ordination. So if the institutional church has reneged on its promises—its promise—how are they to view their own promises to it?

For under John Paul, from their perspective, they have seen their partner turning aside again, revealing her controlling side and forcing them to wonder what kind of men they are to stay with her. They now feel like "kept men," in Father Tod's terms; several of them complain that "the church has got us by the balls." Precisely what they are describing in these metaphors will become clearer later. The overall result, however, is that they are asking, once again, Whose fault is this, and what can we do about it? Do we want to stay with the church, for how long, and under what circumstances? The lure of divorce, for my classmates, is not an issue confined to the married.

3

Once a
Seminarian

*B*y the time the seminary began to reform, I was gone. I left
the seminary without making the final commitment, largely
because I didn't like what I had seen of her by that time; nor
did I like, as we say nowadays, the person I had become in the relationship. I left St. Francis at its most rigid, and I carried the image of seminary—and institutional—rigidity with me for a long time. I used it to
make my break from the church.

That did not happen immediately, however. After my senior year in
college, my own diocese sent me to Catholic University in Washington
for what would have been four years of theology. After one year, I left. In
my current, revisionary interpretation, I left in part because I no longer
enjoyed the security and status I had known at St. Francis, where I had
found a comfortable niche as a top student, a better than average athlete,
and a nice guy. On my weekends home from Milwaukee, my parents'
friends would come up to me after mass and tell me once again what a
wonderful thing I was doing. I felt special, was made to feel special, and
by not seeming to insist on that status, I became even more highly regarded.

But at Catholic University, surrounded by seminarians from around
the entire country, all of whom had been sent there because they seemed
exceptional, I no longer stood out; as far as I could tell, no one was say-

ing, "There goes Ray Hedin." I did not earn a spot on the seminary house football team or on its basketball team. I received no better than average grades in my theology classes. And to top it off, because Catholic University was coed, walking around campus in my cassock made me feel all the more insecure; insecurity as well as awakened desire brought the celibacy issue home to me. I had felt "called" to enter the seminary; now, with no one fussing over me, with no reinforcement, I wasn't sure enough of the "I" to be able to hear the call anymore.

So I left. My mother cried when I told her; my father nodded sadly. I cried too; but when I entered the University of Wisconsin to study literature, I became immersed quickly in a new life. I strained to understand works of literature to which I brought very little training or experience. I read James Baldwin's *Another Country*, with its aggressively existential insistence on the ability—the duty—of every human being to create his or her own identity without aid of convention or law or tradition, and I had literally no idea what he was talking about or how that might be done.

To dating I brought even less expertise; my first kiss, at age twenty-two, was a gingerly peck on the cheek of an undergraduate woman I dated for nearly a year, having met her on the way back to the dorm after church. In my two years at Wisconsin, I did not advance much from that start—ice has to thaw before it can even dream of boiling—which was the major reason she dropped me. I did, however, feel some of the political excitement of Madison in the late 1960s; I thawed socially first, from the outside in. I had plenty to adjust to, all right, but the process was exhilarating. I thought I had left the seminary, if not easily, at least for good—until the dreams started.

I came eventually to teach at a liberal university which, in the ten or fifteen years before I was hired in 1974, had earned a reputation as a place genuinely dedicated to its teaching mission and unusually concerned for the welfare of its faculty. Since then, however, in the process of embracing norms of behavior and achievement consistent with its current, exalted ambitions—looking for more respect and accepting the established terms for gaining it—Indiana University has lost much of what once made it distinct. So I find myself in a situation similar to that of my classmates: What does it mean that I have repeated my history in so many ways? What kind of person am I to need institutions and then to find them unsupportive and indifferent to what I thought were our shared goals? Is it worth staying, and under what terms? What kind of a person am I becoming (again?) by remaining here? Their questions are my questions; after twenty years, our shared concerns drew us together.

I began this project by concentrating on classmates who, like me, had left the seminary before ordination. I assumed that they would have stories closest to mine, would have the most to tell me. In most cases, this did not prove to be true. There were so many of them—128 in our original high-school class eventually dropped out—that it would have taken me years to see if there was the kind of metanarrative at work which I eventually thought I detected with the much smaller groups, the priests and the former priests. Nonetheless, based on those interviews and on the biographical sketches which 68 of us wrote for our class reunion booklet, a few generalizations are possible.

Although a few of my classmates have scattered to the edges of the country—California, Texas, Florida, New York—the great majority have stayed in the Midwest, with three-quarters still living in Wisconsin; geographically, we have not strayed far. The same is true professionally. Out of forty-seven jobs listed in the biographies, twenty are service-oriented: six therapists or psychologists, four high-school teachers, four college teachers (are we a service profession?), and a smattering of others—relatively short leaps from the seminary. Nineteen are businessmen. Nineteen (I am excluding the priests) have advanced degrees or at least have done post-graduate work. The wealthiest, as far as I can tell, are the former mayor of Oshkosh, Wisconsin, who now owns six Burger Kings and other extensive real-estate holdings, and a publisher who, in conjunction with his wife, has turned a program of Catholic reading materials for children into an extensive empire. We have produced no national figures, but in measurable areas—given the fact that the great majority of us come from relatively uneducated, nonprofessional parents—we haven't done badly.

Only one of us, a writer, could be considered a genuine freelancer; a few have shown impressive entrepreneurial skills. The rest of us have gravitated back to institutional or corporate settings. Only seven are single, two openly gay, and one classmate has had a sex-change operation. No one (including me) acknowledged divorce in the biographies, and I have evidence now of only two others. Approximately three-quarters have remained Catholic, at least by their own definition; only two labeled themselves atheists in the interviews. If there is anything common to most of us, it is that we have not been especially daring or deviant.

Otherwise, the closest thing to a shared link among the former seminarians was an intense memory of the seminary. On some, to be sure—usually those who left after only a few years—the seminary did not leave much of a mark. But with most of us who stayed at least into the major seminary, the experience still loomed large in a combination of memory and longing. For us the seminary was the site at which issues of meaning and identity and direction first came into focus and the touchstone to which we return in one fashion or other in order to judge where we are now, how far we still might need to go—and whether we need to find a way to somehow recapture what we had there. For us, the seminary was one of our deeply registered beginnings; and it has now become central again as we try to shape or reshape the middle of our lives. For this subgroup of those who left before ordination, "former seminarian" is an accurate though partial phrase: what we once were remains very much a part of what we are.

Of this group, Derek Hartman, although he would seem to have traveled further from his seminary days than anyone else in the class, is the strongest exemplar. His story, precisely in its extremes, suggests better than that of any classmate the issues raised by a seminary past, issues with which I began this book and which remain with me now, at its end.

I talked with Derek on Thanksgiving weekend 1987, in Minneapolis, where I had gone to see my sisters for the first time since our father died. Derek and I had belonged to different groups at St. Francis; he was a "knitter," even though his mannerisms were not as effeminate as those of the others, and I was a "jock," he reminds me. But in the seminary the lines of division were not as clearly marked or as exclusive as they are in many other schools, and Derek and I had always liked one another.

Derek acknowledges that I was one of a considerable number of classmates to whom he felt attracted; he remembers buying toothpaste for me once and typing an essay for me early one morning to help me meet a deadline. Those gestures may or may not have had an erotic tinge to them; if they did, I was too naive to notice, though I was not so naive that I didn't know what "knitters" suggested in our lexicon. In any case, Derek's gestures were characteristically generous.

My parents and sisters had liked Derek too; he had driven down from Wisconsin to visit several times, and they were drawn, as I was, to his friendliness, his energy, his verbal flagrance—which suggests that my parents were less narrow in their tastes than my memory generally gives them credit for. Now, arriving for Saturday morning breakfast, he sweeps in wearing a beret, one earring, and—this is the shocker to me—a zimarra. I thought those horrendous black longcoats had all been burned in our gleeful pre-graduation revel in the woods. Derek wears it with flair, actually looks good in it—although I cannot quiet a little voice that says, yes, I was right all along about those coats, they fit with the cassock all too well. In any case, no matter how whimsically he wears it, that Derek still has his zimarra is the first clue to me that he may not have traveled as far from the seminary as his surface mileage would suggest.

Derek has thought of himself as a misfit since his youth, when he was acutely aware of his awkwardness and his lack of interest in traditionally male activities. When he realized that he was gay, during middle school, he felt even more estranged from his peers. This pervasive sense of himself as an outsider intensified his appreciation for the community he found in the seminary, which he remembers more vividly and misses more acutely than any other member of our class:

> My sense of community is a group of people who are interested in
> something common other than themselves. There was something that
> we believed in and that was very energizing. We were going someplace.
> That was a wonderful motivator. I was so totally reinforced from the
> outside. That's unique. I don't have that in my life anymore. Now I'm
> on my own. People will say, "It's okay, do your own thing, blah, blah,
> blah." But those attitudes never provide the reinforcement that we got
> there, never. And I miss that. The seminary was a warm harbor. But
> maybe that's unreal. You just don't find that in life.

Yet for Derek, the price of belonging in the seminary was high. For
if sexuality in general was denied, homosexuality was doubly denied:
we were all assumed to be sublimating normal sexuality, not its deviant
forms. The major seminary was at least consistent to its unspoken fears:
we were forbidden to enter one another's rooms. But the minor seminary
acted as if heterosexuality were the only sexuality to worry about: no
girls allowed, therefore, but plenty of naked male bodies available for
observation. Hence, for Derek, life in the dormitory—seventy boys in
one room—was constant excitement, constant anguish, especially at
shower time: "I'd see these wonderful bodies and I'd just want to fall all
over them." His arousal was matched only by his conviction that "there
was something wrong" with him for feeling this way.

His pain was heightened by the fact that homosexuality was literally
unspeakable. For traditional Catholics of our generation, the church had
the mythic, godlike power to name and to judge by naming—saint, sin-
ner; believer, unbeliever; seminarian, ex-seminarian (defined by cancellation, like ex-priest). The church's power to name was the power to give
us identity, to shape us into what we were to become: believers through
baptism, adult Christians through confirmation, priests through ordination, forgiven through confession—and less officially but no less powerfully, "good people" through repeated seminary acclamation.

The church also assumed the awesome power to refuse to name at
all—as in "non-Catholic"; it left those who did not fit its definitions
without any ontological status, with no identity at all—even a negative
one—to cling to. And precisely because seminarians sought to belong to
the church in the fullest sense, we tended to internalize its judgments;
thus its refusal to acknowledge those who did not fit its traditional
standards could be devastating:

> I had a couple of men that I spent a lot of time with. I would say, "I love
> you," and then we would hold each other and do all kinds of things
> that were splendid. But what amazes me is that in these connections we
> never said, "I am gay" or "We're homosexuals." There was no way you
> could even voice this then. It could not be spoken; I could not say the
> words. So through a lot of rosaries and stuff I pushed the fact that I am
> gay away, even though I was madly attracted to many people in the
> seminary.

After two years of college, Derek began to feel that the communal bond was no longer there for him. "I would see these people in groups," he says, "laughing and talking and smoking cigarettes, and I knew that I didn't want to be in those groups. It was time to go someplace." But where to go and what to do was unclear to him. His parents and his pastor, very supportive when he entered the seminary, had little useful advice for him now that he wanted to leave it. He is particularly bitter about his assigned spiritual advisor, whose notion of smoothing Derek's path out of the seminary was to deliver a diatribe against sexuality and marriage:

> He had a newspaper in his hand, it was showing women's clothes. "See this bra, see this lingerie? You get married and all they want is more of this stuff." What a hell of a thing to say to somebody. It was atrocious.

It was as if everyone within his Catholic culture refused to conjure a positive identity beyond the seminary; to name alternatives would be to validate them.

Without much focus, Derek transferred to a small Catholic college and entered a "phase of just craziness." This was 1963, a time when "to be gay was still a disease. It was a sickness, you were mentally disordered." So, like many of us who left the seminary but not its prescriptions, for a long time he concentrated on trying to do what he felt he should do without consulting—or even knowing—what he wanted to do. And because he felt that he should be heterosexual, he felt he could be; God, we knew, never asks the impossible.

He managed to graduate, then entered a midsize midwestern university to study philosophy. He laughs at this choice now, seeing it as another example of his inability to imagine anything not validated by his seminary past. Ill-equipped to make decisions on his own, he transferred to the University of Wisconsin to study German, another subject from his seminary training. He hated the German program, however, and became a "recluse totally focused on my own misery." He describes that year and a half as "horrible"; he slept fourteen hours a day, subsisting on Wheaties, Mounds bars, and coffee.

Listening to Derek's recurring lament that "nobody ever told me what to do," a lament whose tone was self-directed irony rather than self-pity, I remembered an incident which occurred in my own life in the summer of 1968. I had just finished my M.A. at Wisconsin, had signed up to teach at Norfolk State, and was on my way to Boston for a summer conference of all the teachers in the thirteen-college consortium of which Norfolk State was part. I was driving the first car I ever owned, a 1964 Chevy Belair, a car I had picked out in preference to a 1965 Impala because I did not want to show off the newfound wealth of my first job; I was not about to be "of the world" even as I raced to catch up with it.

Halfway across Ohio on Interstate 80, I suddenly came upon a complicated set of underpasses and offshoots. I couldn't read the signs quickly enough, so I sped on through, then pulled over and discovered that I had made a mistake which would cost me twenty miles to correct. I remember very clearly the panic I felt precisely because *no one had been there to tell me what to do.* Isn't someone supposed to be taking care of this for me? Where is Father Busch now that I need him? Am I really going to have to make these decisions on my own? And if this is what traffic signs can do to me, what am I in for?

It took Derek several more years before he accepted his sexual orientation. In the meantime, however, he met Suzanne, a woman he liked more than those he had dated in college, and he married her. The marriage felt wrong from the start; he would look through gay magazines "just to remind myself, just getting in touch, even though I wasn't willing to say that that was really what I was interested in. But at least the possibility was quietly and bizarrely affirmed." It was not until several years into his marriage, after his son was born, that he finally became sexually involved with a man. He describes the awkward beginnings of that relationship with a decided glee at its gothic trappings; yet he was still struggling internally at the time, and his residual uneasiness with his behavior then shows through even now:

> This guy owned an abandoned home near my house. An old house, no power, no windows, stairway was torn out. That's where I had my first sexual experience after many years. I crawled up this old ledge late at night, dark, on this musty old mattress, and there I was—Christ, what was I, maybe thirty-three or thirty-four, and my son was home sleeping and here I am on this mattress. There was an old radio playing downstairs and the house was abandoned. Then he moved up in the attic where my son's bedroom is now. So he was living there even before Suzanne moved out, which is tacky, really. (*laughs*) It really was. (*laughs*) That was kind of crappy.

Eventually he and Suzanne both became sexually involved with this same man. Derek's description of this triangle and of their eventual divorce party—close to a hundred guests, readings from Anne Morrow Lindbergh on "the dance of life," and all in all "a splendid evening"—suggests how far he had swung, at least on the surface, from the norms of the 1950s seminary into behavior more often associated with the liberated 1960s.

The divorce put an end to his attempts to reorient his sexuality; all of his relationships since then have been with men. In the biographies each of us wrote for the class reunion, Derek described himself as "active in gay issues"; to me he spoke openly and with ease of his homosexuality.

Achieving this comfort zone, however, involved a considerable reorientation. He grew up, he says, "thinking that truth came down from the hierarchy," but he eventually came to feel that it is legitimate to trust himself, that "if I try to give things my honest presence and try to be the person I am destined to be, what more can I do?"

> I really do believe that I have within me the knowledge I need to move me through life. I'm intrigued by tapping the larger consciousness which often goes unspoken. I began to realize that significant parts of my life don't fit church structure. I began to see spirituality not as an unquestioning embrace of some external formula, rather as a discovery of the health that lies deep within each of us. In terms of the sexuality issue, these are just expressions of emotions I feel and there's nothing wrong. It becomes wrong only if it's abused, like for any sexual expression. It is an expression of a person I need to be, and am.

On the face of it, Derek's reliance on his own instincts and on the "larger consciousness" within is an extraordinary achievement; the seminary's emphasis on docility to institutional authority did little to foster an Emersonian embrace of our inner impulses. And yet his self-trust is not as unusual as one might expect from men nurtured in the culture of original sin; I discovered a great deal of it even among the priests in our class. For in the seminary, alongside all the talk of human weakness and necessary dependence on the "mind of the church," we received a strong countermessage: that we were the salt of the earth, that we were chosen, that we were good. Specialness is a powerful antidote to self-doubt.

It is also true that the seminary taught us to examine our consciences scrupulously, to look inside ourselves every day to root out our flaws. Within the highly circumscribed lives we led, however, few spectacular corruptions were there to be found; on the whole, we did not become a guilt-ridden lot. Furthermore, once we were out of the seminary, but not free of introspection, many of us became even more inclined to accept what we saw within, especially in contrast to the behavior we often saw around us.

In short, in our post-seminary lives we did not have to discover for ourselves, from scratch, that "I'm okay"; we did not simply learn that message from the mainstream culture of the 1970s and beyond. We had the conviction all along; paradoxically, the authoritative church taught it to us, or at least equipped us to see ourselves that way.

As Derek became more comfortable with his homosexuality, he became less comfortable with the institutional Catholicism which continued to condemn it. As the balance shifted, he did not decide to leave the church so much as he sloughed it off: his newly confident self did not fit his old skin.

> I often see this kind of candle with me; you know how the candle just flickers out when the wax is gone. I see my leaving the church in that way. I could tell the candle was burning down if I ever bothered to look at it; but I apparently never looked at it. It was not a real upsetting thing for me. It just piddled away.

*   *   *

By all external measures, then, and by his own internal standards as well, Derek has moved as far from his seminary origins as anyone in the class. And yet it is clear from his conversation that he longs *somehow* to integrate the self he has become with the church he once valued.

For Derek, the seminary has played a central role in this journey of symbolic return. One of the first things he mentioned in our interview was the immense satisfaction he felt from having been permitted to stay overnight at the seminary several years ago with one of his lovers. Derek's tone in describing this visit was triumphant but not flaunting; he was and still is exhilarated at what he chooses to see as an implicit institutional blessing on his homosexuality. In this one case, at least, he was able to go home again on his own terms:

> I just delighted in this. It was very important to me to spend the night with Larry in Hennie Hall, in the guest room which used to be Father Ledworowski's room where we used to go for permissions, because the whole seminary totally canceled me out as a gay person. It was orgasmic just getting in that room and I thought, "Yeah, I have finally put all my perversions in this whole fucking dump: here it is." (*laughs*) It was a real sacred little pilgrimage for me. It was a great joy. It was like pulling the loose ends of a tapestry together and going back to the home fires to tie those final knots so it won't fall apart anymore.

Derek has been affiliated primarily with the Unitarian Church for twelve years. Yet his desire for reconnection finds an echo in his current activities on behalf of Dignity, the organization of gay Catholics to which he has also belonged for the last ten years. Dignity contains "a lot of people whose journeys are very similar to mine; we're people in exile." And since it is the Catholic Church that exiled them, it is the Catholic Church from which they most want recognition and acceptance.

In 1987, when the Archdiocese of St. Paul evicted Dignity from the Newman Center, Derek, as president of the local chapter, sued for reentry on the basis of a city ordinance banning rental discrimination against gays. He sued not only for the right to use a building but to finish the psychic business left incomplete by his (merely) private pilgrimage back to the seminary: he wanted, at last, to assert his sexual identity publicly in the presence of the church, to be heard in his own voice by the church which has so for so long considered him unspeakable:

> There was a unanimous vote at the meeting that I chaired last year. I said, "You know, I don't care what comes of the lawsuit, but my own self-esteem and my own embrace of myself demand that I pursue this course. I don't give a shit what happens. At least we've made a statement."

And yet, in spite of his conflict with the archdiocese, he finds individual Catholic priests warmer and more receptive than the Unitarian ministers he has known. Crucially, he finds the priests more willing to grant verbal recognition to gays—to grant them the dignity of a name—even in the act of questioning their sexuality:

> My Unitarian minister at church, Ralph, in the twelve years that I've gone there, the words "gay lesbian" have never fallen from his lips. I said to Ralph, "You know, there is something about naming the fact that we exist." The Catholic priest I know talks about gay lesbian people. Just the fact that he is willing to admit the fact . . .

The importance Derek places on being acknowledged verbally would later help me understand the resentment felt by my priest classmates at the church's restrictive naming policies: I am a priest, to be sure, a number of them said; but I am also a man, a human being, and yet the church does not recognize that, does not *call* me human, certainly does not call me a *man*—and hence does not feel obligated to treat me accordingly.

Derek still dreams of an ideal community which would incorporate the sense of mutual support and common purpose he once knew with the sexuality he has since discovered. It would be a place where he could be whole in public and in private; it would pull together what was torn asunder in his past. Appropriately, most of the men with whom he shares this vision are gay former seminarians; what they long for would be, in effect, the seminary reshaped to accommodate them:

> I glorify in my memory that whole context of community. I miss it desperately at times. I know I function best if I'm with other people who share common visions; I do real well. Alone I'm capable of tremendous inertia. I also realize how much we can enrich the lives of one another, and I've become convinced a lot of that is lost unless it finds an appropriate home in a community context. In my memory I see that in the seminary: doing a lot, getting a lot done.
> I have a group of gay men, we are all in our forties and fifties. We talk regularly about coming together in a community when we get older and retire. I think that could be a beautiful thing to come together—sure.

In fact, Derek has taken tentative steps back toward the very center of what he once left, envisioning "the possibility of yet even a larger, warmer embrace." When his children get out of high school, he imagines that he might want to become a priest. As a result, he has investigated the possibility of a marriage annulment, since "I've got to clear the board" before going any further.

How a celibate priesthood would be compatible with the active (homo)sexuality he shows no inclination to renounce is not clear to Derek; he admits, "I don't know where I'm going with this, and I really don't care now. It's a time without thought in terms of plotting." At this point he is simply trying to live out his philosophy of trust, to let go of the controls and allow his "journey" to take its own shape.

Derek's central dilemmas are shared by many of us on whom the seminary registered deeply. For most of his stay, he loved it there; but eventually he had to leave it to preserve himself. Thus he redefined but did not ignore the church's mandate to "save his soul" at all costs. He has learned to trust his instincts—and has thus continued to follow that redefined mandate. Yet those instincts, perhaps more thoroughly informed by his seminary training and by the pervasively Catholic culture of his youth than he would wish, now move him to return *somehow*; because the satisfaction of belonging to something larger than himself is still central even to his redefined notion of salvation.

Many of us have declared our independence from the church; but declarations of independence do not wipe out our memories of the mother country, nor of the needs which were satisfied there. Derek would like to recapture for his present self the church's blessing on the very acts by which he severed from it; he wants the church to say that he's okay—now, as he is.

Listening to him, I recognize (and squirm at the realization) how strong that desire is in me as well. I fantasize from time to time about being invited back to the seminary to teach or lecture; sitting on a beach in Greece in 1971—as far as I ever got from home—I wrote a long letter to the seminary offering to teach there, although I never mailed it. Much later, during these interviews, when some of the priests in my class indicate that I'm doing okay—still okay, complications and all—their acceptance means more to me than I want it to.

I also feel that need in relation to my present institution. I want the university to bless me for doing the very things—teaching, for instance, with more energy than I give to research, or writing this book rather than a more narrowly defined, recognizably literary treatise—that separate me from its central tenets. After a long struggle to know what I really value doing, I want to maintain the sense of myself which those chosen activities make possible; like Derek, I have come to trust my instincts that these endeavors are good. Yet I can't help wanting the institution to value me for them at the same time.

Like Derek, I don't want to change back; he and I would both like our institutions to do the changing, to become the kind of institution which would "embrace" us and to declare us healthy instead of deviant. That approval would put into place—or so we imagine—the final, missing element in a hard-won identity which developed precisely through the process of distancing from the institution, but which remains incomplete or unsatisfying as long as that distance remains. Once a seminarian, always a seminarian: having felt institutional support/validation at our core in our formative years, we continue to need it.

That need has some advantages, to be sure. For it underlies our legitimate hope that the institutions to which we look for support might learn to accept and value things outside their traditionally narrow frame of reference. And even if we are being naive in those hopes, isn't that naiveté potentially useful? How else are seemingly fixed institutions to change if someone does not naively insist that they do? Isn't it possible—the priests in my class will raise this question again—that the desire to feel personally at home in our institutions is the necessary engine of change, the only sufficient (personalist) motivation, finally, for anyone aiming at larger reforms?

The problem, of course, is that the desire to feel at home can be a prod to wistful, passive longing rather than to action; it can degenerate, in psychoanalytic terms, into a regressive fantasy, an unrealistic, futile yearning to bathe the independent adult in the security and affirmation of the child, to recover a pre-Oedipal unity of child and mother.

For those of us who feel that we once had something of value which we need again, where is the line between unattainable fantasy and necessary reconnection? I think about this as I undertake, soon after talking with Derek, to return to the seminary.

4

Stirring Up Ghosts

*I*t is September 1988, and I find myself back at the major semi-nary, where, thanks to the help of Father Frederick, I have ar-ranged to stay for the next ten days. The seminary will provide a base for my first extended interviewing trip, and living there will give me at least a glimpse into how the place has changed since I left it twenty-three years ago. As it turns out, the seminary's uncertainties of identity and direction will make it a fitting place for me to begin.

I arrive with mixed feelings. I feel exhilarated to be away from Bloom-ington and my own tensions for the first extended period in years; but venturing so near to my old turf, the turf of my old self, makes me un-easy. "It looks to me," one of my Bloomington friends said as I was pre-paring to leave, "like you're hoping to put some ghosts to rest." My re-sponse was, "No—I want to stir them up again." I can't be sure exactly what I will stir up, however. I have spent a lot of energy trying to leave this place once and for all, and I can't return to it casually, any more than I could receive communion casually.

I drive onto the grounds from South Lake Drive. It feels odd to be entering that way. As a seminarian I never had a car, would not have been allowed to have one. My wheels announce—I hope—my changed status; they will define me, buffer me. Or so I think until I pull up to park in front of Heiss Hall and see one of the seminarians emerging from his car. I get out, wonder whether to lock (who are these guys nowadays?), decide that I will; I need to feel safe here.

I look up at the entrance of Heiss Hall, built in 1956, which I still think of as the "new" theology building; it is now half-empty, so that I have had no trouble being allocated what was once a student room. The building is Y-shaped, and I am facing its prongs now. I cannot help but think that the arms of the church are extending themselves to—what?—embrace me? Smother me? I'm taking this too seriously already, and I know it.

Sunday afternoons were always depressing for me at St. Francis. Very little organized activity took place at that time, and yet we couldn't leave. I felt particularly enclosed then, cut off, lonely; the protectedness of the seminary was not appealing at such moments. Now as I walk around, I see a young couple pushing a stroller. They look relaxed, with no sense of awe or violation; for them, this is just a nice place to walk. I feel a welcome shock of change—and a residual surge of outrage: how dare they intrude, how dare the seminary let them intrude in my day? And why am I thinking of it as an intrusion?

A couple in a car (Are they married? I wonder. Would mere lovers feel comfortable here?) stop me to ask directions to the book sale they saw advertised in the paper. Why are they asking me? Do I look like I belong here? "I don't know for sure," I hear myself saying, "I'm just visiting. If it isn't in the library, it might be in the gym; they're both around to the right."

I had missed Bloomington's best annual book sale by making this trip, so I follow them to the Miller Gymnasium, the "old gym" even twenty years ago, where I played so many of the games which are still in my head. This is the gym where I once was carried off on the shoulders of my minor seminary teammates after I sank a twenty-five-foot jump shot to send our annual game with the major seminary into overtime and eventual victory. Now the gym proper is closed and locked; through the windows I see storage boxes along the sidelines, spilling out onto the floor.

The book sale is downstairs, in what was once the "smoker," the aptly named room where the non-jocks huddled every day to play cards. No signs of that now; the room is filled with books on jerrybuilt shelves, in boxes, in heaps on the floor. I recognize Father Fetterer, the librarian, behind a cash box; I would have expected him to be dead by now. I introduce myself—I'm Ray Hedin, I used to be a student here, I teach at Indiana University now. (In my journal from this trip I wrote, "I told Father Fedderer that I was teaching now at St. Francis"—and then, months later, looking back at my notes, I wrote in the margin, "No, Ray—you teach at IU.") I barely knew the man when I was a student here, but, irrationally, I expect to be recognized. He nods pleasantly, goes back to his receipts. I notice several books from the old minor seminary, stamped with its seal, books I remember seeing on the shelves thirty years ago, now being cleared out: no audience for them, no minor seminary. I buy a number of books, surprised and elated that in my professorial stage I can find books I want at a seminary book sale.

I leave the gym and walk what was once my regular after-dinner route, through the woods along the path which touches the outer limits of the grounds; this was the seminary at its most secluded, the most attractive side of its seclusion. I find myself remembering an argument I had, walking this path, with Scott Lawson, one of my best friends, who had just announced that he was leaving the seminary after college graduation because he wasn't happy and wanted to be. I argued with him that being happy was beside the point, that if you are called, you have no choice but to respond. Scott, now married and a prominent therapist, keeps reminding me of that argument whenever I see him; he wants me to retract, hopes that I am now freed from what he sees as duty-bound rigidity.

But I don't retract, not wholly; so we revive the argument. It strikes me still that the scholastics had this one right, that happiness is a by-product of doing something worth doing rather than a direct object. The sticking point for me now is not the notion of by-product but the issue of "worth doing." Is marriage worth the effort? Is monogamy worth it? Is divorce worth the pain? Who gets to say what is worthwhile, and in what terms? The church, one's local institution, the self? Is it worth it, for instance, for me to do the kind of writing which is not personally rewarding but is highly rewarded by the university? Is teaching, which I do enjoy, worth it when the university pays it so little regard? Does the question of worth—"worth doing"—circle back inevitably to include self-satisfaction as the essential element, so that happiness, or at least satisfaction-in-doing, becomes central to the definition after all? Yet if something is *only* satisfying but not acknowledged or rewarded externally, can it remain worthwhile—still give satisfaction—over the long haul, against the grain of our larger context, especially for those of us who gravitate to institutions because, seemingly, we want to be part of something larger, we need their reinforcement, we need to feel aligned? I wish these were "academic" questions for me (is that term really synonymous with "meaningless"?), but they are not; I will discover soon that they are crucial issues for my classmates as well.

As I walk past the cemetery in the heart of the woods and look at the gravestones of the nuns who served us and whom we took utterly for granted, I realize with a start that in my three years and hundreds of walks at St. Francis, I was never curious enough to find out who was buried here. It occurs to me that I am trying to evoke for myself a past which was not always very present to me at the time; I am trying now to immerse myself in a world which, in my characteristic removal from my (earthly) context, I skimmed over then. The past, according to Styron, Faulkner, and just about anybody who considers the issue, is never dead; it is not even past. But for me, the problem is that the past was not fully alive at the time; I was not fully alive at the time. I used to be known for a deadpan sense of humor—"It's amazing," friends would tell me, "your expression never changes"—but it was more dead than deadpan; I wasn't controlling my feelings, I wasn't aware of having any. Those I had, I froze; I have been trying to thaw ever since.

I was notorious in the seminary for having a terrible singing voice. I have a better voice now; tension, I have discovered, locates itself in my throat. This trip, this project, is in part an attempt to breathe awareness and life back into an old self which didn't have much of either at the time, to let go of the controls I imposed on myself then and which still have their power over me. I had an intense sense of purpose in those days—of vitality in that sense; but partly because the purpose mandated removal from the things of this world, I had very little presence to my own experiences. Now, twenty-some years later, I have (gradually, with effort—it is an ongoing issue) become more present to my life. I have also lost some of that purpose; going back to its origins is part of the project too.

I complete my circuit of the campus; the buildings are unchanged externally, but inside every one of them are signs of retrenchment, if not abandonment. I walk into the dining hall, where the student body once ate together in a large, open area and the faculty ate separately. Now, at breakfast and dinner, the entire student body eats in the small room where the faculty once ate. The large dining hall is used only at noon, when faculty, seminarians, lay students (mainly women), and staff mingle, violating all the class/gender strictures of the old regime—at least until dinnertime, when the women are gone and the faculty retreat to a different, smaller enclave.

Kiley Hall, the "new" auditorium—where the yearly Shakespeare play was presented; where the St. Thomas Day "disputatio" was always held; where the entire student body sat to listen to Kennedy announce the Cuban Missile Crisis; where I had the leading role in *Arsenic and Old Lace* five days after Kennedy was shot in 1963, in front of the most desperately receptive audience imaginable—was now boarded up. I look hard at it, trying to make it look decrepit, worthy of neglect; it still looks new to me. I had expected to stir up ghosts by returning here, but I had not expected to be confronted so literally with a ghost institution; nor had I expected to feel so depressed at the thought of its demise.

Only in Henni Hall are there suggestions of renovation to counter the decay. Henni Hall was the centerpiece of the old seminary; it was residence hall/classroom building/chapel for the entire college section during the three years I was there. In my first year at the major seminary, I could look from my fourth-floor window and see Lake Michigan past the tree-lined entrance drive. Now no one lives in that room, nor on the entire floor. Most of the building lies in disuse.

Yet parts of it have been cleaned up and taken over by diocesan offices. And in the next two years, after considerable debate about the future of the seminary—as a rediscovered alumnus and potential donor, even I was sent a questionnaire—the entire building would be refurbished to the tune of $4.7 million, and all the other buildings would be sold or leased. In the process, Henni Hall would become the emblem of a seminary system simultaneously shrinking and renovating, without being certain which process would predominate.

The refurbishing would evoke in the priests and seminarians I talked with a full range of responses, often shrill. Some were happy that the seminary could still carry on in stylish if condensed fashion and were grateful that seminary traditions—and their own past—would not be totally lost in a transformation into expensive lakefront condos. Others, at a time when inner-city parishes were at risk of going under and priestly salaries remained frustratingly low, expressed outrage at the expense, at what they saw as the lavish scale of the rector's quarters, the church's continuing anachronistic preference for brick and mortar, and the diocese's refusal to recognize hard facts and simply close up shop. "Whatever we can save, fine, if it's legitimate," one of them said; "but let's cut the shit. We're saving these things as if they're Leonardo da Vinci." When is renovation worth the price?

I cover the entire campus—about fifty acres, heavily wooded, very pretty now as it was then, though even more melancholy; the grounds themselves have changed very little, except that the athletic fields have grown wild. There are not enough students to fill intramural teams anymore. The seminary itself—its physical presence, the limits it set by simply being what we could not go beyond, the possible activities it defined for us to the exclusion of all others—is much less the focus of the seminarians' attention now. They come and go almost at will; on a Sunday afternoon like this, most of them are at home. The seminary (like the priesthood?) is not their entire world now; it is the place where they study, where they train for their careers.

Passing what was once the touch football field, I wallow in the memory of one of my few triumphs there, a sixty-five-yard touchdown run after catching a little swing pass. It was a run during which I was shiftier than I knew how to be, and my classmates, realizing the small miracle they had witnessed, mobbed me afterward. That run, and a number of five- or ten-minute spurts on the basketball court, where I was, again, quicker and more fluid than the slow white guy I usually was, were my most memorable early experiences of transcendence, of exceeding my limits and feeling a consequent euphoria. They never took place in chapel, where I made them the direct object of my concentrated effort and hence failed. In chapel, during mass and daily prayers and mandatory meditation, I was known for falling asleep in positions expressly calculated to keep the human body alert.

Yet after all those years of trying to disconnect my present sense of self from the person I was here, I find myself realizing, as I look at the goal line I stumbled over at the end of my colossal effort, that my abiding concern (if not fixation) with transcendent experiences—an ardent desire for them, a sense of frustration when I don't experience them often enough or intensely enough—has its origin here, where I first experienced them and therefore knew that they could be had on this earth. It is one effect of the seminary on me that I can acknowledge and embrace—although it has its underside as well, in my pervasive discontent with the usual and the mundane, with the people closest to me when they fail (as I see it) to excite me, with "this world," and with my ordinary, day-to-day, decidedly untranscendent self.

Those team games, unlike anything else I did here, engaged my deepest energies and concentration. They were individual and communal at the same time; they activated my best stuff, the self alive in service of something larger. In the process they occasionally raised me beyond my ordinary level. Teaching does that now, occasionally, and in the interviews/conversations I will soon undertake, I will be surprised to see my priest classmates respond by calling such experiences spiritual, comparing them to what they—also occasionally—experience during the liturgy or while giving homilies. I will be surprised also at how satisfying I find that designation (am I spiritual after all?) and at my apparent willingness to regard their approbation as validating.

When I return to Bloomington, I have a long talk with Ivona, tell her that the issue of spirituality has been revived for me, and that I'm afraid she, a lifetime atheist, will have little respect for that revival. But she surprises me, saying that she has always considered herself spiritual and has felt similarly frustrated at not knowing where to go with that realization. It is one of the best talks we have had, the first of a good many.

That first night, I eat with the students, as I will for the next ten days. A Mexican student sits down with me, asks immediately if I am married, nods appreciatively when I say yes. Some of the students ask me who I am, why I am there. A few seem interested; the rest carry on. I had half hoped to be seen as a returning veteran, a man of experience, an envoy from the big world with urgent messages to convey. I want the students to reactivate the sense of specialness I enjoyed as a seminarian, to assure me by their attention that I haven't lost it. But these seminarians know more about the big world than I did at their age, are much less in awe of my past than I am; they do not feel driven to sit at my feet.

During my stay, I find myself lapsing into sexual numbness. This is not what I had in mind by reviving my old self. I'm away from home, freer than usual, uncertain about my marriage; I could explore the city. But in this setting, I can't even imagine doing that; the seminary seems to be icing me down again.

Yet my married status seems to spark thoughts of sexuality in the seminarians. One of them becomes friendly over the next several days, talks with me about celibacy. He tells me he's thirty-eight, has lived with five women for periods of one to five years; he has financed two abortions after threatening to leave otherwise. He knows that at least some of his fellow seminarians have been "around the block" a few times; others haven't made it to the corner. He had the "love of his life" twenty years ago. Now he's been celibate for two years. He expects celibacy to be hard, but not as hard as it would have been twenty years ago. He says he sees at least some wisdom in the church's traditional rationale for celibacy; it would be hard to serve two masters at the same time. He seems to be laboring to endorse this argument; but then I could be projecting my own skepticism onto him. I also realize that in my own life there are analogous tensions between competing claims—between writing and family, for instance—and that I have not been able to resolve them; but I do not admit this to him.

At lunchtimes, if I am not out conducting interviews, I eat in the large dining hall and meet several of the lay women who now make up a significant segment of the student body. They seem energetic, friendly, purposeful, committed to service—a livelier lot, at first and superficial glance, than many of the seminarians. They attract me; but, I remind myself several times, their theology does not. I do not believe; I do not. Yet I admire them for acting on what they believe.

My university colleagues, I realize, are similarly interesting, perceptive, stimulating, often more so; and they aren't driven by a theology I don't accept. They are driven, in part, by the desire to be stimulated, the real lure beneath the more grandly phrased "life of the mind." But beyond that ultimately self-oriented urge, which I share, most academics, careers uppermost, cannot afford to indulge in service; for "service" is a category which barely registers on the university scale. I don't feel that I belong at St. Francis by a long shot, but I am intrigued as well as disturbed by the fact that I feel more comfortable with these women than with my colleagues.

After ten days at St. Francis, I move to Weakland Hall, now the dormitory for the college seminarians attending Marquette University. I make the move willingly to fill out my picture of the current seminary, but also because staying at St. Francis has not reaffirmed my sense of being special. I have no rational claim on specialness, I know that its lingering assumption has been my curse for twenty years; yet I still respond with silent pique when I am not fussed over.

The idea of moving downtown for five days excites me. After all these years, I'll get a glimpse at seminarians living in the world in a way that my classmates and I could only fantasize about. Weakland Hall, named after the current archbishop—a gesture toward the contemporary in itself—sits on the corner of 23rd and Wisconsin, downtown Milwaukee's main east-west street, just off the western edge of the Marquette University campus, in a neighborhood which is considered slightly disreputable and marginally dangerous at night. I park across the street at the seedy hotel which offers space to Weakland visitors like me—the bell captain is friendly; he thinks highly of Father Andrew, the priest who supervises the dormitory—and walk to the entrance. I pound on the locked door, finally catching the attention of the receptionist inside, who lets me in after I explain who I am and assert that Father Andrew is expecting me. Several third-floor student rooms, she tells me, have been burglarized recently by someone climbing in a window in open daylight. The doors of the building are locked at all times; she gives me a key and tells me not to let in any passers-by.

I track down Father Andrew, just emerging from a student conference. He is immediately friendly, as he is on my subsequent visits; Andrew is a former dog trainer who retains the warmth of the genuine animal lover. He takes me into his office, which fronts Wisconsin Avenue and offers a view of the street—and street people—just a few feet beyond the window. He likes this location, he tells me; it's important for the seminarians not to be isolated. He talks to the street people frequently himself, does what he can for them. The building, he tells me, was formerly a Ramada Inn whose owner decided to halt its slide into disrepute by selling it to the diocese. I smile; I enjoy the idea of seminarians living where prostitutes once did business. Like Father Andrew, I prefer to regard this not as a conversion from sin to grace but as an acknowledgment of continuity, that the "world" and the church are no longer entirely discrete, that the business of the latter is in and with the former.

We talk for forty minutes. When I apologize for taking so much of his time, he leans forward, touches my arm, and says, "Ray, my time is not all that important." The gesture seems genuine—and unlike anything I have heard recently on my own campus, where most of us claim to be busy all the time. (When a university colleague, a good friend with a similarly intense Catholic background, read this section, he said that to him this comment smacked of self-hate rather than generosity; it suggested the church's continuing denigration of self under the guise of attention to others. I see his point, and not seeing it earlier makes me wonder about my claims to have put my old ways behind; yet Andrew's gesture still strikes me as sincere.)

He shows me the guest room on the second floor, a student room indistinguishable from motel rooms everywhere. Its one touch of seminary austerity is the thin, creaky mattress; but the size of the room along with its private bathroom and shower puts it in a class beyond anything in my own seminary experience.

My room is across from the student lounge, which is not used very much, since the students have TV's, stereos, and refrigerators of their own. But the lounge does contain the floor phone, and I spend a good deal of time in the next five days taking calls from Sharon, Rebecca, and Sandy for William, Anthony, and Emanuel. I become adept at this: "No, he's not in; he may be in his history class; can I take a message?" I learn not to say, "Oh, is this Sara?" when I hear a voice asking for Richie and sounding much like Sara's did yesterday; it may turn out not to be Sara this time.

I come to enjoy this; I feel like a go-between not only for the students but between my past and their present: I can adapt, I'm not locked into some antiquated sense of what a seminarian is supposed to be. In fact, though, I come quickly to think of the residents as "students" rather than seminarians; "seminarian" carries connotations from my past which don't seem to apply now. I like the change, but need a different term to accommodate it, a term which does not claim to set them off dramatically, to define them as "other."

I eat frequently with the twenty-odd students here, the two priests who supervise them full-time, and the other priests who stop in occasionally to help with counseling. The students, I learn, are not exactly encouraged to date, but are not forbidden either. The unofficial expectation is that by the time they graduate from Marquette, they should be ready to disengage from their dating relationships as part of the move to the major seminary, theology, and an impending celibacy. But while they are here, they live much as other college students do.

The contrast with my own seminary experience is brought home further by a conversation I have with Bernard, a junior majoring in comparative literature. In response to the diocese's partial recognition that the priesthood is becoming a more varied profession than it once was— and, I suspect, in response to everyone's awareness that a "call" to study scholastic philosophy would find few listeners—the students can major in nearly anything.

I ask Bernard what the rules are like here. He looks at me, pauses, and says, "Rules? You mean, like—restrictions?" I laugh; his bemusement at the question speaks eloquently, and I tell him so. Knowing that I run the risk of sounding like an old fart glorying in how tough things were in his day, I go on to tell him how tough things were in my day. He is amazed—as I am, watching him, seeing my old world register its fantastic distortions on someone not already acclimated to them. "It's not like that now," he says, in a triumph of understatement. The students are expected to attend morning prayers and late afternoon liturgy, and the handbook (so they still have one) says that if they miss consistently, they could have their candidacy reconsidered. But that's about it. Many of the students have part-time jobs—clerk, bartender—and lead active social lives. So long as they stagger down to morning prayers, the amount of sleep they have behind them is their business. The general assumption is that they are adults and can be treated that way.

The priests corroborate this picture, but complicate it with their own assessment of the students. "I like these kids," one of them tells me—and from the way I see him act around them, I believe him—"but their conservatism appalls me. Not just the political conservatism [I had already noticed quite a few Bush/Quayle signs on the doors] but the conservatism in their view of the church. They don't ask, 'What can I contribute to the church?' They ask, 'What can the priesthood do for me?' " They are retreating to clericalism, he complains, anticipating a note I will hear repeatedly from my classmates; they want respect, and if the laity will no longer give it to them automatically, they will insist on it.

I think about the fact that my classmates and I, though we may have been drawn to order initially, ended up with more than we could stomach; these students, he suggests, respond to freedom by wanting more order than they have. One of them is on the verge of leaving because of what he sees as Weakland Hall's "air of decadence"; he doesn't like the beer cans he sees in the wastebaskets, is offended by the fact that exceptions are sometimes made to the rules—a senior allowed to miss prayers, for instance, in order to take a class required for graduation. Some of them are becoming seminarians again.

Five days into the trip, I phone Ivona and we manage to avoid our usual tensions; we are light and open and sharp together. Is it that we are on the phone at a safe distance, or am I relaxing up here, letting go, and listening to her? Our conversations always work when I listen well, when I move past self-absorption, when I stop trying to control—something I keep remembering, and then forgetting. Yet whenever I do relax, I react against the loss of control, and get nervous again.

Meanwhile, I am meeting classmates all over the city and throughout the southeastern part of Wisconsin. The interviews with the priests in particular stir me up. Their surprisingly unsettled state draws me to them. I tell a good many of them about my own problems, and they see connections with their own. The linkage of their concerns with mine, of what I do with what they do, of their world and mine, unlocks something in me—and makes me realize that, whatever the feelings I have or may rediscover toward the institutional church, I have strong affinities with and respect for these men—and for their frustrations when they feel that their institution does not support or reward their efforts, when it seems to operate more as an enemy to meaning than as its ally. At the same time, when I find myself oddly irritated by their anger at the church, at the tendency of some of them to fix the blame out there, my irritation only strengthens my sense of connection; I share that trait too, and wonder about it.

My conversation with Father Frederick in particular starts slowly, but takes off when we start talking about God and other sources of meaning. Just after the taping ends, he says that he continues to believe because he is convinced that the desire for meaning has to lead somewhere. I reply, as I have at other times (it has become my standard answer over the years), that the desire for meaning doesn't make things meaningful, any more than hunger produces food, any more than my need for my father means he is still alive. The desire for a God doesn't prove He exists. But I find myself adding—a new note for me—that the desire for God doesn't prove He doesn't exist either.

In my last interview, just before I leave town, I talk with Eliot Grayson, a former priest, now a successful businessman; his bitterness against the institutional church braces me, reminds me of my own grievances against it, reminds me that I don't believe what the church teaches, what the priests believe, for all my newly discovered admiration for them. The people I've met here attract me, but their theology does not. I do not believe, I again remind myself, with relief, as I drive back to Bloomington.

And yet, over the next four years of conversations, I found myself drawn increasingly to the priests and former priests in my class. I was moved more than anything by the history of their ongoing "marriage" to the church, which by now, twenty years into the priesthood, had a weight and complexity to it equal to anything I could conjure in my long-term relationships with my wife and with the university. Priests may not know much about sex—although some of them certainly do—but, I come to realize, they know more about marriage than they are given credit for.

In this context, however, I was also struck by their repeated, characteristic references to the "institutional church," a phrase which, in their vocabulary, had come to suggest everything that was distant, controlling, unappreciative, hierarchical, regressive, and bureaucratic about their organization and nothing that was positive; it was a phrase which had all but replaced the warm, nurturing "Holy Mother" to whom they had once felt they were committing themselves.

The impersonality of that new phrase and the frustrations which they described suggested that their relationship with their organization had undergone a shift of the most basic sort, a shift which affected every area of their lives. Yet most of the priests ordained from my class remain in the priesthood; out of their twenty-nine, only seven had left, an extraordinarily low number in comparison with the classes just before and after them.

I felt a strong need to try to understand all of this, partly because I increasingly saw a connection between them and academics like me. Priests, I was realizing, do not live in a protected world any more than I do, although they had originally expected to, as I had. They too faced the difficulty of maintaining an initially idealistic commitment inside an institution which theoretically embodies those values but which in practice often violates them. They too, contrary to their own expectations, have become concerned with matters of money and professional status. They too are closely bound to their institution—even as they resist it—by varying ties of loyalty, vocational conviction, economic dependence, personal satisfaction with their core activities, and lack of ready alternatives. My fascination with their strategies for dealing with these issues became one of the central prods to this book.

I wanted to understand not only what had changed for them but what had not, how and why they stayed in the priesthood even though they no longer felt obligated by the mere fact of their original commitment. I wanted to see how they accommodated their frustration with the church without moving over the line into total alienation or withdrawal, what they seemed to gain by staying as well as what they felt they had lost. I wanted to understand what they had done to retain and channel at least some of their fervor and satisfaction. These questions drew me to the priests in a way that both energized me and refocused my entire project. Their concerns were more than academic questions to me; it was precisely because they were that I felt compelled to sort them out.

But those concerns also prodded me to do more research than I had done in several years. I knew that I couldn't understand my classmates unless I knew some of the contexts they were operating in; so reconnecting with them reactivated in me some of the academic energy I had not been able to tap for some time.

5

The
Personal
Plight

Priests are always told, "What is it with priests? They're
not married, they don't understand women or married
people." And I say, "Well, what is it with lay people?
What makes you think you understand *my* life?"

—Father Malcolm

Father Tod was one of the first priests I interviewed. I called
him not because I had known him well before, but because I
had not. If there was a new story out there, I wanted to be able
to hear it, and I was afraid that with the men who had once been my best
friends, the old grid I saw them through might interfere. Tod turned out
to be a revealing starting point.

Immediately after greeting me at the door, Tod expressed open glee
at the small but newly discovered freedoms of apartment living. "I love
it!" he said, as he skirted a pile of books in the middle of the floor and
sat in his easy chair. "Just to thoroughly luxuriate in being able to come
down and read the paper in my bathrobe, have a cup of coffee. I could
care less what the furniture looks like. This is my space, I can do with
it what I want." No wonder, I realized later, that having his own personal
space meant so much to him; in so many of the other areas of his life he
cannot do what he wants—or else is no longer certain what he wants.

By his own account, at various times in the last twenty years Tod has suffered loneliness, depression, burnout, and considerable disillusionment with the institutional church. For the last five years, he had been pastor of a parish torn by strife at nearly every level. In the central areas of his life—his sense of the church, of the priesthood, of his own spirituality—where older generations of priests might at least have hoped for certainty and stability, he finds that there are now "no maps" to guide him. And two years before we talked, he had had a stroke—"one hundred percent stress-induced"—followed by a life-threatening leg infection; together, they had left him without his previous "sense of invincibility" and all the more concerned with "figuring out his game plan" for the years that he might have remaining. Not only because of his discomfort but because of the thoughtfulness with which he addresses it, Tod provided me with a good introduction to the newly destabilized priesthood my classmates are now experiencing twenty years after their ordination.

Tod began by describing his troubled parish, to him a microcosm of a current church in flux and showing the strains:

> It's an extremely mixed area. The mix is increasingly black and Oriental. We have rich, poor. It's also grayed. We have six retirement communities plus three care facilities. Apartments, condos, HUD housing. We have a lot of new industrial growth, which is primarily going to be minimum-wage jobs. We've got everybody!

An ideal parish, he said, would involve "the sense that people have the experience of God's kingdom, of something larger than themselves. Community would be a part of it, a welcoming aspect, an hospitable atmosphere." Although his own parish was, as recently as twelve to fifteen years ago, "a good, little, indigenous community" with a tavern as its community center, one of the Milwaukee suburbs burgeoned into it from one end and urban expansion encroached on the other; as a result, "shopping centers, condos, the whole works" ended up burying the town woods and the creeks and the local haunts. The original core community remained intact, but it no longer had exclusive domain; the result has been "warfare on many levels":

> Conservative and liberal within the church. Suburban versus the indigenous community. There was warfare between the pastor and the associates—open, including taking up petitions among the parishioners. Between school and religious education. Honestly, it was going on on many, many levels.

After the previous pastor was suspended, Tod was "parachuted" into the parish with "a mission to somehow bring about some healing and reconciliation." But the old village group, Tod says, was "a well-functioning sociological unit, a dynamite community with well-defined rituals of entry and departure. They knew how to excommunicate people if they didn't want them. I stepped on a lot of land mines. Basically, I was told by quite a number of parishioners, 'Nothing personal, but we're not going to give you a chance. Welcome.' "

Tod had a difficult time with one of his associates as well, a man who already had been a pastor but was now, under the new diocesan policy of a fixed six-year term of office, going back down the ladder. "That's happening more and more," Tod said, and it is especially difficult in a post–Vatican II parish where the laity are much more independent and assertive than they once were. "You've been used to the type of pastoring which many of these men experienced, when their word was law, when everybody asked permission first. Now they're not being asked. And suddenly the loss of power . . . "

Without a cohesive sense of community, and torn by their own specific political and cultural differences, Tod's parishioners started to cross parish lines at will, looking for the best school here, the most congenial homilies there, the most attractive wedding service somewhere else. According to Tod, this pick-and-choose approach mirrors "the consumer nature that has affected us all so thoroughly. We prefer shopping within the little strip malls with exclusive shops rather than in the large department stores." Tod is even less comfortable with this tendency in the church than he is in secular society "because it interferes with the work of the gospel":

> If a person comes to church with the expectation of having his needs met, to get "service," it's very difficult to convince that person that he has an obligation to meet the needs of someone else. Other than "I scratch your back, you scratch mine," which is not the highest level of psychosocial development.

Tod was not alone in lamenting the breakup of the old-style parish. "We grew up in a church where the parish was more like a family," another classmate said, a family held together by ties of geography, ethnicity, and loyalty; now, however, the parish has become a voluntary association in which "like begets like," a political, cultural, all too often economically defined "club" whose leader is more titular than authoritative, because its members can leave at any time. The upside of this reversal, he said, is that the pastor has been stripped of his arrogance and that, as Vatican II intended, the people have come to feel that "they are the church"; the considerable downside is the all but total disruption of community.

Furthermore, many of the laity no longer grant my classmates the automatic respect once accorded at least to their office. Few of them wear the Roman collar anymore except for formal functions, and even when

they do, it doesn't work its old magic. "Going over to the parish school,"
one of them told me, "isn't much fun anymore. The kids react to me with
indifference if not disdain." Parish boards have proliferated—Milwaukee is a national leader in developing lay programs—and they are run
by knowledgeable, educated laymen unawed by Father's credentials. "I
have to acknowledge their expertise now," one priest told me. "I have to
work harder to prove my own opinion. I have to be able to prove it."

Among these new laity, even Tod's willingness to share power has
caused problems: "I see myself as largely very collaborative," he said. "I
tend to enjoy working on projects with others. I enjoy a free exchange of
ideas. I have this deep-seated belief that if we work at this, if we are willing to approach it openly, we can have a good time working together and
do a good job." To his dismay, however, what he viewed as collaboration
was often misunderstood both by his associates and by his parishioners:
"They say I expect *them* to make the decisions. I say, 'No, can *we* make
the decision?' I have been frankly surprised by the number of people
who seem to be totally unable to recognize that as an option."

And yet when he has made decisions—has taken the ultimate responsibility that he feels he cannot avoid—he has stirred up resistance just as
surely:

> A number of people are upset with some of the decisions I've had to
> make. Replacing a deacon and a parish secretary who were very trusted
> by a number of groups in the parish. Decisions to share authority on
> [parish] council and in committees with people who were previously
> not enfranchised, but who then came to the realization that my coop-
> erating with them did not mean that they were now enfranchised and
> others were disenfranchised.

The laity's consumer discontent, according to Tod, often prods them
to shop around for a priest still willing to make decisions for them so
long as he makes decisions which suit them: "They want the power to
decide who has the responsibility to take care of them." Thus, with a
final irony, the pick-and-choose laity, under the guise of promoting their
own rights, end up reaffirming the hierarchical, autocratic church—and
distancing themselves from my classmates in the process.

On the level of stated belief and hard-won Vatican II principle, Tod,
like the rest of his classmates, has come to appreciate and value this new
breed of parishioner, newly risen from the church's underclass, now
more feisty than flock. Nearly every priest I interviewed echoed Tod's
assertion that he preferred collaboration to the old model of the autocratic pastor (which many of them had suffered under as newly ordained associates). They now insist almost to a man that the laity are as
important to the church as priests; several of them put their own slight
spin on the central Vatican II epigram—"The Church is the people of

God"—by asserting that "the people are the church." Father Brent has become a nationally recognized expert on how to "empower" the laity; for him, "collegial" and "shared decision making" are "very much the fiber of the work we do. It shows up in everything." Still another priest asserts, "It's great that I'm challenged by the laity. I love the trend."

It is questionable whether earlier generations of priests had a closer relationship to the laity; a priesthood set apart was central to the traditional model. Yet at the very least, the undeniably greater fluidity of parishes at the present along with the policy mandating a fixed term of office has made long-term relationships with the laity even harder to establish and maintain—all of this at a time when my classmates want more rather than less personal contact. Wanting more, as we shall see, is part of their self-concept.

If Tod finds many of the recent trends in the church difficult in practice if not in theory, he finds many of the more traditional pressures of the priesthood equally frustrating. A few years ago, in fact, when the demands of ministry seemed overwhelming, Tod experienced an intense period of "depression" and "burnout": "I got aggravated living a life surrounded only by males," he says. "Being a kept person. Being paid a salary, living in parish housing, etc. : 'Father, we pay you, you're there whenever we want you.' " At that point, he felt that he was "into ministry in a way that I needed to get out of. There was too much giving, too much work, and not enough time to expand."

In the context of all this strain, Tod's personal and emotional life became all the more important to him; so in spite of his reservations about a need-obsessed laity, he concluded, "I want *my* needs to be met" too. That conviction—one of his few current certainties—has led, for instance, to a series of close friendships with women he has come to consider "soul mates," because he has found that they provide him with a level of understanding he has not found among other priests. It has meant refusing to do some of the traditional tasks of a pastor; "I've written them out of my job description," he says. And currently, it means that "I need to go elsewhere." His stroke, he feels, cured him of "the myth of invincibility": he now knows not only that he could die, but that there are some things he cannot handle, most noticeably "the pressures, the history, the frustrations in this parish."

Tod is much more certain about the need for a change, however, than he is about what that change might be. He would love to "take the shingle down, to play belated easy rider" for a while, to say, simply, "I'm in between things" and in the process of pondering his goals "for the next twenty-five years." He is skeptical, however, about "how much of that I'm going to be able to negotiate with the home office here," especially in the context of a severe shortage of priests.

Tod's confusion is understandable. He was drawn to the priesthood, he says, because it was a "helping profession." But how is he to help—to minister—today? How is he to hold his parish together when it has no internal cohesion and his parishioners have no qualms about going elsewhere? How, in his words, can a priest "prophesy"—i.e., tell the uncomfortable truths that sometimes need to be told—to a laity who can either vote him out with their pocketbook (at a time of great financial strain on most parishes) or simply move out of his hearing? How can he effectively share authority with parishioners who cherish their independence but still want him to make the hard decisions—and then bristle when he does so? What does it mean for him to be "pastor" to the newly elevated "associates" who are not exactly his equals but are no longer his clearly defined "assistants"—especially when they may well have been pastors already?

Furthermore, how is he to feel comfortable inside an institution which, as he sees it, has changed much less than he has in the last twenty years? Tod has worked very hard, he says, "to change in my own behaviors toward women. I've shucked off some old ways of viewing things. It's become second nature." So he now finds himself "embarrassed" by being part of "a clerical culture that has denigrated women" and frustrated by "the presumptuousness of Rome to not even give women's place in the church a serious consideration." And more broadly, to what extent can a priest who has "never felt part of the institutional church" in the first place operate comfortably within an institution which he considers basically compromised by "a European understanding of what is church, religion, and everything: male-dominated, authority as power versus authority as service, a church that recognizes class and to some extent tends to promote class differences"?

How can he regard as "holy father" a pope who seems to him, as he does to many of Tod's classmates, "almost a caricature of his office," especially in his tendency to avoid some of the most important issues facing the church—the status of women, issues of divorce and celibacy? Pope John Paul's basic strategy, in Tod's view, is to say simply that "it's a problem that shouldn't exist." And overall, how can he see to it that his increasingly important "needs" are met in the context of an institution that directs the priest to serve but seems to him to pay little attention to serving the priest?

Tod admits that on the night before ordination, he was unsure about going ahead, especially since he felt he "never fit the mold" of the traditional priest:

> Tomorrow, everything was focused on tomorrow. We sat in Bill Schuit's living room and finished his liquor cabinet. I stopped in the chapel on my way back to my room at about two in the morning, a little bit buzzy, and I remember sitting in the darkness and saying, "I don't

know whether this is what you want or not, but I've done the best I can.
If you've got any objections, you've got about six hours." (*laughs*)

Yet he felt, he says, a "definite sense of call." It was that sense of call
that got him through the ordination, and it is that sense that he referred
to again when he told me that it still seems "more or less right" that he
continue as a priest. But if the call is still there, what, specifically, today,
is the answer? What, even, is the call?

Tod was not so naive as to anticipate that the priesthood would demand no adaptation on his part; but his own puzzle metaphor suggests
the manageable kinds of changes he anticipated:

> I expected something like what I went through shortly before ordina-
> tion. The only way I've ever been able to describe it in imagery was:
> When I was a little kid, I got a puzzle from my grandparents. It was a
> red barn with a pony and a fence and a tree. It had very large pieces,
> and I'd put them together. This was a series puzzle—each time I had a
> birthday, I would get another box. And that box would be added to the
> puzzle. They were smaller, more intricate pieces. But what used to be
> blue in the creek now became sky. So the picture itself remained some-
> what the same, but all the pieces rearranged themselves. Just the time
> that I could put the pieces together blindfolded, another birthday would
> come and I knew that I'd have to put them all together again. There are
> going to be differences, but it's going to be basically the same scene.

Instead of piecemeal and controllable change, however, he has found
something far more pervasive and jarring: a priesthood whose shape
and direction are no longer discernible, within a church simultaneously
insisting on and feeling the strains of liberal Vatican II changes in some
areas and reverting to pre–Vatican II conservatism in others. Inside a
church whose contours he cannot readily recognize or easily endorse, he
no longer inhabits basically the same scene:

> I see the church changed. I'm in the last stages of grieving over the
> death of the church I was ordained in, with beautiful sunsets and sun-
> rises, where all things were possible. I see the death of that dream. I
> find myself at times putting myself in the position where I say, "You
> know, God, I really don't approve of this."

Tod's current uncertainties have reshaped his spirituality, which has
now become for him not a haven of eternal truths or a refuge from this
world, but a means of validating human processes and needs and, perhaps most important, of accommodating what he cannot understand
or endorse—without relying wholly on the traditional terms of "God's
mysterious ways":

> I'm intrigued by Jung's idea of a collective unconscious because for me
> it's a lot less restrictive than id, ego, superego. It leaves me a place to

put grace or, to use the theological terms, "divine inspiration." It also
gives me a place to put what the new-age religioners call "positive men-
tal energy" (*laughs*) or the impact of human desires. There's a freedom
there, there's room for something I can't quantify. I think that moving
more into the intuitive, creative, contemplative is something that allows
me to live with the paradoxes that I see as being a part of the church
and a part of religion. You preach one thing and we do the exact opposite. Part of me is just beginning to say, "So?" We're looking at thousands of years. So there are difficulties.

Tod is no longer confident about how to envision a heaven or hell or a
deity ("I've run out of definitions; I wait to be surprised"), and he finds
himself no longer motivated "in the sense of reward/punishment; that
was earlier." The only image of an afterlife that he can conjure is of "a
country that I hope to visit or a place I want to call home":

> I think part of that [desire for home] has come from my moving. With
> that moving, I've done a number of leave-takings: the moving out of the
> seminary, basically a leave-taking of pretty much the whole class. Get-
> ting immersed in a lay world, and being in that first parish for years
> and moving on from there; that was a leave-taking. The close brushes
> with death. Also, the sense of distancing. Suddenly I said home is a place
> I've never really been. That's a cliché; but it is someplace that I'm still
> hoping for. The story that stuck with me is the Abraham-Sarah story.
> The sense of people who had finished their life. Now they were being
> invited to move someplace else, to a place they wouldn't recognize, by
> a God they didn't know. The sense of leave-taking, the choosing be-
> tween Sarah and Hagar. Choices and movement, all with consequences,
> always that sense of the needing to move on. (*pause*) I recognize that
> whatever I've called home, also whatever I've called God, is something
> that I've had to leave behind. Home is left behind.

The heaven Tod envisions suggests the costs he has paid and continues to pay on earth for a life of unsettling changes. His heaven is a de-
ferred version of what he would like here on earth, something neither
he nor most of his classmates have found in the contemporary church
and the contemporary priesthood: home. Their specific dislocations vary
from priest to priest, as we shall see, but what they have in common is
a landscape unmapped and ridden with faultlines.

All post–Vatican II Catholics find themselves in an uncertain religious context. To most current theologians, the Bible is no longer a source
of timeless dogma but a document which can be understood only tenta-
tively in its own historical context. Theologians, newly attuned to epistemological trends, are modest about what human beings can know in
general, in particular about what we can know of "human nature" (or

whether there is such a thing), and consequently about the nature of both religious truth and ethical norms.

This makes for a doubly confusing situation. It's bad enough—or exciting enough, or both—not to know with the old certainty what to believe and how to act. But Catholics also don't quite know whether or not this new spirit of inquiry and openness has been sanctioned by the church. The theologians are headed in one direction, while the highest levels of church authority—the pope, Cardinal Ratzinger (the ultraorthodox head of the Vatican's Congregation for the Doctrine of the Faith), and many bishops, especially those appointed by Pope John Paul II[1]—are resisting these changes. Of course, in the new view, these latter are not necessarily unquestionable levels of authority anyway. As part of the new historicism, the pope's claims to infallibility and the hierarchy's claims to pervasive authority over the laity have themselves been seen as products of those earlier periods of discredited absolutism. The "mystical body" of Christ once had a clear "head"; the newly empowered "people of God" do not.

According to the *New York Times* (August 23, 1987), in the last twenty years, American Catholics have exceeded the educational level of all Christian denominations except Episcopalians and Presbyterians. A higher percentage of Catholics than ever before are attending state colleges and universities, where the authority of the church is at best a muted force in their lives. They live in an age in which "taking control of one's own life" is the reigning ideology; they are no longer eager to concede that control to any institution, not even the church.

In *Tomorrow's Catholics, Yesterday's Church*, Eugene Kennedy argues that old-style, "culture one" Catholics, who are emotionally tied to the institutional church and derive their definition as Catholics from it, are being replaced by more sophisticated, "culture two" Catholics, who no longer look to the institution or its official representatives for authoritative criteria on what to believe and how to lead their lives. They look instead to themselves, make their own judgments, and define the church in their own terms. In the spirit of Vatican II, their loyalties are to the church as a community of believers, not to the church as institution.[2]

Much has been written lately about the restless independence of these Catholic laity. According to Andrew Greeley and Mary Greeley Durkin, nine out of ten American Catholics no longer accept the church's official position on birth control, yet they still consider themselves Catholic.[3] The dissenters include four out of every five weekly communicants. In 1960, before the Vatican Council, 15 percent of Americans raised Catholic no longer considered themselves Catholic; according to Greeley, that percentage has remained constant over the last quarter-century.[4] The church's reaffirmation of its traditional stand against birth control has

not cost it many Catholics; but it has contributed to a new type of Catholicism.

What is less well known and yet abundantly clear from my interviews
is the extent to which the uncertainties and possibilities of the post–Vatican II church have affected priests as well. No less than the laity, Father
Tod and many of his classmates reveal their own penchant for independence from institutional control; for selective adherence to traditional practice and belief; and for basic redefinitions of their own spirituality, of their role as priests, and of the terms of their membership in
the church.

Unlike the laity, however, the priests find that their new independence
is complicated by the nature of their institutional ties and responsibilities: no matter how thoroughly they may choose to think and act freely,
they are a part of the institutional church in unavoidable ways. Like dip-
lomats who continue to "represent" countries whose policies make them
uneasy, they are neither wholly in nor wholly out, neither "culture one"
nor "culture two." In this, as in so many other ways, they are a generation caught in between, defined by their ambivalence.

Father Frank, who now teaches theology at the major seminary, com-
pares the current situation of priests to that of married people. Marriage
among Catholics, he says, was once assumed to involve a total package:
children as a matter of course, sexual fidelity, financial support from the
husband, emotional support from the wife, an overall commitment to
being married for the duration—like it very much or not—and general
societal respect for the undertaking. Now, however, couples tend to see
marriage as one menu among others, a menu from which they can select
certain items and send them back to the kitchen if they don't satisfy:
We'll take the sex and the companionship, thank you, but not necessarily
the children. I'll have this career and she will have that one; our bank
accounts and our lives will remain distinct. Ask us again about children
after the rest of the meal is finished. Separate checks, please.

My classmates entered the seminary at a point when, in an American
Catholic church whose outlines had been largely intact for decades, the
priesthood was also considered a "total package." That package was presumed to include a predictable set of satisfactions and a nonnegotiable
set of tradeoffs and deprivations; as Frank Sinatra asserted about marriage, "You can't have one without the other." The package included the
right to feel special, chosen by God Himself for the highest calling available to man, and hence rightfully immune from worldly pressures. It included a sense of inherent authority and mission: the priest was God's
spokesman, the designated savior of a specific, local world, his parish. It
also included instant respect from a relatively uneducated, largely immigrant laity who would function willingly as "flock" to the priest's
"shepherd."

The priest's considerable power and status were dependent, of course, on his lifetime subservience to the authority of the church and to its representatives in the hierarchy. Subservience meant, among other things, that the priest would publicly promote the church's official positions, a relatively light burden for priests trained to believe that there was no real alternative to those positions. In exchange for working several years as an "assistant" in a rectory (whether or not you liked your boss or rectory living itself), you would eventually become a boss through the same seniority system. And in accord with the benefice system that had been intact in the Western church since the Council of Trent in the sixteenth century and in this country since the end of the nineteenth, once you became a pastor, you would all but own your parish. Becoming pastor was the equivalent of academic tenure, only more so: you could move up or laterally, but not down, and you could not be squeezed out for reasons short of persistent public scandal.

You would have a very low, direct salary, to be sure: in Milwaukee, $500 a year in 1942, the year most of my classmates were born; $2,400 a year at the time of their ordination in 1969. You would have very little independence in lifestyle; "lifestyle," in fact, with its connotation of alternate choices, is a term you would not be likely to use, a concept not yet born in clerical consciousness. You would be expected to live in the rectory, to wear your collar in all but the most private moments—because always and everywhere you "represented" the church—and to be on call twenty-four hours a day. On the other hand, you would have steady room and board; and after retirement, you could remain "emeritus" in your parish until you died, with undiminished honor and fewer cares. You would feel nurtured from ordination to grave by what you thought of as "Holy Mother the Church." In a real sense, a sense largely perceived as positive, then, you would "belong" to the church. The church would serve as your home.

The heaviest price for many was celibacy and the loss of family life; but there was at least the "fraternity of priests," it was thought, a ready-made network of comrades fighting the same fight, to compensate in part. And in the long run, there were the rewards of an afterlife, in which total, never-ending intimacy with God—the perfect lover—would more than compensate for a mere lifetime of emotional and sexual deprivation.

If you didn't like some of these things, you had twelve years of seminary preparation to think about it, to bring your own ideas into accord with "the mind of the church"; but once you made the commitment, you were "a priest forever." The only way you could leave was in total disgrace. Besides, as one of my minor seminary teachers (now in his early sixties) said, "Where are you going to go?" The church was *the* holy mother, and no surrogates were available. If you stayed, you stayed on the church's terms. Like the traditional marriage, the priesthood was not open to alterations; it was a ready-made suit, whose specifications had been in place for centuries. You were expected to fit it or live with the discomfort. In the traditionally defined "vocation," God did the calling and the church wrote the contract; the only answers available were yes and no.

A broad caveat here. This constellation may or may not accurately reflect the realities of what my classmates—and I—refer to as the "old church." It may well be that the old church is more a construct useful for establishing generational differences and for sharply defining current dilemmas than a reflection of hard fact. Surely previous generations of priests had their complexities, their (hidden) ambivalences and frustrations. As Leslie Tentler points out throughout *Seasons of Grace,* her study of the Detroit archdiocese—and as my own memories of my strong-willed, empire-building pastor remind me—many of them certainly found ways to assert their own individuality and to brook authority in their own ways. But at least in broad terms, the constellation I have just described had public currency in previous generations; it was the myth of the priesthood, and I heard something like it from the older seminary faculty I interviewed as well as from my classmates.

Whatever its ultimate accuracy, for my classmates at least, that myth no longer holds, for a number of reasons. Their final years in the seminary took place in the midst of the civil rights movement; they came to cherish what they see as their own rights as vigorously as they defend the rights of others. Later, after their ordination, Vatican II's theology of empowerment predictably reached beyond the laity to affect the very priests who were called upon to be its agents. And as they moved enthusiastically toward greater engagement with the world, they lost some of their putative immunity from the world's values. They felt the pull of humanistic growth psychologies, for instance, which raised personal development to the level of moral imperative, denigrated the notion of docility to external authority, and called into question any seemingly lifetime commitments which smacked of excessive self-sacrifice. When Rembert Weakland was appointed archbishop of Milwaukee in 1977, his own relative independence from Rome—his public call for the ordination of women, for instance—provided a further context for autonomy; why be totally docile to Rome when Rome's own representative is not?

Whatever the conjunction of reasons, many priests in my class have become as selective as the laity and have gravitated toward similarly independent criteria for their choices. That includes, first and foremost, the right to think for themselves. "The way the 1960s affected the seminary," one classmate told me, "was to convince us that we were to question the very existence of any type of authority." That questioning quickly extended to their own institution: most of them now feel free to differ with the church's stated positions on birth control, the ordination of women, the infallibility of the pope. Some do this publicly, others—dissidents but reluctant to rebel—do so more discreetly in private conference. They feel similarly free to redefine their theology, and not all of their redefinitions have originated within the church.

In matters of their own morality, for many of them the right to think for themselves included from the very beginning the right to see celibacy as "a personal, private decision." The more open study of church history which infiltrated their later seminary years alerted them to the fact that celibacy (arguably) was not required of priests until the eleventh century and did not take full hold until the sixteenth century; hence, as one of them put it, celibacy "is not integral to ordained ministry even though the church now requires it." One classmate, no longer a priest, says that even at the very moment at which he took the vow of celibacy in the spring of 1968, he had no intention whatever of living a celibate life. He crossed his fingers behind his back during the ceremony in silent cancellation and a year later fell in love with the first nun he met in his first parish. More telling, Father Jeff (an articulate spokesman for a noncelibate priesthood) puts his ongoing refusal to live a celibate life in the political terms of our generation—which are, of course, traditional American terms as well, though not in the Catholic tradition: celibacy was "an unjust law" and he was a conscientious objector. As Father Tod asserted matter-of-factly, "Celibacy is optional. It's presumptuous of the church to assume that anyone who is called to ministry has the charism." As members of the 1960s generation, my classmates demand the right to keep their options open.

Their sense of commitment to the priesthood itself is similarly provisional. For the great majority, "a priest forever" does not resonate with the force of former days. Only two of them stated categorically that they would not withdraw that commitment under any circumstances; most of them, however, more attuned to developmental psychology than to canon law, assert that commitments made at a given stage of life should not necessarily bind someone moving through a different stage. The early church, several of them reminded me, did not demand a permanent priesthood, and as one priest put it, "Not everyone is cut out to be a priest forever." And since the church has changed its mind a good deal during Vatican II and since then, shouldn't they have the right to do the same? Worst of all, "forever" smacks to them of institutional control— the great bane of their rights and one of their abiding fears—and denies the validity of their own changing needs, which have proven to be much more insistent and less readily satisfied than they expected. "Needs" are as important to them now as "rights"; the two terms have become, for some of them at least, all but synonymous.

The provisional nature of their commitment has been intensified as the notion of vocation has elided for many of them into "career" and "profession": careers can be redefined, renegotiated, abandoned. In fact, as several of them asserted, careers *must* be abandoned if the only alternative is personal stagnation. Father Ralph, described by one of his classmates as an "ideal priest," told me that five or six years into his priesthood, he found himself seriously considering whether to leave simply because he was "getting fed up with taking care of everyone else's problems. I wasn't letting anybody take care of mine." He did not fear eternal retribution if he left the priesthood, nor did he anguish over ascertaining "God's will" in the matter, as if that were an extrinsic and readable entity. "Strange as it is, I don't know how important God was in the whole thing." What was important was whether he could continue to be happy doing the work of a priest. As another priest says, "If the day ever came that I got up one morning and said, 'I'd like to skip today,' then it would be time to get out."

Within the priesthood itself, many feel free to select some of its traditional duties while rejecting others. Increasing numbers prefer to live in homes and apartments—"alternative housing," as the archdiocese has reluctantly come to call it—rather than in rectories. They do so largely because they insist on the right to time on their own, a space of their own, an identity apart from the church. "I like to live around people who are not churchy," one of them said, "normal people with real concerns." Living away from the parish, another told me, "allows priests to be functioning Christian citizens rather than kept persons. Rectories institutionalize priests too much." Living in an apartment, Father Herbert said, "gives us independence from other celibates who want to control us in the two areas where the church has always wanted control: sex and money."

In general, if my classmates don't like a task which has traditionally been part of their "job"—another term which has crept into their vocabulary, less august than "career" but equally far from "vocation"—they are more likely to find a way to avoid it than to accept it as "God's will." Father Tod, dissatisfied with the longstanding assumption that he would double as bookkeeper in his own parish, said simply, "I've written them [such tasks] out of my job description." "I don't pay bills," Father Eugene says simply. "I've gotten out of that."

The same assertiveness characterizes their stance toward assignments. When one of his first pastors contradicted him in public, one of my classmates reacted quickly:

> I called the personnel board the day after Christmas and said, "I want out of here and I want out of here fast. I'm going to be out of here by the fifteenth, and if you don't have a place for me, I'll give you my address." I was out of there on the seventeenth of January.

In short, for many of my classmates, the priesthood is no longer a ready-made suit; if it doesn't fit, they try to alter it.

It is important to note that the generational/priestly idealism which characterized them at the point of ordination has not been replaced for the most part by cynicism; like Tod, they still see the priesthood as a "helping profession," and they share his conviction that the church is the right place, or at least the best available place, for them to practice it—even if that means ignoring the church as institution in the process. They do not reject the notion that a priest has a "role" which precludes certain forms of behavior. But they want a hand in shaping that role; and in any case, they refuse to equate role with self: as one of them put it, "I think of myself as a human being who is also a priest."

At the very least, like the more literally married members of their generation, they have come to want more independence within their commitments—and to fantasize extensively about independence from those commitments. When I asked them about what they imagine themselves doing in an alternate life, they pictured themselves as cowboys ("I'd love the freedom of it all"), forest rangers, bakers ("in my own business"), writers, pop singers ("I'd love to be able to control a huge crowd like that"), restaurant owners, winners of the lottery ("where I'm independent"), full-time downhill skiers, even Superman: men who (seem to) call their own shots, men in charge, with no one to answer to directly.

Most of them now bristle at "belonging" to the church even as they remain its most visible representatives. Just as Tod has turned toward more intuitive philosophies, many of them have turned to painting, writing, and other forms of long-buried creativity; they want to give play to their right brain, the part of them they feel the church has neglected, the part the church does not own. They would prefer to be their own men, affiliated but not subsumed; it is precisely the difficulty of keeping that balance which defines most of their characteristic tensions.

But if my classmates resist some of the traditional definitions of priesthood in the spirit of their cherished independence, it is also true that many of those old definitions have simply crumbled around them. The post–Vatican II priest no longer wears distinctive garb to set him off as different; he now, literally, speaks the same language as his parishioners. With a more intelligible, vernacular liturgy, he is no longer so obviously a cult figure, presiding over the mysteries—and hence no longer so inherently an object of wonder, awe, and deference. More practically, as we shall see, the lifelong job security my classmates anticipated in the priesthood is gone; the church has proven to be less the nurturing mother and more an impersonal boss. Overall, their sense of themselves as special, important to the church and valued within it, has been badly shaken. It is also true that my classmates and the archdiocese of Milwaukee are engaged in forging new definitions of the contemporary priest and of his relation to the church; but these definitions are much less certain than the old, they are not yet firmly in place, and they raise as many questions as they answer.

Metaphoric Loss: The De-facing of God

The "paterfamilias," the King—today these symbols have lost their magic for us. In future our age can only worship something more penetrating, more organic, vaster, something that rises above every human value.
—Pierre Teilhard de Chardin, *Christianity and Evolution* (1969)

"Is there a God?" asked the Marxist.
"Certainly not the kind people are thinking of," said the Master.
"Whom are you referring to when you speak of people?"
"Everyone."
—Anthony de Mello, S.J., *One Minute Wisdom* (1986)

Father Eugene was willing to be interviewed but less evidently eager than many others. Described by other classmates as "laid-back," he sat with his legs crossed and eyes half-glazed throughout most of our conversation as he spoke calmly, even drily, of the "tradeoffs" inherent in the life of a priest. He spoke repeatedly of the "one hand" that registers his frustrations and of the "other hand" that tallies his more or less equal satisfactions; his consistent two-handedness suggests a man seeking—or at least accepting—balance rather than intensity, a man not easy to rattle, or to excite.

He is, however, a published poet and short-story writer, a man sensitive to the implications of language; he is also someone who gives great weight to the personalizing moments of priesthood—moments of direct contact with teenagers, for instance, or a good homily, when "you know you've touched people's hearts." So I should not have been surprised that his one moment of evident agitation came when he relived a conversation from twenty years ago which had challenged his personal image of God for the first time; for that challenge threatened the very heart of his spiritual vision:

When I was in first-year college, somebody said to me, "Do you think when you die and go to heaven, you're going to see God?" And I said, "Sure." And he said, "No, you're not. You can't see God." I said, "What do you mean, you can't see Him?" "Well," he said, "God doesn't have a body, head, and arms and legs." That didn't make sense to me. Yet it kept bouncing around in my mind, not in any painful way, but I was always saying, "I wonder what he meant; I wonder what God is like?" So that anthropomorphic God was with me for a long time, embarrassingly so. He was still there when I was ordained.

Within three years of ordination, however, Eugene experienced a moment of epiphany which replaced his old God with something new and reshaped his entire theology. "People would come in," he says, "wanting to talk about the pain in their lives. And it always became the absence of love: a marriage that broke up, somebody that died, problems with their children, alone in town and not knowing anyone—whatever." What surprised him was that his parishioners would invariably talk about "how God seemed very far away" at such moments. "At first," he said, "that struck me as curious, because you'd think that's when God would be closest. 'You go to God' and so forth":

> Then all of a sudden it clicked. I said, "*That's* what John is talking about when he said that God is love. He says God *is* love. People who experience love experience God, and if you haven't experienced love, then you won't experience God because God is love." Well, once I had made that leap, it spiraled, just generated quickly into seeing God as much more like an energy, a cosmic force, a divinism that pervades all creation. And that redefines heaven and hell, redefines sin, it redefines the church.

But although Eugene's redefinition of God rescued the love he considers central to his spirituality, he acknowledges that "this theology has its own problems, just as that theology had its problems." For love as a cosmic force does not quite do what a loving Father did:

> The difficulty I end up struggling with is that it seems kind of impersonal. How does that cosmic force know or care about Eugene? How am I an individual in that cosmic whole? Yet all the gospels say that Eugene continues to live. I'm not sure how to put that together. . . . But that's who God is for me.

In this context, it is not surprising that Eugene is one of the priests who feel most abandoned on Sunday afternoons, when he is left alone in the rectory after the peak, interpersonal energy of the liturgy. For he now must look to the people for the personal connection which God Itself no longer offers; when he doesn't find it, his sense of abandonment is sharp:

> Loneliness comes when I'm alone, and I know that everybody else isn't. It comes on a Sunday afternoon, when the image is that everyone else is together and I'm by myself. Put it on a Monday and it's no problem. . . . It hurts. Sometimes I'll read, or I'll write, or I'll go on a walk. I'd rather do it with someone. The antidotes are—loving somebody, caring about people, not living for yourself.

To Eugene, "the church is the frustration," the abiding source of his grief; for in its perceived impersonality and increased remoteness—"the things it talks about seem so separated from life"—the institutional church now mirrors the God who presides over it. An impersonal church

is especially painful for a man who needs personal recognition and support—for himself and for others—all the more intensely now that the
God he believes in does not provide it.

Eugene's comments touch on one of the most basic changes my classmates have experienced since ordination: the loss of God. This is not to
say that they have embraced the "death of God" or turned to disbelief
in any fundamental way. But their post–Vatican II God is no longer the
anthropomorphic Old Man in the Sky. Nor, in spite of the efforts of feminist theologians, is the God they now refer to a She; one form of projec-
tion is no more sophisticated than another, even if it is more politically
attractive. As a result, in accord with current trends in theology—Protestant as well as Catholic, Jewish as well as Christian—but very much
against the grain of their intense desire for a personal priesthood, God
has become for many of them not wholly impersonal, but somehow less
personal, less involved with them as individuals, less the motivational
center of their ministry. He is, for Father Ralph, for instance, "a force,
energy, being, a live being I don't know how to define" whose residually
anthropomorphic sense of humor—"He laughs and doesn't take life all
that seriously"—conveys at the same time a new degree of distance from
human concerns.

Of course, the Old Man in the Sky was an easy target for contemporary theologians, and I must admit that I jumped gleefully on the decon-
structive bandwagon on my way out of the church; but my classmates
show signs of missing Him, and for good reason. For He was the center
of the old package, a caring presence, terrifying because He set the rules
and knew everything, but validating and affirming because He paid a
lot of attention to each of us. He was appealing because He was engaged;
all the force of a nurturing church derived ultimately from a personally
loving Father whom, in conjunction with the Holy Mother, we could all
imagine. So how, after all, does one go about retaining a powerful, motivating belief in a personal God unless he is free to *imagine* Him—or
Her—as a person *somehow* like those persons we know?

The answer, for some classmates, is to focus on Jesus, God-made-man,
rather than on the Father-reduced-to-life-force. Nonetheless, the Son
takes his nature from the Father—in the Trinity, at least—and the Father's transformation into something less readily imaginable or approachable has resulted, I believe, in a similar reduction in the personality of Jesus. To Eugene, for instance, "Jesus is no longer the little boy
that was out there, that came in and got into human flesh; he becomes
'the one who is totally loving.' "

Listening to my classmates, I heard very few confident references to a
traditionally personal Lord as one of the foundations of their belief. Consider, for instance, the vacillations of Father Thurman, a theology pro-

fessor who teaches a course in Christology and has given a good deal of thought to the subject:

> I sometimes think of God as personal, but generally I don't think that I do. I think of Jesus as personal, but I don't really sit here and pray every day like, "Oh, Jesus . . . " Well, I do, but I'm not picturing Him or imagining Him in any way. It's a concentration of my energy, intellectual and emotional and spiritual, and a giving of that into some place or into the hands of some force or energy that has nothing but my health and benefit in mind.

Before this is a matter of theology, it is a question of metaphor. Although it may be hard to claim sophistication and still retain belief in the Old Man, it has proven just as hard for my classmates to be moved by a God whose metaphoric personality has been impaired. Surprisingly few of my classmates claim an active and satisfying prayer life, and even when they do, they describe it more often than not as getting in touch with a higher power rather than as praying *to* a personal God. "Sometimes my praying takes the form of creating," Eugene says, "like writing poetry. Sometimes it takes the form of drawing. Sometimes just walking through the woods or walking to the lake. My praying is certainly not a talking to God."

How could it be, if God is no longer a person for him? God as "cosmic force" or "life force," to quote just two of the phrases I heard from classmates, might be something to be reckoned with and responded to; but it is a God they can no longer imagine influencing or readily feel close to. Nor is it so easy to imagine being rewarded by divine pleasure or punished by divine anger when there is no person to attribute those emotions to. For most of my classmates, what Father Tod calls "the heaven/hell punishment thing" has receded dramatically in force; "I don't know what an afterlife means anymore," says Tod. "Hell may exist," Ralph told me, "but I can't imagine anyone actually in it." "Hell," says Eugene, "is ceasing to exist," while heaven becomes merely "that part of the cosmic force that I enflesh." In any case, he asserts, understandably enough, "That's not the reason I do stuff."

Perhaps closest to home for priests, this less personal God is also less easily conjured as some*one* who selected them, who *chose* them from among others to be His representatives, who rendered them special by that choice. If God is less personal—or, more accurately, less easily imagined as a person—then the very basis of the priest's traditional claims to stature are undermined.

The transformation of the old God may be a gain in intellectual sophistication, in short, but on the emotional level it is a loss which leaves my classmates lonely and unvalidated at the heart of their theology. It is a loss which reverberates throughout their lives, forcing them to direct elsewhere their still-intense need for a personalized religion, for personal appreciation, and for confirmation of their original specialness. It is a loss which opens up a whole range of frustrations when these personal needs are not met.

Loneliness and the Need for Intimacy

Vince Dwyer, a Trappist, dedicated the last part of his life to priest support groups. I remember years ago he came to Milwaukee to make a presentation on this. His conclusion after dealing with many, many priests was that something like 88 percent or 95 percent of us do not have a close friend with whom they are intimate about anything. I remember, I was a pretty young priest at the time, I thought that was absolutely insane. I couldn't believe it, because I thought I had everyone in the world. But I see now, at the age of forty-five, that it is very difficult to maintain friendships that are really nourishing and sustaining and supportive.

I remember feeling so bad when Ted Johnson left active ministry and I lost contact with him. I knew that I had lost a large part of myself; I had lost my history. There wasn't another human being around that I ever related to that had known me for more than two or three years. They never knew me the way I used to be. They didn't know my struggles or my experience. I felt that was a great loss; it is a great loss. So I have tried over the years to keep people like that around. But I haven't always found them in priests.

—Father Thurman

In the seminary, the one thing Father Malcolm and I had had in common was our interest in baseball; he was fanatically devoted to the Braves before they broke his heart by moving to Atlanta, while I countered with a melancholy but unswerving devotion to the Chicago Cubs. So when he answered my first phone call in 1987—except for a brief conversation at our 1985 reunion, I had not spoken with him in more than twenty years—I said, without introducing myself, "Malcolm, what was the National League's most memorable thirteen-inning game?" "That's easy," he said quickly: "Harvey Haddix's extra-inning no-hitter, all in a lost cause. 1959. A tragic event. Of course, the Braves did win. . . . What can I do for you, Ray?"

In more substantive matters, Malcolm was equally quick to respond every time I talked with him over the next four years. He was usually available for lunch or dinner, even on short notice. Twice we talked in his rectory well beyond the end of a normal work day. Twice he invited me to his apartment, mentioning each time that he had not gotten to know anyone in the neighborhood. Wherever we were, he would keep his eyes focused on me throughout and would register my comments and questions immediately; he always seemed to be totally present.

His parents both died several years ago, and he is reluctant to depend too heavily on his one sister for emotional support. His parish, like Tod's, is in turmoil because of political divisions among the laity; caught in the crossfire, he feels more distant than he used to from the people he still sees himself as serving. Nor has he felt any easy connection to other priests. As an associate in his early parishes, he suffered from a "lack of support" from his pastors, and even with his peers he has never felt any automatic attachment. "I wish we were closer as a class," he says. "We never get together." Overall, he seemed to need a good deal more human contact than he gets.

"I decided that since I wasn't great at anything in the seminary, I would at least be a nice guy," he told me. "So I worked at it." To my lights, he succeeded; he came across then, as he does now, as one of the gentlest, most decent men in our class. He is also the most articulate classmate I talked with on how lonely the priesthood can feel on a daily basis, and what that loneliness can drive a priest to.

Ten years ago, Malcolm fell in love with Jessica, a parishioner who was "in dire straits" emotionally. "I'm a rescuer," he says, and so without fully realizing what he was getting into, he began seeing her regularly. Counseling sessions turned into drives in the country, dinners together, shopping expeditions, long conversations in the car and in her apartment. Up to that point, celibacy had been for him an unpleasant but unavoidable reality that he didn't think about very much. An affectionate person by nature, he had always known that between "Punch and Judy," the traditionally defined pitfalls of the priesthood, "it would be Judy for me." But that possibility had been an abstraction; now the strength of his emotions caught him by surprise:

> I never thought that I would find somebody as a priest. I really never did say, "Could I be attracted to somebody?" All of a sudden I find myself being attracted to someone and it blew my mind. I didn't know how to handle it.

Malcolm was equally mystified by the effect of this relationship on his priesthood: "I began to fall more and more in love with God and the mass, and I began to fall in love with a woman. I said to myself, 'What the hell's going on?' " Although he insisted several times during our conversations that he and Jessica never had intercourse, they were physically intimate to a considerable degree. More to the point, he says, they began to see one another two or three times a week and became emotionally intimate: "We became so accustomed to one another that we were like husband and wife, just getting to know one another, almost taking one another for granted." In his late thirties, a period at which, he says, "you lose enthusiasm," Jessica seemed to bring him alive, to bring out of him things he thought he lacked: "I've never met a human being in all my life who lives and loves fun so much—and to come to me who was so afraid of fun!" After several years of such close and satisfying contact, "I didn't know if a wanted to be a priest anymore, or would I want to marry this woman."

Malcolm does not deny that sheer sexual attraction played a role in his relationship; Jessica, he said, is "a really beautiful woman, you can't believe how beautiful. And although you love God, even emotionally, your testicles still yearn for what God intended them to do. Some days you just want to screw anything you can see, and so you suffer." Prodded by his own heightened enthusiasm for God and the mass, he is certain that although "the priesthood and sexuality is a difficult thing, if it could be lived out ideally, it would be a wonderful thing." But Malcolm also felt that he could not continue as a priest if he had a sexual relationship with her—"I don't know how I could have offered mass"—so for several years they lived on an uneasy border: psychologically and emotionally intimate, yet technically chaste. The result, for both, was as much torment as satisfaction—and a good deal of social awkwardness:

> I was always paranoid about being seen. So if we'd go out to eat, I'd make sure it was far away, far away. She never got used to that. I'd say, "I'm sorry, but I'm doing something that I'm not supposed to be doing." Once I walked into a restaurant with her and five priests were up there. Can you imagine that? I got up and left. The waitress didn't know what the hell was going on. I literally ran out. That was painful. Funny things happened too. She lived in an efficiency. One night she got a visitor. I had to hide. Where did I hide? Under the sink. There I am, Roman collar on, scrunched under the sink, wondering, "What the hell am I doing?"

Father Tod's story provides a further gloss on Malcolm's, highlighting the tensions inherent in celibate intimacy with women. Tod is unapologetic about his relationships, which he finds "nurturing, extremely helpful"; "that kind of psychological intimacy with women," he says, "takes a hell of a lot of the edge off the physical, because the relational needs are being met." He pays a price nonetheless, because "the expectation that priests don't have women friends is very much the same as that married couples don't have friends of the opposite sex." As a result, "it gets a little awkward at times," he says, "when one of them calls and a secretary answers and begins to recognize a voice." When he regularly attends Milwaukee Symphony concerts with a woman friend, "I can look diagonally from my seat and there's a group of priests up there. I stand up at intermission and sense a little awkwardness."

In his case, such intimacy produces unofficial but real signs of disapproval from the church—or at least from churchmen; it intensifies his own resentment at mandatory celibacy; and it makes him all the more aware of the limits of clerical living, of being "surrounded only by males." Thus, Tod's most satisfying remedy for loneliness and alienation becomes at the same time an additional source of discontent with the institution whose stresses he had hoped to soothe. This circular pattern, in which the antidote to priestly loneliness and frustration ends up distancing my classmates even further from the institutional church, is pervasive; it constitutes one of the central emotional configurations of their lives.

Another man was also in love with Jessica during this period, although Malcolm insists that she wanted no part of him; when he discovered that Malcolm was coming to her house, he slashed Malcolm's tires, threatened to beat him, and came close to choking Jessica in his rage.

None of these complications prodded Malcolm to end the relationship, however, because for all its prices, it offered him respite from his loneliness. The relationship ended only after Malcolm told her that he could never leave the priesthood:

> It was a terribly painful thing. I really wanted her to go on. But I knew I couldn't stop her from achieving another relationship with another person, and I told her that. It was quite the opposite of any movie you might see, with the priest or the monk riding into the sunset leaving the woman crying. *She* went into the sunset, leaving the priest crying. I couldn't have my cake and eat it too.

The break came several months before I talked to Malcolm the first time, and he was still reeling. He was convinced that loneliness was the basic pain now, just as relief from it had been his most intense satisfaction earlier. "Loneliness is not sexual," he said. "The overall loneliness is that you'd like just once in a while for someone to talk to." At present—a present that has extended over the four years of our conversations—he simply tries to get through the day:

> Some days are better than others. Some days I can cope with it, and some days, no. Some days I desire to make love something terrible, and I fantasize about it, I wonder about what it would be like to make love to a woman. I've been in love . . .
> During the day, I'm pretty busy at work, but at night, it gets pretty lonely. I might stay here till 9:30. I'm tired, I go to bed, I turn on cable TV and watch a movie maybe, at least to get my mind off something. Should I pray? I should pray. Do I pray? No.

The loneliness is terrible sometimes. The older you get, the more it is. You're not lonely all the time, and not everyone lives in life not being lonely. I'm not saying "poor me," don't get me wrong. But you know, you get lonely.

I'm not saying that as an excuse for what I did. It's just part of the life that is difficult. Many times I say, "Gee, maybe I should have married, because I enjoy the companionship of a person, especially of a woman." But then I also realize that one day doesn't last forever, that the hours do slip by and before you know it, you're in bed, and there's another day, and you say, "Well, I got through that."

When I reached forty, what bothered me the most was—I said to myself, "Gee, I'm never going to have a child that will be mine." That hit me, that hit me. There will never be another me like that, a part of me walking around. Now he may turn out to be a bum, but nonetheless . . . I always fantasize if I were to die and get to heaven, God would say, "You fool! You were supposed to marry her, you'd have these kids!" And I say, "Oh, I didn't know that. Why didn't you tell me that?"

In retrospect, Malcolm refuses to see his experience with Jessica as positive. "I deserve my punishment," he says, "because I had no right. I had no right." He repeatedly expressed intense regret for the pain he knows he has caused her; it was his own sense of shame about his unfair treatment of her more than any fear of exposure that made him initially reluctant to let me use his story. Besides, at this point, he cannot detect any increased wisdom in himself: "I can only hope and pray that I've become a better person, but right now I don't see it. I am not proud of myself." Nonetheless, when I turned to the different, predictable question about whether a priest can understand marriage or sexuality, his answer suggested to me that the experience had indeed affected his priesthood:

I don't think a priest ever will understand completely, any more than a lay person will understand the celibate life and the frustrations of a priest. I'll never know what it is to reach orgasm with a woman unless I fail in my vow. I'll never know what it's like to be able to change my child's diapers. But as long as you have suffered to some degree, you will understand suffering. That's the main thing. You will understand a woman or a man who comes in and says, "I'm lonely because my husband or wife is not intimate with me." I can understand what it means not to be intimate.

Malcolm's ten-year relationship with Jessica has left him no more certain about his stand on mandatory celibacy than he was before. "Do I agree with it? I don't even know," he said. "I don't even think about it, because I'm not going to get more frustrated than I am now. It isn't going to be changed in my lifetime, so why even ponder?" Malcolm is left, then, with a celibacy he feels he cannot avoid and a continuing affection for a woman he cannot marry. He is left, above all, alone.

True to their training, my classmates did not expect to need a lot of emotional satisfaction as priests. In the seminary, the church's hierarchies were made clear to us: religion had nothing to do with emotion; the love of God rose from the spirit, not from the flesh. The "flesh" linked together emotion and sexuality in a connection that spoke less of an integrated relationship between the two than of a hostility toward both as twinned opposites of rationality—and the elision of the two (rather than their interrelationship) persists in many of us today.

Just as we resident students were superior to the day students because we were more removed from the world, the celibate life was superior to marriage because it was more removed from the flesh, and the rational life was superior to feelings because it was—more rational. Sex was "necessary for procreation," it was conceded reluctantly. But if you didn't plan to procreate, you didn't really need sex; and according to the ascetic, minimalist ideal the church had retained from early monasticism, it was always better to do without things that you didn't absolutely need. In spiritual terms, less was always more.

Not that doing without would be easy. We were told often of St. Jerome's grim formula for sexual restraint: "between a man saint and a woman saint, a wall two feet thick." The ideal, as Hans Ziegler remembers, was "to weed that out. To be perfect was to be nonsexual." Or as Malcolm put it, "I'm really supposed to be in love with Christ and Christ only." And since we knew—because we were told—that God never asks the impossible, we knew that somehow God would give us the strength, the spiritual "muscle power," in the now-skeptical words of one of our former faculty members, to restrain ourselves.

Intimacy with God, of course, was necessary, the highest good; in heaven, blessedly purged of our bodies, we could enjoy a spiritual union untainted by emotion. But with man or woman it was suspect, dangerous. We heard a good deal about St. Simon Stiletes (the book on seminary heroes is waiting to be written), who demonstrated his sanctity by spending twenty years on top of a stone column. The forty feet by which he removed himself from human connection presumably brought him that much closer to God.

What modest amounts of emotional satisfaction we might need would be readily available, we thought, through institutionally provided channels, as they had been in the seminary. In our few unscheduled hours there, we rarely retreated to our rooms. Instead, we would stand outside the dining hall and talk, take walks in the woods in small groups, play cards in the smoker, or participate in intramural sports. We expected such easy camaraderie to continue forever, through the "fraternity of priests" into which we would be initiated at ordination. The seminary was our home away from home, and the rectory would take over that role after ordination. We would get further satisfaction from being as central to the world of the parish as we had been to the world of the seminary—appropriately so, in our minds, because we were, after all, central to the church itself. As one classmate put it, "I had everything very cleanly laid out. I was there to administer and to bring the archdiocese to the parish. The world was going to jump to see me come; great things would happen in the wake of my presence."

After the security of the seminary, loneliness came to my classmates—as it did to me, in different circumstances—as a series of shocks; they felt pain in areas where they did not anticipate any sensation at all. For one thing, many of them experienced the sense of being left out for the first time, of not being at the center of things. Not that everyone felt that he resided at the heart of the seminary; but since to study for the priesthood was in itself to reside close to the center of the church, marginality within the walls was a good deal more secure and prestigious than stature outside the walls. Even those classmates who felt peripheral on the seminary grounds testify that they were kings in their home parishes.

And since the seminary had been such a small and tightly scheduled world, we felt, accurately or not, that we knew everything that was going on at any given moment, even if we weren't there doing it. There was, after all, a limited range of activities available. If one class was in study hall, so were the others; if some of us were playing basketball, others were playing cards or taking walks. Inside our own world, we never had the sense that others might be doing something of an entirely different order, or something about which we had no clue whatever. We knew that people in "regular" schools were dating and doing God knows what else. But in our own surroundings, we had colonized all the available spaces. They held no mystery for us, no unknowns to tantalize us or make us feel deprived.

This history helps to account for the intense depression classmates such as Father Eugene felt—and still feel—on Sunday afternoons. On Sunday morning, their role in the liturgy confirms the sense of centrality which they internalized in the seminary. The response of the people energizes them; their mixing with the congregation afterward reaffirms in them the sense of personal connection which they entered the priesthood wanting and expecting. "What human being," Malcolm asked rhetorically when recounting the satisfactions of Sunday mass, "has one hour or more a week when they are the center of attention, when a large group of people are totally theirs?" Yet Sunday afternoon often finds them abandoned in front of the TV set, on call but rarely called, feeling peripheral instead of central, unwanted instead of indispensable.

No one in my class is more eloquent on this subject than Mark Klugman, for whom the loneliness of Sunday afternoons was a major factor in his eventually leaving the priesthood:

> Like they say, Sunday afternoons were the pits. Even if the Packers were playing well, they were the pits. If it was the pastor's Sunday off, and you were on, you went to your room, you turned on the TV and watched a double-header of football, or read a book. A lot of it was in contrast to the fact that in the morning, you were among the people, pouring your soul out to them with whatever little message you have for the day, talking to them after church. And they went off with their families. Maybe they went and stayed in front of the TV. But in your mind, gee, there was a family, they're going on a picnic, going to a movie, or home scrubbing the car. They probably thought, "Yeah, Father's sitting there and nobody's pestering him, he's got it made. You know, he doesn't have three kids screaming at him when he's trying to see the last play of the fourth quarter."
>
> During the week you had kids in school, you went over there. You were busy. At night you maybe had someone coming in for pre-marriage talks, or convert classes, or somebody with a problem wanted to come and talk to you. You were in contact with people; but on Sunday afternoon, boy, if you pulled the rectory duty, you were alone. You were hoping somebody started dying—you know, get me out of here; I want to talk to somebody.

Eventually, when the leveling effects of their own liberal theology had begun to take hold, my classmates would experience an even greater sense of being less important to the laity than they had expected to be. But for most of them, the sensation of diminished importance began immediately after ordination, when they finished their official Sunday morning business and then found themselves left, in many ways for the first time, to their own devices, with no community around them.

Not incidentally, Sunday afternoon also offered them no schedule to give them comfort. What to do with their own time? That freedom—exhilarating after years of structure, terrifying after years of structure—emerges intermittently throughout their week; but it is unavoidable on Sunday afternoon. On the immediate level, it offered them one of their first tastes of an undefined priesthood. "There is no structure to the priesthood," Malcolm told me. "You can make something of it or you can sleep." He cites the example of one priest who did just that, returning to his bedroom every day after mass and not emerging until dinner. A few of my classmates are self-starters, but many, by their own description, are not; they were not trained to be. "I don't know that I can make myself do something new," Father Eugene admits. "It's almost like when the diocese says, 'You've got to do this,' then there's the pressure to produce."

Feeling left out of parish/family life might not have been so difficult if the parish rectory had lived up to its billing as surrogate home, as their haven in the heartless "world," the place where the institutional church would live up fully to its billing as a nurturing, supportive mother. To the contrary, traditional rectory life comes across in these interviews as the clerical equivalent to an arranged marriage: an arbitrary bringing together of strangers with the expectation that they will make it work whether they like one another or not. For earlier generations of priests, that expectation was part of the package. But in an age of tentative, serial relationships predicated on continuing satisfaction, my classmates did not take to the arrangement eagerly in the first place, nor did they like what they saw when it was handed to them.

No doubt, generational stress has always been part of rectory life, often coalescing around the long waiting period endured by associates before they became pastor.[5] Such tensions were further complicated for my classmates, however, by their status as 1960s liberals who found docility especially distasteful (even as they found freedom discomforting). One classmate, who does not drink, tells of his outrage when his pastor ordered him to serve as bartender for older priests after the yearly Forty Hours devotions; another tells how his pastor would sweep into the dining room every day after mass, hold out his cape, and wait for his associates to take it from him. "He expected that kind of service. That was his expression of priesthood." It was the associate's job to answer the phone, while the pastor answered the door: the better to facilitate non-contact. In the two years my classmate spent in that parish, he and the pastor ate two meals together—both during the bishop's annual visit.

A great number of my classmates across the full spectrum of temperament echo Malcolm's complaint about a "lack of support" and trust from their first pastors: the pastor's public denigration of his associate's choice of reading material for grade-school children, for instance, or the pastor's cancellation, without consultation, of his associate's popular folk mass for youth. Their desire for such support harks back to their roots in the traditional church, in which the pastor was expected—however unrealistically—to serve as father figure to his associates as well to his parishioners. Yet to a significant degree, my classmates undercut their own chances at such trust through their resistance to established authority of any kind and their generational scorn for anyone over thirty. Since those suspicions were often matched by their pastors' equally intense distrust of upstart radicals, their early encounters were often classics of confrontation.

The conflict between Father Frederick, now a seminary professor, and his first pastor is typical. Frederick was one of the most interesting priests I talked with, a soft-spoken, gentle man with a wonderfully wry sense of humor—and a considerable store of stubbornness. His four years studying theology abroad during and immediately after the Vatican Council gave very definite shape to his sense of what a contemporary priest should be. Frederick arrived at his first parish afire with the latest Vatican II theology, only to find an old-time pastor more interested in brick and mortar. Further, Frederick had once been an obedient seminarian ("The thing for me was, don't do anything to get kicked out. I wanted to be a priest, and I wanted to do whatever that entailed") whose conversion to the questioning mode of the new theology left him little taste for docility. He recalls his first meeting with his pastor with full acknowledgment of—and only partial regret at—the intransigence he displayed then. His account reveals our generation's proud initial disdain for the material conditions of life, a disdain which has modified considerably. It also shows Frederick's lingering if limited deference to his pastor as pastor, along with his overriding conviction that he was—and still is—right in his theology. Today he would change his tactics, but his 1960s attitudes are intact:

> I came back into a very clerical church, where the pastor was the pastor, and the pastor was to be obeyed in all things. Now, of course, I can see some of the mistakes I made when I first came back, where I challenged the pastor, and it was a matter of talking at two different levels.
>
> I can remember when I first visited the parish, the pastor was interested in showing me the facilities, a really nice rectory. Well, I'm not interested in the rectory and I'm not interested in the living conditions; but that was an important thing for him. You know: "This is where you're going to be living, these are your rooms."
>
> He showed me the church and everything, and he showed me the school. Then he said, "We don't give the sign of peace here." There was no question in my mind that I was going to give the sign of peace—absolutely not. I thought to myself, "Well, you're not doing it, but I'm going to do it." Now, I think I would say, "Why not? Why don't you do it? Do you think that that's right? That the church is wrong in saying that this should be introduced? How does this fit in, what's the reason for it?" But I didn't challenge him, I just thought to myself, "Well, you do your thing and I'll do mine, and I'm right and you're wrong."
>
> After all, he was the pastor. So either I had to do what I did, or I'd have to get angry—and I didn't want to get angry. I didn't have the maturity to say, "Well, we can talk about this and disagree, and that won't bother me. I mean, you're wrong, but you're still a human being." But it wasn't that way with me. It was, "You're wrong."

Twenty years into their priesthood, the majority of my classmates are still not comfortable with older priests, most of whom, they feel, continue to reside in the old church; very few of them have found friends or mentors from that generation. And as we have already seen, they feel equally cut off from younger priests, whom they regard at best as retrograde conservatives and at worst as cynical careerists. Only a few have younger priest friends, and very few give evidence of providing mentoring to the next generation any more readily than they seek it from the previous generation. Their sense of 1960s uniqueness keeps them going and cuts them off at the same time.

Among members of their own generation, many of them want close relationships but find them hard to maintain. Father Thurman, for instance, finds that priestly friendships are complicated by the "very mobile society and very busy, fast-paced life" which priests, like others, now live. Father Tod is aware of a "sense of competitiveness" among priests that makes him "a little reluctant to take that step and trust." For Father Herbert, "workaholism"—an interesting reevaluation of the total commitment to the job traditionally expected of priests—is a "major disease" affecting priests as much as it affects others, making impossible the leisure and spontaneity necessary for friendship.

This isolation is all the worse for the fact that classmates such as Father Spencer see themselves, accurately or not, as the first generation of priests who do not accept loneliness as part of the package, who now openly acknowledge their need for intimacy:

> Older priest friends would deny that they need that intimacy, or they would phrase it in different ways. They need their buddies, maybe they need their friends. They get it a lot of times in booze or in getting together with the guys and drinking. I don't think that everybody who left [the priesthood] necessarily left because of intimacy questions. But I think that those who are around know that they've got to have something more.

A minority of my classmates, including Spencer, say that they do have at least one or two close priest friends. For the majority, however, finding "something more" with other priests—the first sanctioned place they looked—has proven almost as difficult outside their assigned rectories as it has inside.

Partly in response to the busyness of their lives, a number of priests belong to support groups which meet on a regular basis to "talk about what's going on in our priesthood," as one priest put it. Several of my classmates belong to Caritas, a similar, more formal program of support groups which meet periodically for overnight sessions. Caritas meets with mixed reviews: some value it; others shun it either as "mushy sentimentalism" or as window-dressing, a superficial institutional attempt to smooth over deep problems of priestly isolation. A few fear it as a form of surveillance.

In short, for most of my class, the promised fraternity of priests never materialized. Father Albert, who mourns the disappearance of his early hopes in a number of areas, says that there is "not as much [priest companionship] as I had expected. I don't have a group of priests that I would go out with regularly. I don't sense that cliquishness that we were told in the seminary would be there, this club of priesthood that would always be there." Some, in fact, have a positive aversion to the company of priests. Although Father Malcolm admits that at present, "my loneliness is so acute that I don't mind their company," he is convinced that in general, "a lot of priests don't like being with other priests. One of our former teachers used to say that when you gather priests together, it's like manure. You know, manure is good if you spread it out." I heard that phrase from more than one priest; it seems to have achieved the status of folk wisdom.

Father Tod, for one, suggests that this disdain of priests for one another and the isolation it produces is rooted ultimately (as so many issues are for my classmates) in institutional attitudes: since the church does not treat priests with respect, they have a hard time regarding one another highly. Fellow priests become reduced, in their own eyes, to the working class out of which most of them came:

> There was always a lot of talk about that, the fraternity of priests, the esprit de corps, second only to the marines. Fine. That, I don't think by far and large, has really happened. I and a number of other men went through a bit of disillusionment with that, realizing that we're just a bunch of workers.

That Special Feeling: The Aura That Isolates

> Catholics seem to imagine their clergy differently than do members of other denominations. Despite themselves and the crisis in their morale, priests are nonetheless perceived as sacraments of a world that transcends our own. They are the sacramental persons par excellence. They want to be, if one is to credit the passionate assertions of some priests, "just like everyone else." But the Catholic imagination, fully aware of the human limitations of its clergy, still imagines them as "different," as hints of what the ever-lurking God is like, as rumors of angels, as men who point to a world beyond themselves, as signals of the transcendent God.
>
> —Andrew Greeley, *The Catholic Myth* (1990)

An additional factor in my classmates' isolation is the sense of specialness which the seminary inculcated in us, the conviction that as priests we would be somehow more than human, "all things to all men," an "alter Christus." The priest could handle his baser urges (urges were inherently base) with greater ease, sublimate them more smoothly than the rest of men. He either was cooler at the core or had readier access to the coolant of grace. He was, in short, different—and hence, for instance, capable of a celibacy that most men would consider beyond them.

The traditional church to which my classmates and I gravitated in the 1950s did everything it could to perpetuate the notion that priests should and could maintain an inviolate center untouched by everything around them—and as a corollary, not communicated to anyone else. Our seminary faculty played their part; they were there to prepare us for the traditional super-priesthood, and it was consistent with that aim that they tried to conceal from us any serious tensions they might feel. We had little evidence that celibacy might be an anguishing thing for them, that living on campus and being on call twenty-four hours a day might cause strain, that they might need more time away from us, that they might need anything apart from us—or ultimately, that they might really need anything at all apart from more chances to serve God fully.

We were the centers of that world, after all, and we assumed that they were content to be our supportive periphery. And although we did see evidence that some of them were not happy—specifically, that they were lonely—the fact that they bore their unhappiness silently seemed to imply that they bore it willingly; we read that willingness as a sign of their otherworldly spirituality, which added to their mystique. And of course silence itself is part of the mystique; the cultural ideal of the stiff upper lip is built into the model of priesthood through the seal of the confession. The priest, like the cowboy of movie fame, is a man who can keep his mouth shut;[6] what the church denied us in one area of traditional masculinity it instilled all the more emphatically in another.

In the traditional seminary, in the traditional priesthood, as in the (relatively, ostensibly) more traditional marriages of my parents' generation, the prevailing ideal was not to let the strains show. The effect on those of us raised in those settings was to suggest that there were no strains. Family systems psychologists have recently explored the tendency of family members to replicate the structures and behavior patterns—negative as well as positive—of their immediate and extended families: patterns lived through and deeply felt etch themselves in our memories and become our behavioral maps, whether we like it or not.[7] My classmates and I are the offspring of a seemingly flawless priesthood, and we suffer from the analogous, residual, guilt-producing conviction that we should be flawless too.

As seminarians, we bought that image eagerly because we saw ourselves as special; to accept the necessarily flawed humanity of priests would be to give up our own aura. It would be to give up taking for granted the deference that priests and seminarians (we felt) had coming to them. So if celibacy was a superhuman demand, we felt we could meet it, because we were selected out. And if God expected us to be "all things to all men" and yet simultaneously to deny our own impulses in the process—no need to be all things to ourselves—we knew we could do that too; God never asked the impossible.

On the level of their experience, my classmates now *know* that they are not immune, that they are not essentially different from the rest of men, and they resent the way that the illusion of difference continues to produce unrealistic expectations—and hence to isolate them further from the laity. "Everybody expects you to bat a thousand," Father Malcolm complains:

> You can never blow a homily, you can never be too tired to do something. You always have to be there for the people. You can never say, "Geez, I'm too tired tonight." Maybe you've got a hemorrhoid, or a toothache. But they say, "God, your homily wasn't very good." And you say, "Do you get up and always hit a homer?" A priest has got to be Robert Schuler or Fulton Sheen or Jimmy Swaggart every time.

More than one of them went into a tirade specifically against the Bing Crosby, *Going My Way* image of the priest[8] as a man who evokes admiration but never feels passion, the no-sweat priest whose humanity is reduced to his charm, his most endearing, least problematic side; such a priest, as Father Albert describes him, "could come up very quickly with a response to every situation. He was a person who was in many ways removed from reality."

By contrast, my classmates' desire to be seen as human, flaws and all, was one of the most intense and eloquent wishes I heard in our conversations. When I asked one priest who had recently moved into a new parish what he would most like his parishioners to understand about priests, he responded at length and with considerable passion on the laity's tendency to ignore a priest's common humanity and on the loneliness which he suffers as a result:

> I don't think people really know their priests very well. They see us in a role. Rarely do people really understand us, or take time to want to understand us. Rarely does anybody ever sit down and ask you questions about how you are inside; the kinds of questions you ask—rarely does anybody ever ask them without some other agenda going on.
>
> We're an enigma to many of them, I think. We're much more like them than they realize. Much more. Part of me enjoys the role of priest and pastor and having "power" and the ability to make things happen. But that's not all of me. There's another part of me that likes not to make any decisions and likes to just be able to shift gears completely and do something totally different. I like vacations where my lifestyle is totally different from what it is here. I need that. There are very few people who really see that side of us or take time to see it.
>
> I remember getting here to this parish—the reception was cool. I'm sure it was because of other things that were going on here in the past. But I don't think people realize how hard it is for a priest to come here,

or anywhere. To uproot yourself from where you were for eight years, get plunked into a new place. I don't know if they think about it or not. That when a priest comes into your parish and it's brand new for him— what a trauma that is. You know what a trauma it is just to move from one house to another with your family, staying in the same job maybe. It's big stress. For us, we move where we work, we move who we work with. It's a complete uprooting. You come over here and get plunked down, and that's really hard. It's probably harder on you as you get older and you long for someone who's going to be a real friend.

If we ever told them how we really were—how often we were shaken in our own faith or how often we felt like quitting or how sometimes we'd like to tell them what we think of them—they probably wouldn't like it too much. Whatever it is that makes people like Ronald Reagan— maybe it's a similar thing about their priests. They prefer an image or a veneer. They don't really want what's underneath or somebody who's going to disagree with them.

Tell people that in many cases they are much holier than their priests. [Tell them] not to be so terribly shocked when they hear a priest getting into trouble. And not to be too sad when a priest leaves. Because if a guy has done a good job and helped people, you ought to thank God for the good work he's done and not think about what he's not going to do.

Bring the priest a cupcake or something. Anything. Sit and chat for a while. Anything.

Their desire to have their humanity acknowledged helps to explain my classmates' recurring insistence that the pressures of celibacy are similar to the pressures of marriage rather than essentially different: we are all in the same boat. Of course, I was told repeatedly, we would like to have an intimate relationship, and we find it frustrating not to. But isn't it frustrating for married men like you not to be intimate with more than one woman? We're not so different.

Many of the priests in my class, however, suffer from the residual assumption that they *should* be above it all even though they know they aren't. Though Father Albert, for instance, vehemently resents the *Going My Way* image and insists, "I don't feel that I'm a different person," he still admits that "in the back of my mind I wish I were one of those ideal priests." The assumption of specialness and difference dies hard, even when it exacts a price. Its persistence is one of the strongest indications that the "old church" still has a considerable hold on many of us who have consciously turned away from that church's definitions and dictates.

Another reason why my classmates have a hard time letting go of that ideal is that their parishioners yearn to keep it intact. The laity, according to Father Albert, "still want to consider priests special":

Very often with kids that I take hiking or whatever, they're still surprised to find that I'm normal or natural. They would prefer to have a hero. Even adults still want to have the church like it was in *Going My Way*. They would be more comfortable if priests were that way.

Although surveys of lay opinion in recent years have made it clear that the laity want "human" priests, my classmates' comments confirm what these studies suggest: that the humanity found desirable involves friendliness, accessibility, humor, understanding—traits which make the priest an appealing, effective dispenser of services.[9] Such surveys focus almost exclusively on what laity expect from priests; there is no comparable emphasis on what priests might hope for from the laity, nor on what the laity might contribute to priests in the way of understanding or attending to *their* needs. Andrew Greeley has similarly suggested that married women who receive counseling from priests strongly support mandatory celibacy;[10] the priest's celibacy gives such women access to an understanding listener without their having to consider his needs in the process.

The priest's humanity in this context does not include flaws, problems, or intrusive desires—for privacy, on the one hand, or sympathetic companionship, on the other—which might interfere with those services; hence my classmates' lament that the laity, accustomed to twenty-four-hour shopping, still expect them to be on call at any time yet will otherwise leave them alone and lonely—on Sunday afternoon, for instance.

The accessible priest thus becomes a provider/product to be used and judged; as one priest complained, "We get put into roles, and people don't want us for ourselves." In the new church, another priest told me approvingly, the priest is more a "sign" of the church than its privileged embodiment; yet on the negative side, in the bitter words of one of our seminary professors, "priests are treasured many times for their sign value, not for their real value—and certainly not for their personal value." This ironic, veiled functionalizing of the relationship between priest and laity constitutes, I think, one of the crucial elements in the transformation of the personal, nurturing church my classmates expected into an impersonal "institution."

Such functionalizing also helps to explain the recurring note of self-reference (inclining at times toward self-absorption) in my classmates' comments on what *they* need or, as we shall see in the next section on sexuality and celibacy, on what would fulfill *them* or how relationships with women do or could make *them* whole. The laity's expectation that priests will serve them provides the only concrete model my classmates have for how relationships work; hence they too talk of how others might serve or fulfill them, without much emphasis in either case on mutuality.

It is precisely in setting priests off as different, that is, that the church has shaped men whose very longing for genuine relationships reflects the distortions of those who are set off; a noticeable degree of self-referentiality in regard to relationships is, I would argue, one of the very effects of celibacy, even in men who want to escape celibacy as a way of escaping the confines of the self. "Priests are selfish," one of them told me, acknowledging what he saw as a regrettable inevitability. "Our structure has not liberated us yet as men," another acknowledged; "that's what we're fighting for."

Even if sympathetic laity attempt to understand a priest's frailties, hostile outsiders are more likely to hold him strictly accountable for any significant violation of the ideal. One priest in my class who had had a long-term sexual relationship with a woman sent me a front-page clipping from the *Milwaukee Journal* to explain why he was reluctant to let me use his story, even in disguised form. The article described allegations that a prominent Jesuit had had an affair with a woman eight years earlier. The Jesuit was named in the article, the woman was not, and he had been summarily suspended by his order, pending further investigation. I know nothing about the merits of this case, nor am I trying to defend sexual exploitation, if that should prove to be true. What is clear, however, is that in the context of aggressive media—my classmates see the Milwaukee press core as sharks in relation to the church—the image of what a priest should be or might aspire to be becomes, as it often is now for politicians, what he must be, or claim to be, to maintain his position. The murkier areas of complex behavior and mixed motives are not allowed him.

In *Our Inner Conflicts,* Karen Horney suggests that "the most unyielding neurotic solution to anxiety is the self's creation of an 'idealized image' "; to her, perfectionist impulses invariably veil an unacknowledged self-contempt.[11] It strikes me, however, that in relation to my classmates, the process is reversed. It is not their individual, personal anxieties which cause a compensatory, perfectionist ideal; the longstanding, idealized image of a priest did not originate with my classmates, after all. Rather, the established model of superhuman perfection, internalized by them even if they reject it rationally, causes their anxiety and self-doubt precisely because the church has linked that model with its definition of (otherworldly) holiness.

No wonder, then, that many priests find it impossible to tell outsiders of their failings and difficulties. Father Malcolm, for instance, has never told anyone about his relationship with Jessica:

> I had no right to get involved with that woman. And what's even harder is that you cannot share your grief with anyone unless you go to confession. I can't go home and tell my housekeeper that I am more lonely now because a woman I fell in love with has decided that she just can't take our relationship. What do you say? I can't tell my sister, I can't tell anyone. I can't share that with anyone!

Perhaps the most damaging result of the residual notion of priestly difference, however, is that it tends to isolate my classmates from one another. Many of them do not speak openly of their problems to their peers, because they still cling to the assumption that other priests are immune even if they are not.

"Do you tell your classmates?" Malcolm asked himself after relating his story to me. "No, I couldn't. If some people really knew what was going on in my life, they would probably be surprised and shocked." When I suggested that if they knew what was bothering him, they might tell him what was bothering them, he replied, "That could be, because I'm as ignorant about their lives as they are of mine." It would be difficult to tell other priests if he fell in love, Father Tod said, because "we've had that saintly model so ingrained in us, the saintly models that have become part of our own image of what it is to be a priest." If they cannot live up to a flawless image—not one of them claims to—they keep the ideal behind it alive by projecting it onto their peers.

As a result, however, they induce much of their own considerable loneliness. One of the reasons that the "brotherhood of priests" has never materialized for many of them is that they tend to see other priests as colleagues (if not rivals) across the table rather than as brothers under the skin. If rectory life has not been a haven in a heartless world for them, this is partly because it is a place where men just as troubled and needy as other men tend to deal with one another "professionally" without ever touching on their personal problems. In this regard, the rectory mirrors the boardroom and reinforces once more the model of reticent, controlled masculinity in men who desperately need and want "something more."

For a few classmates, a change of assignment has involved the forced separation from true companions; for most, it has meant the trading of one set of tense relationships for another. In that sense, their comparisons of celibacy with marriage make painful sense: they know what it is like to be distant in the midst of anticipated intimacy. Better to live in an apartment, as Malcolm does, as so many of them now do, and have the advantage of privacy, than to suffer isolation without privacy.

Several of them told me things which, they said, they had never told a priest outside of confession. They did this, I think, not only because they assumed that I was still "good people," but because I did not hold back from them the complications of my own life: I was not immune, and so they did not have to claim immunity. Malcolm, for one, was visibly relieved when I assured him that, although I could not give him any names or details, I had heard comparable problems from other priests as well. "Is that right? Really?" he said, with open amazement. In one of the many ironies of this project, I became, to some of them, their confessor, precisely because I was not a priest.

My classmates' loneliness, like their seminary immersion in change, has gone a long way toward reshaping their sense of themselves and of their relationship to the church. They were ordained expecting the priesthood to be personally satisfying. It was in the relatively self-contained arena of the rectory that they experienced their first personal dissatisfaction as priests and in which they first expressed their discontent at the perceived insensitivity and rigidity of the church's official representatives. Their present, pervasive frustration with an impersonal, indifferent institution was born in the house which proved not to be a home.

Similarly, having felt left out by the bulk of their parishioners and not as close as they would like to be with other priests, they would move increasingly away from the parish as sole center of their lives and learn to look to themselves for satisfaction; hence their movement to "alternative housing." Hence too their eventual espousal of personalist philosophies of growth to articulate their conviction that the needs of the individual must take precedence over his institutional role. These philosophies would give form to what had already begun to emerge: their felt need to look somewhere other than to the institutional church for the "something more" they long for. As we shall see in the next chapter, that impulse would make the restrictions of celibacy all the harder to accept.

Celibacy and Sexuality: Competing Spiritualities

> Man has an essential nature of his own. . . . Full health and normal and desirable development consist in actualizing this nature, in fulfilling these potentialities, and in developing into maturity. . . . By this concept what is good? Anything that conduces to this desirable development in the direction of actualization of the inner nature of man. What is bad or abnormal? Anything that frustrates or blocks or denies the essential nature of man.
>
> . . . The healthy man is all of a piece, integrated, we might say. It is the neurotic person who is at odds with himself, whose reason struggles with his emotions.
>
> —Abraham Maslow, *Motivation and Personality* (1970)

> [The perspective of this book] accepts health as our best criterion for the soundness and rightness of religious experience.
>
> —Eugene Kennedy, *Tomorrow's Catholics, Yesterday's Church* (1988)

> I'd have to give more thought to squaring intimacy with priesthood. But I have human needs too. I'm far enough along that I can make my own decisions. I wouldn't want

an external judgment or body to determine my decisions
in this regard.

—Father Herbert

When we were ordained five years, someone got several
of us together for a retreat. It was a pretty good experience. The first guy started out all pious and everything
was wonderful. I remember one classmate, who was still
a priest at the time, saying, "Jesus Christ, give me a
break. I don't know what the hell you're talking about,
but that ain't the life I led. Let's get real." So we did. It
was great, because we went around that room, and almost to a man, every prostitute or massage parlor from
Pittsburgh to Minneapolis had been hit by us. Somewhere along the line, we had all acted out sexually, almost all. So it was a very affirming kind of thing. We
never redid that experience. Maybe it was too much. We
broke up into small groups after and never got together
again.

—Father Rupert

In a generation of (often) lonely priests who do not accept loneliness
as part of the package, who know that they've "got to have something
more" and do not find it for the most part with other priests, and who
no longer give automatic, overriding weight to institutional mandates,
how does obligatory celibacy fit? In what terms do they deal with a celibate priesthood, and how do those terms affect their relationship to a
church which continues to insist on it?

"Celibacy is a real difficulty for me," Father Edmund said, "and I
think for all priests. I have some wonderful woman friends, and there
are times when I think this is the most wonderful thing that could happen, just being with a woman, sharing, and the sense of intimacy."

Father Edmund's distress over the issue of celibacy is unusual only in
the degree of thoughtfulness he brings to it and the evident intensity
of—not too strong a term in his case—his anguish. Edmund is a man
both very warm and very thoughtful; during our several conversations
over a four-year period, he showed himself to be a careful listener with
an open mind, a man who tries hard to think his way through his problems instead of following his immediate impulses—although those impulses are very strong indeed. If I said something he found worth attending to, he would do just that, for several seconds, before responding;
he ponders more evidently than anyone I know, though his quick grin
and ready sense of humor keep him well short of ponderous.

Edmund and I had several conversations over a three-year period. He
does not specialize in small talk; he has real issues to discuss, and he
gets to the point quickly—partly by temperament, and partly because,
as he said, "I can't talk about these things with ———," citing the most

likely candidate among his colleagues. Once in particular, by the time we had reached the freeway on our way to a restaurant, no more than three minutes after I picked him up in front of his rectory, he started in right where we had left off a year before on the subject of Anna Maria, the woman he has loved for several years and whom he would love to marry—if he could do so and remain a priest.

Edmund's pain over mandatory celibacy was all the more moving because, although he certainly gives Anna Maria her due—he showed me her photograph in evident confidence that I would be struck, which I was—he also tries to give celibacy its due. He acknowledges the costs of intimacy ("the effort it takes to be sensitive to another person"), the limits of human love, and the advantages of the "solitude" which psychiatrist Anthony Storr has described eloquently: positive time alone to be creative, to think the thoughts which might never come if energy is channeled into personal relationships.[12] Ultimately, Edmund tries to subsume his loneliness in his relationship with God, who remains a personal presence for him:

> The thing that comes to mind is Augustine, who said, "Our hearts are restless until they rest in you, O God." The human heart cannot be filled with human love alone. In my best moments, I try to say, "Don't try to run away from the loneliness, because the loneliness is also where you're going to find strength." I feel in my deepest moments that loneliness is something that I chose in order to do other things. I feel that loneliness is part of the ministry, at least as we know it. The thing that I've been trying to do—I struggle with it—is to have time for the Lord, when I really bring all my loneliness to the Lord and say, "I struggle with my relationships with men, I struggle with my relationships with women, I experience satisfaction and dissatisfaction with both, and I have to find the source of the unity of all my relationships in You." I find a certain peace and integration in that.

And yet he is nonetheless convinced that intimacy with a woman could benefit his ministry because "the women who are really closest to me can understand what priesthood means to me." Specifically, he would love to be able to marry Anna Maria because "when I'm with her, I feel really graced. She is very perceptive, very spiritual." Perhaps uppermost in his mind—gauging from the number of his references—she seems to offer him the only route he can see to the psychological integration he seeks for himself and for his work as a priest: "We can't say that humanity is just composed of Adam and it's not composed of Eve," he now realizes, fully aware of how exclusively male our training was. "It's a matter of integrating the feminine and the masculine. . . . I'm really struggling with that—to say, 'Well, what is the feminine part of me and how can I draw on that?' Anna Maria is so aware of feelings, and of my feelings. It's like a mirror; I couldn't see it without her saying it this way." As a result, all his concessions to celibacy to the contrary, "if there was an option of choosing a different priesthood today, I would choose it."

Edmund has made several transcontinental trips to see Anna Maria over the last six years. His movements back and forth from Milwaukee to the West Coast reflect his own ambivalence: drawn to her and yet unable to leave the priesthood behind; drawn to the priesthood yet unable to leave her behind. But because "this is the only priesthood that we have," and because he feels strongly committed to his work, he had concluded the last time we spoke that "I've got to let go of Anna Maria emotionally." He finds that prospect "very, very hard."

Ultimately, he knows that a celibate priesthood has traditionally been based on the model of sublimation, and he knows what this model demands of him: "I need to take some of the emotional energy that I want to give to Anna Maria and see how I can incorporate that into what I'm doing here" in the parish—to direct his emotions into his homilies, for instance—but this too is "very, very hard." This is not, for him, an eager embrace of the traditional (male) claim that work comes first and other complications—human beings, for instance—be damned. For him, as for Malcolm, the reason the energies of love and the energies of work do not readily mix is that the church forces apart what he would love to join together.

Similarly, he is convinced that the traditional claim that grace will always suffice to help a priest cope with his desires simply fails to take human nature into account; many priests, he says, discover after ordination that "it [celibacy] is not my charism"; they realize too late that "I can't do it, I can't do it. If it's not this woman, it's another woman. I don't have it, I can't do it." He is also convinced that the ultimate damage for such an unhappily celibate priest is that "I put so much energy into being celibate that I don't do a damn thing. I'm not productive at all because all of my energy goes into coping with this." Since he feels very strongly "the need to be creative and productive" as a priest, his worst fear is that giving up the woman he loves will damage him and thus impair his priesthood, leaving him with neither source of fulfillment.

Edmund's willingness to wrestle with these questions fuels his resentment at the church's unwillingness to do the same. Echoing Tod's complaint that the church skirts the celibacy issue by asserting that "it's not supposed to be" a problem, Malcolm laments the willful silence of the institutional church:

> It's not easy to be honest, to say, "What are the structures that really can't be productive, and where does this structure have to change?" I find that's where the church is today. We have to be honest about what structures are helpful and what structures really have to change be-

cause they're not serving anybody. I don't think that we're willing to
do that. Celibacy is absolutely taboo to talk about.

During the course of our conversations, Edmund vacillated over what
to do: he could not imagine not being a priest—beyond his considerable
devotion to his work, he was also well aware that he has no readily mar-
ketable skills—and yet he could not muster whatever it would take to
put an end to the relationship. The last time I talked to him, he had decided that the work of a priest was paramount for him; he told me that
he had put Anna Maria on hold. Yet he was obviously still struggling;
even in the act of explaining his decision, he talked about her with great
affection and energy, his voice softening as he explained, as he had several times before, what a wonderful woman she is. He remains convinced that the two of them would be a good match emotionally and
spiritually and that married to her, he would be a better priest.

Of all the priests I interviewed, Father Jeff (about whom I cannot provide many details, for reasons which will quickly be clear) reveals most
compellingly the connection suggested by Father Eugene between a
newly impersonal God in the heavens and a heightened drive for strong
personal relationships here in this world. "I don't think of God," Jeff
says, "necessarily as some individual somewhere who's running all of
this, and I have a good relationship with Him. It's like a cosmic energy,
and I'm in harmony with that energy." Specifically, he lives out his own
claim that sexual intimacy—homosexual intimacy, in his case—is a principal means of connecting with that energy. Hence, consistent with
Eugene's notion that whatever promotes love is good, Jeff argues that
sexual intimacy is positively related to spirituality and ministry. The co-
herence of his argument offers the greatest challenge to a listener's inclination to judge quickly or categorize easily on the issue of sexually
active priests.

By his own admission, Jeff came to the seminary to escape "a miserable family situation"; both of his parents were alcoholics and his father
was physically abusive to his mother and sister as well as to him. He
thinks now that "I was a natural for religion because I needed a father.
I was always being cut down by my father. I didn't have a 'dad,' so I
could get into God. I needed a mother, I got it in Mary. I needed a brother,
I got it in Jesus. I wanted to be a saint; I wanted to be someone that people could look up to and imitate." In the seminary, partly because he was
a good athlete, he found "all the positive strokes that I did not get at
home. I had a great need to be accepted, and so did all the things that
I needed to do in the seminary to be accepted, and I was. I was very
happy."

But in the early years of his priesthood, he became radically lonely once again:

> In my first parishes, no one knew me, and even after they did, they didn't particularly care. They weren't very impressed. I never have thought more seriously of suicide than I did in those years. Many nights being up till four or five in the morning, I really did want to die. If I could have thought of a way of killing myself that didn't hurt, I might have done it. People used to ask me if I had ever thought of leaving the priesthood. I would say, in a joking manner, "Oh yes, about once a month, every month, since I got ordained." Basically because of loneliness. What I wanted was relationships. I loved the work, but had I found a relationship that would have worked for me, I would have left. That was always my bottom line.

It is not surprising, then, that every element linked to Jeff's notion of spirituality—from extrasensory perception to his vision of what the early church was and the present church should be—is characterized by an intense need for close and positive human relationships. He sees nothing radical about this; he considers his emphasis on personal growth through mutual support a return to the model of the early church. For him, the church's more recent emphasis on mandated behavior is a lapse from that ideal:

> I really do believe that I can sense spiritual energy, and that other people who are attempting to communicate on that wavelength pick it up, and we communicate. It no longer surprises me at all that I'll begin thinking about someone and a day or two later, about the time it took the mail to get to me, I'll get a letter from them. I feel such a tremendous sense of unity with people all over the world who want to get together and pray and talk about their lives.
>
> I've often felt that that's exactly what the primitive church was. It was a group of people who were free to get together and share, like your men's support groups. Where they could really share life the way it was, with all the shit and how messed up it was. Somewhere along the line, the church got out of that. It was no longer self-help through acknowledging our weaknesses, but became a group of people who tried to be good and show how strong they were.
>
> Oftentimes, when I go into church, I am filled with a lot of sadness because I see people sitting there in these pews, in a great deal of pain, for all sorts of reasons. I would like to be able to say to them, "Oh gosh, if we could really acknowledge how weak and helpless we all are. There is such power and energy here that is available here for us, but it won't force its way in. Until we let go, it's not going to barge down the door."

For Jeff, the need for closeness is inseparable from the need for sexual intimacy, of whatever kind:

> When you talk about relationships, we're also talking about sexual fulfillment. We now seem to be claiming for married people that there is no conflict between love of a woman and love of God. Love of your wife is love of God. So I have not found any opposition, really, between the love given and accepted between me and another man, and my ministry and priesthood or my relationship with God. It seems to strengthen it and fulfill it and motivate it and encourage it.

His theology, which is simultaneously Christ-centered and growth-centered, is consistent with his actions. In the seminary, he was drawn to the priesthood so he could become an "alter Christus"—specifically, a priest who could nourish others by his contact with them:

> I was really turned on by his healing ministry. Jesus was the model for us in the way he used power. Here was a man with absolute power, but his absolute power did not corrupt absolutely. He was the only one who ever succeeded in always using power to heal and strengthen. I have a great desire for that. I like to focus my sense of power in my hands. Whenever I touch another human being, and my life comes in contact with theirs, that somehow that touch would send them away stronger, healed, more powerful, more confident than they were before they met me. Because I would allow myself to be a vehicle, as Jesus did, for this positive cosmic energy flowing through me. That's very exciting.

For Jeff, the counterculture Christ who emerged from the 1960s is an "anti-institutional figure" who provides us not with prescriptive behavioral norms but with the example of a man who "valued his own experience," most notably his perfect relationship with his Father. "His own experience of His love for His Father," according to Jeff, "that sense of being in touch with a cosmic energy, was his dominant claim to authority"; this is Jeff's claim as well.

By extension, behavior which fosters relationships is healthy; behavior which damages relationships—as Jeff remembers all too well from his childhood—is harmful to the spirit. So by those standards, Jeff is convinced that his compulsive gambling—an addiction it took him more than ten years to shake—was spiritually damaging and made him less of a priest not because it violated an abstract code of conduct but because it obsessed him, made him a "bastard" who relegated people to the periphery of his vision, thus impaired his humanity. Conversely, he feels his sexual intimacies are spiritually sound and have made him a better priest because "they never seemed to draw me away from people, or take me away from my work, or my studies, or God. They seemed to draw me closer."

Taken together, priestly ministry and sexual intimacy allow him to express his central traits ("Every inch of me is a priest, every inch of me is a human being") and are therefore complementary rather than contradictory forces in his life. If the church says otherwise, the church can be ignored:

> I have never felt from the day that I took the promise of celibacy that it was really something that I believed in. They always called it a gift. I guess they still do. But I never felt that I had received that gift. [I felt] that it was an unjust requirement that I was forced to sign. Sort of like the making of a confession when you're in prison or captive. It was not something that I had truly chosen. And so consequently, I'm not in conscience bound to follow an unjust law. You know, Martin Luther King or whatever. I made sure that my public life was scandal-free, so that I could maintain my life as a priest, but I didn't feel that I needed to be celibate. So for a lot of years, I had my relationships within the priesthood. I didn't need to leave the priesthood to find them. . . . Because if you want to get into typical church language, your conscience is your ultimate guide.

Yet if Jeff is consistent with his own stated standards, he pays his price for adhering to them. He is by temperament an expressive, verbally open person who admits to "a great desire, a great need, to be accepted." In spite of his evident reasons for caution, he was eager to talk with me—originally in the rectory, even though one of his associates might well have wandered in on the conversation, and again for a second session, far beyond the time I had originally estimated for him. When he had finished, he was openly relieved that I was not shocked at his disclosures. "I'm glad," he said. "That's great."

Yet in order to keep himself "scandal-free" and able to function as a priest, Jeff cannot speak openly about himself except in a few private enclaves. Here the isolating effects of priestly specialness come home with terrible irony: Jeff believes on the one hand that there is great power waiting to be tapped if we would simply acknowledge our universal human weakness; yet he does not tell other priests of his problems because he still assumes that other priests are celibate. "You don't go around asking people about their sexual lives or their sexual practices," he said. "You kind of assume that if someone is a priest he is celibate." So in spite of his conviction that his sexuality is central to his identity ("I am held and I hold. I kiss and I am tender. I love and I have fun doing it. I am this warm, sexual, loving person. I don't think I could ever be other than that. Nor do I want to be"), he must keep that identity secret and hence run his own risk of diminishing his humanity.

More specifically, although Jeff had recently suffered a "major blow" in the breakup of an intense two-year relationship—"I feel that I was divorced, here I was a priest getting divorced"—he could find no way to alleviate the pain: "I thought, 'Jesus Christ, this guy needs support, and where am I going to go to talk to somebody about this who isn't going to freak out?' "

Ironically, although it was the need for approval which led him to the seminary, where he could get "all the positive support and strokes I did not get at home," he has now replicated his family system: his sexual behavior renders him once again marginal, an outsider who knows that "my way of loving is never going to be accepted by the three major valuing institutions in the world: family, church, and civil law. So who the hell am I going to go to for validation?"

Not to the general public, he realizes, for "80 percent of the world's population would be severely critical of me and probably reject me." That leaves him, in his search for validation, only with his conviction that he is acting according to his own conscience. Yet my classmates and I are good evidence for the claim that conscience is never totally independent of the social contexts which shaped it—one reason we stay in institutions is that we still feel their defining power—and Jeff admits, "I feel guilt at times":

> Maybe once a year I have this horrible nightmare of dying and going to God. It is scary because everything in which I ought to invest trust and belief tells me that what I am doing is terribly wrong. So who am I to stand against this? Who am I? I want to be a good person. I don't want to be the kind of person who would cause other people to say, "This church is just full of hypocrisy and bullshit." But I know that if some people knew who I was, they would come to that conclusion. I try to be authentic and real, and my experience has told me that people find out around me that it's okay for them to be who they are. Knowing that I could or would be rejected helps me be more understanding of other people and the ambiguity of their lives. They see me as credible and helpful. But if there's a source of ambiguity in my life, of anxiety, that's it.

The progress of our conversation itself suggested the levels of his discomfort. Early in our first talk, he told me about his gambling problem; he did not feel defensive about that trait, even with someone he had not seen in years. He began discussing his sexual activities much later, in our second talk, after a good deal of mutual self-revelation (I found myself as grateful about his nonjudgmental stance toward me as he was about mine). Only toward the end of that second, lengthy talk did he pull his current copy of *The Advocate* out from under a notebook and acknowledge that he was actively homosexual.

Jeff's position is inherently tense: he is still in the church, and the church is still in him. He cannot rid himself of it, nor does he want to, since he is "every inch a priest." Yet he can never feel a full part of the church so long as he continues to seek an intimacy which it forbids him:

> Am I comfortable in an institution? I suppose my answer is yes and no, but I feel like I don't live in it, exactly. I'm always somehow on the edge or on the margin.

> I don't see myself as religious. Religion for me generally means institution or practices that build up a way of living. I see myself as spiritual. And I find my spiritual nourishment sometimes in the church, but often outside it. In a sense that's a tragedy. Churches exist for one reason only, to put people in contact with what's real and meaningful and to provide spiritual nourishment. But for many of us, they're not doing that. That's a tremendous failure. So we search it out in other ways.
>
> I continue to think that maybe one of these days I will find this wonderful, rich man that I can go and marry, and then I'll be happy forever. I'll marry a doctor or lawyer or something. I probably won't, because I still find largely that other priests are the kind of people I'd rather give to for a relationship. So I'm not going to die rich. I hope I don't die alone. My vision of heaven would be holding or being held. Forever.

As Edmund's and Jeff's stories suggest, in regard to sexuality, my classmates are not torn simply between desire and obedience, between the imperfect, suspect "self" and a life dedicated to others, between earthly drives and a higher ideal—not that such a conflict, even in those traditional terms, was ever really simple. They are torn, rather, between a conflict between two competing kinds of spirituality, both of which have a real hold on them: between integrity to the demands of their institution and integrity to the newly validated self, a self whose actualization is seen not as the enemy of the spiritual but as its potential, even necessary ally.

My classmates take a variety of stances toward celibacy. They see it as a "charism," a spiritual gift given to some individuals—but not available upon demand, and not given to all priests—which can be put to good use in the service of the community and which can provide the independence necessary for a risk-taking kind of prophecy. Some see it as a source of solitude which, however painful, can be made productive for a life of study; others see it as the basis for a domestic peace rendered attractive by contrast to the troubled marriages they often encounter. It suits only a few of them; most have made at best an uneasy peace with it as one of their nonnegotiable "terms of employment," a "tradeoff," in Father Eugene's terms, reflecting a world in which, as Father Ralph says, "you can't have everything."

Yet whatever their particular fit, not one of them sees celibacy as a necessary element in priesthood. They see it instead as an entrenched requirement which, in Father Malcolm's terms, "is not going to change in my lifetime" and against which active agitation would be hopeless. At worst, they see mandatory celibacy as yet one more display of the church's unwarranted and counterproductive control over their lives, one of the central proofs that the church as "institution" is hopelessly out of touch with and indifferent to their needs.

But what makes mandatory celibacy an especially difficult problem for their generation is their conviction that by imposing it, the church violates the true nature of spirituality and undercuts the effectiveness of their ministry.

The great majority of my classmates, by their testimony, entered the priesthood because it was, in Father Tod's words, "a helping profession"; their 1960s idealism heightened their commitment to the traditional priestly spirituality of service. Yet the longstanding Catholic emphasis on self-abnegation as the key to service ("Not I live, but Christ lives in me") has given way for most of them to more personalist, growth-centered theologies more akin to therapy. Influenced during their theology years and beyond by the same kinds of holistic, humanistic psychology which had earlier infused the pastoral training of Protestant ministers[13]—Abraham Maslow, Carl Rogers, and their predecessor Carl Jung were frequently invoked in our conversations, along with Father Eugene Kennedy, who has linked this brand of psychology directly to Catholic spirituality—they came to believe that the self is not to be denied in the interests of holiness. Rather, the self is to be developed in the interests of wholeness: in Edmund's terms, "integration" is the key rather than denial; in Jeff's words, "holiness is wholeness."

Many of them have also embraced a corresponding resistance to law and rules, seeing them as external, authoritarian restrictions, the enemies of growth from within, an "escape from freedom," in Erik Fromm's terms, rather than a positive expression of order. The comments of my classmates on seminary life confirm Father Alex's conviction that "they didn't nourish us. They considered us just as bodies that they had to mold, and spirits that they had to mold. . . . It was at a time when society was figuring out that you don't mold people. You rather bring out the self, and I think that caused a lot of stress and a lot of conflict."

My classmates have worked very hard at "unmolding" themselves, at recovering or freeing or—to risk the jargon—getting in touch with those aspects of themselves which the seminary ignored or actively suppressed in the interests of shaping them to fit a rational, celibate priesthood. Hence, for instance, their hesitant but eager steps toward painting, writing, and music. Their resistance to the institutional church is heightened by the fact that at the very period in which they have moved increasingly away from the Freudian model of sublimation on which their seminary "training" was based (although no one ever dared to invoke Freud openly) toward the more Jungian/Rogerian/Maslovian model of integration, the church has escalated its attacks on such personalist psychologies.

The language with which they describe their sexual involvement with women (or men) makes it clear that they see these actions not as delayed sexual awakenings (the developmental model) nor as the eruption of passion after all those years of control (the return of the Freudian repressed), but as a belated discovery of the need for emotional connection, for wholeness, for "something more" than the camaraderie we knew in the seminary. They do not see themselves as adolescents getting something out of their system at last, but as underdeveloped adults trying to get something back into their system which they had too long denied.

Attuned as they are to the changing culture of their own generation, most of them have come see their own fulfillment not just as desirable but as a moral imperative. For them, developing their "humanity" has become a kind of vocation in its own right which overlaps with their priesthood but is not identical to it. "What I've tried to do," says Father Spencer, "is to see myself as a human being who struggles with what it means to be a meaningful kind of person who also happens to be a priest." When the calling to become what Spencer describes as a "well-rounded person" makes demands not necessarily fulfilled through the institutional church, my classmates try to find ways to meet those demands on their own. "I don't have to look to the church to make me what I am," says Father Alex. "I look to self-actualization rather than to the church." Under no circumstances, for instance, would he let his priestly work take him away from the development of his long-neglected imagination:

> If I had to change to a different role, to a pastor, I'd still paint, but I'd do it at different times than I do it now. I'd still watch my westerns, but I'd do it at different times. They would not stop me from doing that. They would not stop me from reading my novels, they would not stop me from going to Walt Disney World. It's not like they wanted to do that. I would find time for it because I know that I need it.

Such activities are imperatives because for my classmates, a healthy self *is* a holy self; to Father Jeff, "If it's psychologically true, then it is theologically true. Spiritually it's true." And the healthy (i.e., growing, fulfilled) self is the conduit of grace to others, not its obstacle. The central value for one priest, for instance, is "to see importance in myself, self-esteem. Also to try to establish that in others. I think if I feel good about myself, then it is going to reflect in the way that I treat others." In discussing his peak moments as a priest, he connects the satisfactions of administering the sacraments and of engendering personal growth in others in a manner which suggests a larger elision of priesthood and therapy, and of their priesthood with Protestant models:

> The highs for me are when I am celebrating the sacraments, especially the sacrament of reconciliation with young people or people who haven't been healed in a long time spiritually. Anointing of the sick and working with the sick and the dying, and weddings and their celebrations. Helping people come to a greater sense of their own capabilities or helping people sort out who they are and find the goodness in themselves.

In most of the areas of their lives, my classmates see no conflict between service and self-fulfillment. To the contrary, most of them value what they tend to define as the central acts of ministry—the saying of mass, the giving of homilies, the one-on-one contact of counseling, the administration of the sacraments—precisely because those actions provide them with immediate personal satisfaction while promoting their parishioners' psychological and spiritual growth at the same time. This suggests a basic redefinition away from priest as self-denying conduit and toward priest as mutual beneficiary; they expect their ministry to nurture them as well as their parishioners.

Conversely, most of them are reluctant to exercise institutional power or to have it exercised on them because they fear that at either end of the stick, institutional power inhibits growth instead of fostering it. "If I don't want the church to dictate to me who I am," Father Alex says, "I can't do that to anybody else either." "Power," insists Father Eugene, "is a dead end."

In regard to celibacy, however, the distinction between the vocation of service and the vocation of self-fulfillment breaks into open conflict, a conflict which is all the more galling to them because they see it as arbitrary and unnecessary. For they regard sexuality as an inherently healthy aspect of human nature; they regard emotional intimacy as a positive, even essential element in human growth, a force which "plugs them more deeply into life," as one of them put it; and they regard both sexuality and intimacy as positively related to ministry. "I know what it is to love a woman," Father Herbert said. "Going through that experience could enrich me—could enrich my ministry." A few people, they acknowledge, are called to celibacy for the sake of ministry; for the rest, it is only the church's prescriptions which keep sexual intimacy and ministry apart.

The voice of the institutional church on the issue of celibacy is still powerful for most of the priests in my class, however, not because the church's authority on the issue is absolute or its wisdom beyond question—not one of them endorsed those traditional positions—but because they feel that their *personal* integrity demands that they act in accord with the norms of the institution as the price of retaining affiliation with it; celibacy is part of the "terms of employment," and as such has at least a contractual power for them. Furthermore, affiliation with the church is still desirable to them because the institution provides them with the authority to perform those personally satisfying acts of ministry which remain central to them.

So although celibacy exacts a heavy price, by their own testimony most of my classmates continue to pay it so long as—but only so long as—they remain convinced that the personal cost of leaving the institution and losing the satisfactions of priesthood would be higher. They are borne out in this calculation by the evidence of some classmates who have left the priesthood in search of growth through marriage and have found less rather than more. Yet to accept a stifling celibacy runs the risk, they feel, of diminishing their humanity and thus undermining the very ministry for the sake of which they endure celibacy in the first place.

So they find themselves in a bind: Which kind of integrity shall I give more weight to—and how can I live without the other? Why should I have to choose at all? Why cannot the church see that it is acting not only against my personal welfare but against the congregation's spiritual welfare in demanding of its priests a dehumanizing denial of their full potential? "Maybe the price of celibacy is too great," Father Edmund wonders, "not for the individual but for the church."

None of my classmates has found a simple answer to this dilemma. Some, like Tod, have had intense friendships which veered toward something more, and have eventually pulled back. It has not been easy for them to do so, nor to forget what they have given up; they have remained in the priesthood but with a heightened resentment of the church. Others, such as Father Herbert, have been involved with women and have then withdrawn, not out of duty but because the relationship simply didn't work for other reasons. It is interesting that Father Malcolm, whose relationship never became explicitly sexual, is the only emotionally/sexually involved priest I talked with who reaffirms the traditional notion that what he did—what he felt he needed to do to cope with his overwhelming loneliness—was simply wrong.

In most cases, the source of my classmates' frustration is the breakup of the old clerical package without anything fully developed to take its place. In relation to celibacy, however, the reverse is true: the old package remains officially intact while, from their perspective, the rationale for it has crumbled and a more positive alternative, linking human growth and spirituality, is ready and waiting.

A Secular Priesthood

My classmates' elision of therapy and ministry is worth reflecting on further, for in many ways it is emblematic of their redefined stance toward "the world." In *Habits of the Heart*,[14] Robert Bellah and his colleagues, drawing on examples from all areas of American life, conclude that for most Americans of our era, "a distinctly religious vision has been absorbed into the categories of contemporary psychology. No autonomous standard of good and evil survives outside the needs of individual psyches for growth" (232). With nothing objective, nothing apart from the self to look to for direction, we are left, according to Bellah, with only subjective standards of judgment: the sole basis of our most important decisions is merely what promotes our own self-actualization. Such judgments, he argues, are essentially suspect, shut off as they are from any inherent reason to consider others or from any sense of a larger social good distinct from the self.

In spite of the fact that a good many Protestant ministers have assimilated therapeutic norms—he quotes one who asserts that his role is to "help them [his parishioners] take the scales from their eyes and experience and see their magnificence" (229)—Bellah implies that the traditional American religions, with their insistence on an objective ethics and communal responsibility, still offer the best hope for an effective antidote to insularity and self-absorption. He has particular respect for Catholicism in this regard.

Habits of the Heart offers a compelling cultural analysis; but in the light of what my classmates have to say, its implied prescriptions are problematic. The very possibility of "objective" ethical standards, after all, has been questioned by many theologians convinced of the cultural relativity of all such standards. But more directly to the point here, what happens when Catholic priests themselves, the church's official representatives, become convinced that many of the church's standards are inhuman and hence antithetical to true spirituality? What happens when priests—for whom the central, traditional meaning of being "in the world but not of the world" was that they would remain above the influences of their culture and keep their eyes focused on the eternally valid—begin to look increasingly within themselves and, to a considerable degree, outside the institutional church for their sources of meaning, their criteria for conduct, and—as we shall see in the next section—their standards of achievement?

Where are their parishioners going to find "objective," detached religion if those thought to embody it no longer espouse it? And to the extent to which they do not espouse it, is this shift toward personalist spirituality and assimilation of secular, cultural norms a sign of decay or a sign of an incipient, healthy redefinition of religion itself? Are my classmates losing touch with immutable standards, or are they out ahead of institutional structures, the harbingers of change by virtue of their own dissent?

To these large, institutional questions I have no easy answers. In relation to my classmates, however, I can say at least two things confidently. One is that the spirituality which they espouse is not unadulterated therapy per se. Most of them, instead of abandoning their established beliefs, have infused them with therapeutic implications. If the self has become a sacrament for some of them, they still believe in other sacraments as well; they advise getting in touch with the self and thereby keeping in touch with God. Furthermore, most of them still believe in a

God who, however impersonal He may have become, is not reducible to their own inherent potential. And granted the considerable degree of self that they retain in their formulations, they consistently imagine growth as interpersonal and communal rather than merely individual-istic; in that regard, they bear out some of Bellah's hopes.

But whatever the balance at which they aim, a second thing is also clear: the religion that they espouse, and which the laity experience through them, does indeed contain considerable elements of the culture which both Bellah and the institutional church would like it to counter. Theirs is not a religion abstracted from the people who live it or from the communities that embrace it; it is a humanized, contextualized re-ligion which is, in part, both in and of the world.

Their movement toward personalist psychologies, that is, touches on but does not exhaust the complexities inherent in a phrase I had heard a thousand times but had never considered carefully before listening to them: that they are truly *secular priests,* that this is not merely a literal description to distinguish them from cloistered monks, as we were taught in the seminary, but a live and accurate paradox which captures the complicated position of men who are both "in the world" and, to a significant degree, "of the world" as well.

This is not to suggest that they are, as we used to say with a curled lip, "worldly"; that term implies all too well an inherent disjunction be-tween spiritual and earthly, a disjunction which most of them deny. It is rather to acknowledge what should be a given: that they are not, cannot be, and no longer choose to be totally immune from their culture even while they retain a strong allegiance to nonmaterial values.

6

Finding a Place
in the World

The wound of loneliness in the life of the minister
hurts all the more, since he not only shares in the human
condition of isolation, but also finds that his professional
impact on others is diminishing. The minister is called
to speak to the ultimate concerns of life: birth and death,
union and separation, love and hate. He has an urgent desire to give meaning to people's lives. But he finds himself standing on the edges of events and only reluctantly
admitted to the spot where the decisions are made.
—Henri Nouwen, *The Wounded Healer* (1972)

Don't you mess with Mr. Inbetween. . . .
                —from the song "Ac-cent-chu-ate the Positive"

*T*he great majority of the time, Father Frederick comes across as
a good-humored, temperate man who speaks slowly and carefully, giving even his occasional devils their due. So I was startled
when, in the middle of a measured discussion of the current status of
the priest in the church, Frederick's voice rose markedly:

The other day a woman was leaving the church where I said mass on
Sunday, and she said to me, "I told the altar boy to tell Father, 'Where's
the bell?' " [during the liturgy]. I thought, "Who the hell are you? He
should tell you, 'I'm the pastor and if you don't like it, go someplace
else where you can have it your way. You don't know what this is all

about. You don't have a right to that complaint; that's unsubstantiated.
If your grandmother had said that, maybe I could understand.' "

No priest I interviewed has a more exalted notion of the priesthood
than Frederick, whose tensions with his first pastor, as we saw in the
previous chapter, turned partly on Frederick's adamant refusal to accept
mere brick and mortar as his central concerns. Yet no other priest feels
so wide a gap between his sense of the inherent stature of the priesthood
and the diminished status and uncertain definition of the priest within
the current church. As a faculty member surrounded by confused seminarians in an underdefined seminary, all of it leading to a priesthood in
which few things are clear to him except that priests are undervalued
by both laity and hierarchy, Frederick is doubly well situated to reflect
on the troubled place of the priest in the current church.

Frederick comes from working-class parents who urged him toward the priesthood as a dignified way of avoiding his father's life of
drudgery:

> My father was a glazier. He was always working with glass and sash
> and puttying. It really was a very difficult job; he always had cuts. I can
> remember my mother telling me, "You don't want to go to work there.
> You don't want to do that with your life." She always respected sisters
> and priests. She didn't know exactly what it meant to be a priest, but
> she thought that would be worthwhile and it wouldn't be as hard as
> manual labor.

During his minor seminary years, Frederick's notion of priesthood
clarified under the influence of his eighty-year-old pastor, a "refined,
dedicated man" who had studied theology abroad and whose scholarship fund would later make it possible for Frederick to do the same.
Frederick remembers the two of them excitedly paging through a copy
of the Gutenberg Bible, exulting at the Latin passages they could identify
in spite of the German script. He emerged from such experiences convinced that the priesthood was "a life of prayer, a life of scholarship, a
life of culture."

His four years studying theology abroad during and immediately after the Vatican Council gave further shape to his sense of what a contemporary priest should be:

> I had classmates who could read Greek, who would get a newspaper in
> Greek. There were people who could speak Latin. It was a completely
> different environment from St. Francis. The student body was really in-
> tellectual. There was a sophistication; they were aware of ecclesiastical
> limitations and politics—they were informed. I felt that they were all
> the things that we weren't. Vocation—people didn't want to be just a
> simple parish priest. They had aspirations, even if they were going to a

parish, to continue reading. It was important to be an intellectual even
if you were going to a parish.

When he returned to the States after ordination, he wanted to stir
things up: "I wanted more controversy, I wanted to have things in flux.
I didn't want everything black and white, I wanted gray. Let's live with
the gray." He found himself, however, back in "a clerical church, where
the pastor was to be obeyed in all things," where learning and asking questions did not seem central to the operating definition of priestly
work. One particular occasion brought home to him the sense that he
was in a time warp where "the things that really mattered in church
people weren't interested in, and things that I thought were really secondary they thought were primary":

> *Humanae Vitae* was published in 1968, and I thought it was regrettable.
> When I was ordained in 1970, Pope Paul VI was still pope; I was in
> Rome and you could see the papal apartments, you could see the light.
> I was with a friend of mine from Rome, and he said, "Those are the
> papal apartments, and the pope is up there, he's reading. I hope he's
> not writing." I remember thinking, "Right, I hope he's not writing."
> I came back to the States and told that story on a retreat and nobody
> laughed. I thought, "Did I leave out something, or are these people just
> so unaware of what's going on in the world in theological circles?" I felt
> I was in a different world.

After two parish assignments and a stint as a high-school teacher,
Frederick was sent once again to Europe to earn his doctorate. Since then
he has been teaching at the "new" St. Francis, where, theological liberal
though he is, he feels particular satisfaction at carrying on the best of
the seminary's traditions:

> When I get my books together in my briefcase and walk into class
> and take things out, I think, this is what Albert Meyer [former semi-
> nary professor, rector, later archbishop of Milwaukee and then Chicago]
> did when he taught here. He took all these books into class and he un-
> packed them, and he showed them to his students. When I go to the
> library, there's a reproduction of the Gutenberg Bible, a donation from
> my old pastor—the one he and I used to look through—and now it's in
> the library. I go into the library, and at times I feel, if I can just study in
> the presence of these Bibles. I go up to that floor, and I think, "There's
> a tradition that I'm part of. These people have made what I'm doing
> possible, because they valued it"—so I really have to do this seriously
> and well.

As I discovered during my own stay there, the seminary is no longer
the isolated, rule-bound bastion it once was. Nor is it characterized by
the old forms of docility and deference in preparation for a lifetime of

automatic clerical authority. Frederick wears a sport coat and tie to class instead of a Roman collar; the students refer to him easily as "Frederick." During the two classes I sat in on, he engaged their many questions eagerly, validating their willingness to challenge as much as their specific concerns; he likes to go over to the student lounge in the evening and talk informally with them.

To Frederick, who relished the considerable mixing he found among students and faculty in Europe, this lessening of the distance/distinction between professor and student is all to the good. Yet he is troubled at the same time by the breakdown of distinctions among the students themselves. For the seminary now admits women as well as men, lay candidates for master's degrees in theology as well as seminarians, future permanent deacons as well as future priests. The seminarians no longer dress differently, live much differently, or learn a different, cultic language in anticipation of a priesthood set apart.

Frederick has no quarrel with this inclusiveness on a theological level, since his own research in church history has convinced him that the clergy/laity distinction as we have known it is "basically useless," grounded as it was on the attempt of entrenched clerics to designate themselves as inherently superior to a "flock" defined a priori as ignorant and thus conveniently in need of direction—and control—from above. In the church of the people of God and in the face of an increasingly sophisticated laity, such claims make no sense to him; "the term 'clergy and laity,' " he insists, "really is detrimental to community."

Nonetheless, Frederick sees this blurring as the source of an acute identity crisis among current seminarians. Under the old regime that he and I spent considerable time castigating, our self-concept as seminarians was constricted and immature but clear. We had a sense of community in part because there was no one else around but us. We had a clearly defined (if inadequately explained) priesthood ahead of us. And we were made to feel special all along the way, coddled (in most cases) by our parents and lionized in our parishes both before and after ordination. We thought we knew who we were.

By contrast, not only has the present seminary's move toward openness and inclusiveness weakened what Frederick sees as its tradition of scholarship, it has also shaken the seminarians' traditional sense of themselves; where we once felt special, Frederick is convinced that they now feel indistinct and undervalued:

> We have a problem in United States seminaries where we're doing everything. We're putting everything into the seminary—the deacons, yes, they can study at the seminary, and then lay ministries, yeah, put them in. The students are confused. There's no distinction between the

spiritual renewal days for the priestly formation and for lay formation. Academically there's some overlap between lay formation and priestly formation, so you have those students together. Because of all the emphasis on pastoral work rather than intellectual rigor, we tend to "graduate" priests who feel their "training" is completed instead of feeling they are entering a lifetime of study.

The seminarians sometimes resent the presence of women in these courses, and I think they're not legitimate in their objections. But they want to have a sense of identity, they want to be appreciated. They don't want to be just tolerated. And many of them have the feeling that the seminary exists for the lay formation. "Those are the students who are appreciated—they're older, they're women, they're mature, and we're just tolerated." It's not really a seminary, it's a pastoral school.

So Frederick hears the seminarians asking, in effect, Who are we and what is the church doing for us? What genuine, usable distinction is there between the lay students and us, between the laity and priests— and if there is none, why must we be celibate and commit ourselves for life as if to uphold it? Why isn't the church doing more to encourage us now and to reward us later while it lavishes attention on the laity? Aren't we (at least) part of the newly empowered people of God, too? All right, no more "Holy Mother" from cradle to grave, but is there an occasional pat on the back—or maybe a little higher salary—to replace her embrace? Okay, no "anything you say, Father" anymore; but will there be a handshake, a nod of appreciation to balance off the questions and complaints we can look forward to? If we can't tell what our place is here at the seminary, which is supposedly our turf, what will our place be in the parish, in the church itself, in the world at large?

These issues of identity and status trouble Frederick not only because he sees the seminarians suffering from them but because he and his classmates suffer from them as well. "The people know," Frederick said, "that their level of understanding and sophistication is encouraged in the council. Fine. [But] what have we done for priests? We have done nothing for them, practically speaking, and so a lot of priests are confused." Thus the seminary that Frederick is part of, that he is implicated in, does not so much prepare students for the priesthood as it previews for them its frustrations and uncertainties. This leaves him doubly vexed: the next generation of priests looks to him for help as he looks around for help from the church—and not finding it, he cannot give as much of it as he would like.

Frederick is not alone in confronting these issues. Most of my classmates entered the priesthood with a taste for change and an appreciation of complexity and ambiguity—give us gray, after all those centuries of black and white, we want gray—but in the central arena of self-definition (Who are we and where do we fit?), change has brought confusion, gray has turned into fog, and living in that atmosphere has turned out to be less exciting than unnerving.

"It is a matter of making the priesthood more attractive," Frederick said. "If celibacy is a drawback, what are the advantages?" He runs off a substantial list, on which status, high salaries, professional recognition, and a sense of the value of specialized ministry are central, all held together and propped up by a willingness on the part of hierarchy and laity alike to "come to grips with this human thing, to see the priest as a human being" with earthly needs as well as spiritual values. As we shall see, most of his classmates read off essentially the same list. What is striking, however, is not so much the items themselves but that they so clearly constitute a wish list rather than a description of present incentives.

In the old church, as Father Frederick describes it, the communal parish structure, the microcosm of a nurturing church, did indeed take care of most of a priest's needs:

> There were so many priests and so many parishes that you didn't have to worry about anything because the Mother Church was going to take care of you. You got a salary, not much, but you had everything. In a sense your entertainment was all of these people. There were always activities in the parishes. People are inviting you to dinner. Take a vacation, go to a ball game. If you had a car, the gasoline was twelve cents a gallon. The community was your whole life, it was like another monastery.

But when community gives way to consumer mobility, and personal relationships with the laity either fade or never materialize, what is left on the social level are status and power (if I am speaking in decidedly earthly terms here, it is because I am echoing my classmates). And status and power in a given system are relative, an uncomfortably secular realization for men who started off convinced that "empowering" the laity was simply an inherent good in itself.

Yet twenty years into their priesthood, if the laity are up, many of my classmates undeniably feel down; both personally and professionally, they feel slighted, taken for granted, displaced. "Restructuring the diocese," says one priest, "puts lay people in the master role and priests in the continued servant role. Priests naturally resist that structure."

In the context of their own diminished stature, and given their original expectations of centrality, one available response is to revert; it is not surprising, according to another classmate, that priests of his generation "still have the tendency to press the clerical button when push comes to shove":

You are given the idea for so long in your formation that your role is, well, kingpin, that basically you make the final decisions. Then all of a sudden you have this group that is called a governance body, with whom you set the policies. Unless you're very secure, it takes time to get yourself together.

But reversion is too simple a term; even priests who have no urge to bring the old church back nonetheless can feel nostalgic for the position of prestige and influence priests enjoyed in the old days. Father Leo, for instance, is outspoken in his anger at the church for not moving far enough fast enough, for clinging to outmoded ways of acting instead of embracing a genuine spirit of renewal, for insisting on its own authority instead of being "responsive to people." Yet his distress over lost stature and power prodded him to give me a "case in point" about the world my classmates thought they were entering, a world where, as another classmate says, "we would be respected leaders who would have a great impact":

Twenty-five years ago, fifty years ago, the priest was exploited by the system, but you had an environment where the priest had a certain respect and credibility and appreciation. St. Monica's in Whitefish Bay is on Santa Monica Boulevard. There was a real row about naming that street, because they wanted Richard Boulevard, which would be a continuation of Richard Street in the city of Milwaukee. But the pastor of the parish had the political clout and the respect of the aldermen in Whitefish Bay as well as the people. So he was able to railroad that through. As a result, the whole neighborhood is named Santa Monica Boulevard, from Whitefish Bay through Fox Point. The political environment, the social environment had much more respect for a priest then. But that's not true anymore.

Leo's comments suggest the complexity of my classmates' ambivalence. For although the notion of sharing power at all may be residually distasteful to some of them, their recurring lament at not being able to get things done ("You know darn well that you could get the end results twice as fast if you could just do it yourself," one of them said) is more often than not fueled by regret that it is harder now to get the *new* business of the church done. For as my classmates see it, they are characteristically the advocates of progress, which the laity often obstruct: parishioners may enjoy power but, according to one classmate, "they don't like change."

Father Albert, for instance, who feels that he has not changed much since his younger days as a "radical not finding the accepted norm the end of the discussion," opened his conversation with me by telling a painful story about how conservative lay opposition ultimately undercut his hiring of a woman as associate pastor. He was attacked in a conservative Catholic newspaper, received enough negative letters to make the archbishop nervous just before going to Rome, and ultimately was forced to narrow the job definition so drastically that the woman felt she could no longer serve in the position. Thus the decisions that the priest is forced to work out with the newly assertive laity frequently reflect—or reinstate—the old church.

But however complex its effects on them, the post–Vatican II raising of the laity would be much less problematic for my classmates if the institutional church had not seemed to slight priests in the process. Many of them now see the mandated proliferation of lay councils, for instance, as a sign that the diocese has passed them over to hand authority to their former underlings. Similarly, more than one classmate expressed resentment that former priests and nuns are given preference for high-paying diocesan offices, thus providing those who have resigned from ministry higher income and direct power over priests. "We're even pretty sure," one priest told me, "that there's a lady working for the diocese who's married to a priest that she met in the central office, and we're pretty sure she's not married in a church. Does this bother us? You bet, because she's making more than we are. We're making sacrifices and we're sticking with it, we love our work, and now we have these people telling us what to do."

Several diocesan officials acknowledged to me that such impressions are widespread and harmful to morale. Meanwhile, my classmates find what they see as a constant stream of dictates—"all the idiotic stuff that comes out of those archdiocesan offices," offices that are often administered by laymen—as overbearing and peremptory, while their own priestly committees remain advisory to the archbishop at best and are often ignored.

In short, my classmates' genuine willingness to share power with the laity, whatever its costs, is complicated by their resentment over the hierarchy's unwillingness to share power with them. "The hierarchy," complains one priest, "acts like hierarchy. They dictate. They dictate that on the lower level we need to be collaborative." "The laity does not respect the priest as a professional," another complained, "because the church does not respect the priest as a professional." Most of my classmates used softer rhetoric, but nonetheless they repeatedly emphasized that structurally, the hierarchy's power over them has remained undiminished while theirs over the laity has all but disappeared.

And while most of them express great personal admiration for Archbishop Weakland, whose prominent liberal voice among the American episcopate reflects their values well, their one recurring complaint about him suggests their basic sense of being neglected: many of them feel that he is so involved with national and international affairs that he has little time for them, little patience with their concerns. Weakland is to Milwaukee, one of them told me, as Father Hesburgh was to Notre Dame: a man of international stature all but unavailable at home. So in some ways, their relative sense of themselves is made worse by their own archbishop's prominence: he has risen even higher than most other members of the hierarchy in status and influence, and they feel the distance between him and them all the more keenly.

Overall, their frustration and resentment at being taken for granted by both the laity and the hierarchy are intense. As one priest said, "I don't mind being celibate; I don't like it but I knew what I was doing. I'm happy to put a lot of effort into my homilies. I want to collaborate, but I still need to be respected. And I don't expect to make as much money as I could in another profession. But at least acknowledge that this takes effort, that I'm a professional, that I'm making sacrifices." Most of my classmates share the twin convictions of another classmate, however, that "too many of the laity do nothing else but think all day on what you should be doing and how you should be doing it," and that "we don't receive recognition from higher up" either. Consequently, for motivation priests are left, he says, only with "the satisfaction you get from the work."

The inherent value of their work has not diminished for most of them. In a way that I found touching and inspiring, after twenty years of ministry they remain convinced, on a spiritual level, of the *absolute* worth of what they do. Yet their anger at not being appreciated by the church has cut into even that satisfaction: "You want to know why people complain that there aren't any decent homilies?" one of them asked rhetorically. "I can work like hell on a Sunday homily, or I can make one very slipshod. It doesn't make a damn bit of difference to *me*. That becomes really disgusting."

All of this suggests that beneath my classmates' increased desire to negotiate the terms of the job for themselves lies their sense that more is demanded of them than it was of earlier generations, and that they are not getting enough in return—and our generation expects "enough" to include quite a bit. They find themselves uncomfortably in between in two different ways. In matters of doctrine and policy, they often find themselves squeezed between a conservative hierarchy and a liberal—or at least more entitlement-oriented—laity; but in terms of their position in the church, they feel empty space above them, no one below them anymore, and they don't feel much cheering coming from anywhere.

So on the earthly level—for that is where they have their problems— where are my classmates to go for a *relative* sense of their worth? It is in the context of that increasingly urgent question that their intense interest in money makes sense.

The "Value" of Ministry: What Is a Priest Worth?

Those who proclaim the gospel should get their living by
the gospel.
—St. Paul, 1 Corinthians 9:14

A concern for the spirit of poverty exists among the pres-
byterate of Milwaukee. A desire to maintain and
strengthen this important Biblical value is a clear testimony to the spiritual health of the priests. . . . Nonetheless, a spirit of poverty is not served by under-compensat-
ing priests or supporting an unfair or unjust
compensation system.
—National Association of Church Personnel Administrators, *Consultation on Priests' Compensation for the Archdiocese of Milwaukee* (1990)

In the professional middle class, which once fought to secure the autonomy of its occupational redoubts, there is
today no larger question than: What are we worth, and
who will buy?
—Barbara Ehrenreich, *Fear of Falling* (1989)

When I phoned Father Herbert in the fall of 1989 and asked him how
he was doing, his first comment was, "Pretty well. I grossed over $22,000
last year working part-time, which isn't bad. I've had a lot of calls from
parishes to help. I should come out of this with an adequate income."

In the course of the several conversations Herbert and I had over a
four-year period, he had a good many things on his mind: a history
of conflicts with pastors, the lingering memory of a long-term relationship with a woman, midlife loss of energy, a sense of disconnection from
other priests, career uncertainty. But surfacing in nearly every talk we
had, and exacerbating his other frustrations, was his intense financial
anxiety. "I don't have a lot of money," he told me, "and that bothers me.
It comes from family origins, my father worrying about money a lot:
'You should have money and you should not be a pauper.' That's a real
pressure point, at middle age particularly."

Money has been an issue for Herbert from the early days of his priesthood, partly because he has often had to scramble while between parish
assignments; partly because, he says, "I enjoy going on trips and buying
nice clothes, though I never overspend" (he drew my attention to his
modest but tasteful wardrobe a number of times); and partly because,
like most of his classmates, he is convinced that priestly salaries are woe-
fully low.

In the summer of 1974, after he lost one of his first parish jobs in a
dispute with his pastor, Herbert worked part-time at a downtown de-

partment store, selling major appliances. "I was good at it," he says, "but I did feel uncomfortable. I was defensive when parishioners saw me. They would say, 'Don't you get paid enough?' " Herbert says that he was angry at this time over losing his job, and "sad at not ministering more," but because "I had had it with the salary and living arrangements in the parish, I was glad to be in a secular environment with my job separated from my residence."

The following winter, he became an assistant army chaplain in the reserves and reentered parish work at the same time. He made $200 a month in the parish, plus $150 in stipends; together with $130–170 a month from his chaplaincy, he made enough to "get along," in his terms. His double occupation did cause tension, however: "The pastor felt that the parish should get all my energy. He didn't like my getting extra money; it was a control issue."

Since that first job in sales, he has moonlighted at other times as well; in the summer and fall of 1988, for instance, he was a telemarketer for the Milwaukee Symphony for four hours a day, three days a week. "I made $20,000 for them," he says. "That didn't make me feel as guilty. It was uplifting, I was selling an interesting product. I enjoyed working in another medium." Nonetheless, he admits, while he worked his way through the phone book, he would skip over the names of his parishioners.

"Do you want me to say what has been the most irritating thing in my life?" Father Malcolm asked me suddenly in the middle of a conversation about something entirely different. "My income. My income should not be based on someone who takes a vow of poverty. I'm not under any vow of poverty. I can't report all of my mass stipends because my social security tax is so expensive as it is. Otherwise I couldn't pay my bills." "The other thing that bothers me a lot in the church," Father Frederick volunteered after talking about the church's treatment of women, "is finances. My financial problems are much greater than I expected. It's terrible." Father Ralph, one of the most soft-spoken priests in our class, had just finished serving on a task force on priests' salaries and benefits when I talked with him. The experience had galvanized him. His comments are representative both of his class's initial resistance to thinking about money and of their eventual immersion in the issue:

> I was more cautious when I went into that whole thing, but by the time we got done and came up with a proposal, I had no guilt in saying, "Hey, I'm worth something. I think I should be paid more than the janitors. I should be paid more than the teachers in the school. I should be paid more than a lot of these people." And I'm not. So it is a morale issue.
>
> The archbishop was honest with us in admitting that he's coming out

of his Benedictine, protected life: He doesn't go shopping. He can spend any amount of money he wants. He can go anywhere he wants. He just puts it on the tab. I can't. I don't go a lot of places.

The newly ordained come out with big education debts.[1] You're asking them to prepare for their retirement. I went on social security this past year. I had not been on it before. I figure I do have to think about it.

We proposed a substantial increase in pay but then more personal responsibility for it to pay for our things. I said, "Hey, we are now giving all the nuns lay equivalency. We just did it. No questions asked. We just boosted up the salaries of all the nuns. Why should it be different for priests?"

To my initial surprise, I heard more anger in the priests I interviewed over the issue of money than I did over mandatory celibacy. My classmates consider the requirement of celibacy to be arbitrary, controlling, and counterproductive to priestly effectiveness; but they also feel helpless to do anything about it. They know that the requirement comes from Rome, and they consider the Rome of John Paul II beyond their reach. They see their salaries in much the same negative light; but salaries are a local, diocesan issue and hence negotiable here and now.

Furthermore, they at least expected celibacy; it was part of the package. They did not expect to have to think about money, however; when the issue blindsided them, their shock and resentment ran deep. Some of the mildest priests I interviewed became irate as soon as the subject came up—or to be more accurate, as soon as *they* brought it up. Only later, when I realized that it was one of their major concerns, did I begin asking about it. Only then did I begin to see money as one of the focal points for their characteristic tensions of identity, self-esteem, status, even sexuality.

Money has become important to my classmates for a number of reasons. On the idealistic level, one of them insisted, "I would like to do more good, I'd love to be able to do more for kids"; he paraphrased Aquinas's assertion that "one of the virtues of money is that it makes magnanimity possible." More basically (having to deal with basics is itself a surprise and irritation to them), many of them insist that they cannot pay their bills under a system which, at the time of most of these interviews (1988), paid them a salary of $711 a month, room and board at the rectory, a car allowance of $150 a month, and stipends from masses and weddings which might total $150 a month. One priest spelled out where this leaves him:

> I have to pay insurance for my automobile, which is six hundred dollars a year. Life insurance and taxes and other things, that's another month's salary. I already give up one month's salary for my [diocesan] pension. They told me I should be in some kind of tax-sheltered annuity,

which would take two months' more. Now I'm down to living on five
months' salary a year. I can't do that. I can't make it.

Beyond subsistence, classmates like Herbert also want to be able to
buy clothes; a black suit and a handful of Roman collars no longer constitute a wardrobe. They want to take vacations, eat in restaurants, buy
books, go to concerts. A priest is educated to be a cultured man, Father
Frederick reminded me, yet without more money, "you end up being so
narrow in your possibilities. So who goes down to Chicago to see some
plays or musicals or the opera?"

In general, my classmates consider that for the church to deny them a
range of earthly pleasures which are seen as legitimate in the laity is to
deny their status as men who also walk this earth. It is to deny the validity of their post–Vatican II embrace of the world. It is to deny them
the "wholeness" which they have come to value so highly. Ultimately,
it is to deny their humanity. And just as they resent that denial in relation to sexuality—and the lack of understanding of their needs which
goes with it—they resent this one as well. "People have this phony notion," Father Malcolm complained during his discussion of money, "that
priests don't need anything. I'm not given carte blanche. They don't give
me a car. They don't pay my car insurance. I don't walk into a restaurant
and say, 'Well, here's Father.' Understand my life a little bit."

But if their desire for money argues in part for a spirituality no longer
inherently opposed to pleasure, it also reveals their earthly yearning for
recognition by a secular society whose values they do not fully endorse
but cannot ignore. In this way, money is a prism which reflects my classmates' ongoing negotiations between their 1960s/priestly idealism and
the more materialistic culture they find themselves in. For although they
continue to find it offensive that money is considered a measure of a person's worth and that even spiritual endeavors are gauged by a financial
calculus, they end up not only resenting the calculus but feeling embarrassed at how they measure up according to it.

Father Leo, for instance, who was in the act of leaving the priesthood
when I interviewed him, largely because he felt undervalued, was outraged at being regarded as "just a bastard priest in the parish" by a lay
minister who worked for him but was paid more than Leo. He was offended that "because the homily is 'given,' is free, it's looked upon as
cheap and not taken seriously." He resented being called to the hospital in the middle of the night to anoint a dying patient, only to be kept
waiting for two hours. "There's all kinds of abuses along these lines,"
he says, "where priests have to be available. (*Snapping his fingers*) 'Come
on, you slave, I want you.' Because we give free service, our activity is
looked upon as cheap and not worth anything."

Several priests irritated at their salaries nonetheless insisted that money is not the basic problem of low clerical morale; the overarching need is to feel validated, to feel that they are operating at full capacity and are being appreciated for it. One of them quoted Maslow to the effect that "if an upper-level need is not being supplied, you go down to the level below and complain about things on that level." In effect, because they want the stature and recognition which they expected to find as priests but which is no longer automatic, they now want more money; their anxieties over money circle back to their anxieties over the newly uncertain status of priesthood itself.

"According to our culture," Father Frederick acknowledges, "what we can afford means an awful lot." To another priest, "One of the ways in this country that we engage the acceptance, the credibility, of a person is through the financial." My classmates are all too aware of how they fare by that standard. "I had a hard time getting a credit card," Father Malcolm complains, "not because I don't pay my bills, but because I don't make enough money. God, that ticks me off." "The point is," Father Leo acknowledges, "you're discredited. Part of the working world says, 'Well, you make a pittance, so therefore you're worth a pittance.' "

But my classmates also resent what they see as inadequate salaries for much the same reason that they lament their diminished authority and status with the laity: because the need to make money risks diminishing the quality of their ministry. I was told more than once that priests within a parish often compete for baptisms and weddings, which confer status—and a little extra cash. Some, like Father Frederick and Father Herbert, are driven to saying extra masses on weekends as a form of moonlighting. Milwaukee now has a detailed policy and wage scale for such "help-outs,"[2] without which many Catholics would lack services they have come to expect and that my classmates want the church to provide. Yet according to Father Frederick, "You end up being a mass-saying priest" not for its spiritual value but because "you need the money. You go out to maybe two parishes and you make all your money saying masses. I don't want to do that." "We have come full circle," another priest told me. "In our last years in the seminary, we were told that it was not enough to be sacramental dispensers. We must meet people, get to know them. But with fewer priests and our low salaries—I have said four masses on a weekend for money—that's what we are being reduced to again."

When my classmates were ordained, they assumed that, as Father Frederick put it, "the Mother Church is going to take care of you." They were characterized by the peculiar blend of idealism and naiveté often found in men dedicated to "higher" goals (I know the feeling all too well) and therefore inclined to expect—trained to expect, in the case of priests of their generation—that their material needs would fall into place for them, that they would be kept free by the church's nurturing care to direct all their energies to saving the world. In this regard, their traditional Catholicism and their 1960s messianism dovetailed—and led them toward a rude awakening.

For underneath all their specific grievances over money lies a basic sense of shock that the old package no longer holds, that the old contract has been broken, that they are no longer as immune as they expected to be from the mundane concerns and tensions of this world. Their problem was supposed to be how to save souls, not how to save money; thinking about both at the same time has not proven easy.

Nor, I must admit, was it always easy to listen to their comments, even though—or more likely because—I have comparable feelings toward my university salary. For financial anxiety activates in them, as it does in most of us, an inevitably less appealing side: complaints, outrage, and occasional self-pity. To listen to their comments on money, like listening to their insistence on their own emotional needs, is a test of a listener's willingness to accept their humanity in its less endearing but no less genuine moments.

To understand just how dramatic a change their new sense of financial insecurity represents, it is necessary to look at a bit of church history.[3] For the parish system itself, the very structure on which the nature and security of the diocesan priesthood has traditionally rested, was defined from its inception by the stable financial support it offered to priests and the relationship of dependence it established between them and their benefactors. In the early centuries of the church, large landowners granted to priests parcels of land which became both their realm of spiritual responsibility and their source of revenue. In a financial sense, priests did not work for the people they served; they worked for the lord who provided them their land. Without land, the priest was without portfolio or income.

The parish thus belonged to the priest, it became his "benefice"; but the priest also belonged to the lord who had established him there. Later, when dioceses came into being and took over the role of provider, they also took over the lord's ultimate responsibility for—and control of—the parish priest. (That responsibility is still reflected today, for instance, in the fact that if a priest is sued for sexual abuse of a minor, the diocese can be held accountable.) More directly, the system ensured that the priest would honor and obey his assignments; not only his spiritual well-being but his financial survival depended on it.

Up until the ninth century, the parish as property attached, strictly speaking, not to the individual priest but to his office; the parish was his only so long as he was resident there. But by the twelfth century, the priest himself had come to be seen as "permanent" in the parish and had perpetual rights to the benefice. In effect, the pastor owned the parish and all its revenues apart from the portion the diocese might demand.

Although this system had built-in potential for abuse and was the object of countless attempts at reform, it became solidified in the sixteenth century when the Council of Trent ratified the notion of permanent pastorates; it became even more entrenched through the 1917 Revised Code of Canon Law, which universalized widespread, long-standing practice by declaring pastors "irremovable." And although permanent pastorates were not established in this country until the Third Plenary Council of Baltimore in 1884—the church in the United States was still considered mission territory at that time—the concept eventually took hold here as well. The pastor stayed in his parish for life, and the diocese was responsible for his care. When my classmates and I entered the seminary, these tenets seemed as fixed as any of the other semi-eternal truths by which we identified the traditional church. They were intrinsic parts of the priesthood we were drawn to, major elements in the security we anticipated.

Milwaukee Archbishop Moses Kiley introduced a few local reforms of the benefice system in 1947. Flying in the face of customary practice by which American pastors had come to assume the right to a wide range of moneys, Kiley forbade pastors from taking total control over parish collections, pew rents, and stipends for baptisms performed by his assistants. In Milwaukee and elsewhere, however, such piecemeal reforms were often honored more in the breach than in the observance; to cite one story I heard, even after the reforms, an assistant might be ordered to slip an envelope containing his accumulated stole fees for the week under the door of his pastor's bedroom every Sunday afternoon, while the pastor slept.

No fundamental attack on the benefice system, however, was made until Vatican II. Where the parish had traditionally been defined in terms of the rights and welfare of the pastor, it was now redefined in terms of the welfare of the people. And in order to implement more quickly the new thinking which would promote that welfare, the council abolished the concept of the "irremovable pastor"; the pastor would no longer have lifetime tenure (*Presbyterorum Ministerio*, #20, 31). Yet in the same breath, the council asserted that "priests are worthy of receiving a just recompense" for their work (*Presbyterorum Ordinis*, #20). The two moves were connected; the source of income which the church took away with one hand, it gave back with the other, more or less. The pastor would no longer own the parish; but he and his "associates"—replacing the old, more subservient "assistants"—would now have the right to a just wage.

In using language which implicitly linked priests with other workers instead of setting them off in a separate category, the council, wittingly or not, revealed the essential paradoxes of this new stance. Priests would now have "rights" which they had not claimed before—because they would now need them. They would be working for wages—and hence would suffer some of the anxieties and resentments of the wage earner. Without making any proclamations to this effect, the church would now become the priest's employer more than his nurturing mother; the priest would have to stand up for his rights and negotiate with the church instead of resting secure in her care.

Theology aside—or, to put it differently, precisely because the council addressed practical matters without developing a new theology of priesthood to accompany them—these two documents heralded a series of basic changes in the relationship of the priest to his parish and to the church. His position would inevitably become less of an ethereal "vocation" and more of a "job" tied to the terms of this world. In this way too, as with the less official but nonetheless pervasive elision of spirituality and therapy, priests would move closer to their Protestant counterparts. They would also begin to suffer similar anxieties insofar as their tenure depended increasingly (though less pervasively than it did with Protestant ministers) on lay evaluations to which they were once relatively immune.[4] My classmates' heightened interest in money must be placed in the context of these larger changes; what is specific to them is their particular, generational response, rather than the newfound concern with money itself.

In Milwaukee, priests have now been actively engaged in issues of compensation for the last twenty years. Having been given access to the files of the Priests Senate, a body formed in 1968 to convey the concerns of priests to the archbishop, I found that the thickest individual file in the records was that of the "Temporalities" subcommittee, a term which reflects both the archdiocese's willingness to address such issues and its lingering tendency to define them as residually "worldly," still somehow separate from the essentially spiritual issues of priesthood.

Since 1971, that committee has addressed such matters as salaries, cost-of living increases, minimum wage for priests, fees for "help-outs," car allowances, pension plans, health insurance, dental insurance, mass stipends, stole fees, travel expenses, and severance pay for priests who resign from the active ministry. The attention to detail is impressive, and the debates are sometimes finely focused: whether, for instance, car allowances should be given for any use of a priest's car or, as with salesmen, only for those duties carried out on behalf of the parish (1970); how much to pay per weekend "for confessions and bination (saying two masses), exclusive of stipend and travel costs" (1971). At some point, presumably at the height of ongoing deliberations (this particular memo is undated), someone on the committee introduced a mock resolution parodying what obviously seemed to the writer an obsession with money:

RESOLUTION FOR TEMPORALITIES COMMITTEE:

WHEREAS: No provision has been made either by the Archdiocese, the Parish, Institution or Agency by which the Priests are otherwise reimbursed for the soaring costs of tonsorial services:

BE IT HEREBY RESOLVED, THAT AN ADDITIONAL FUND BE SET ASIDE BY EACH PARISH, INSTITUTION OR AGENCY FOR THIS PURPOSE.

BE IT FURTHER RESOLVED, THAT SAID FUNDS BE SENT TO THE FINANCIAL MANAGER OF THE ARCHDIOCESE TO BE CONTROLLED, INVESTED, AND OTHERWISE MAINTAINED BY HIM UNTIL SUCH TIME AS NEEDED BY EACH INDIVIDUAL PRIEST.

AT SUCH TIME, THE PRIEST NEEDING FUNDS FOR TONSORIAL SERVICES WILL MAKE OUT AN APPLICATION IN TRIPLICATE, SUBMIT A RECENT PHOTO OF HIMSELF AS PROOF OF HIS NEED AND MEET WITH THE STANDING COMMITTEE ON HAIR CUTS TO COLLECT OR NOT COLLECT, AS THE COMMITTEE DECIDES, THE NECESSARY FUNDS.

The Vatican Council had left the details of the church's new policy toward removable pastorships and priestly compensation up to individual dioceses. For several years, Milwaukee contented itself with making minor adjustments to a salary system seemingly still based on the traditional assumption that priests were not of this world in the first place, and that in any case the church was still providing ordination-to-grave care for them. From 1974 until very recently, for instance, percentage increases in salary were derived by reference to the Metropolitan Milwaukee Index, a standard cost-of-living gauge. The base itself, however, remained unquestioned. In 1969, my newly ordained classmates received, in addition to room and board at the rectory, $197 a month in salary, $5 a month car allowance, and up to $150 a month in mass stipends. In 1979, the starting salary was $320 a month; for my classmates, with ten years of experience, it was $405. In 1988 they were getting $711.

Meanwhile, throughout this period, the fees for mass stipends remained unchanged; directly spiritual activities are presumably the hardest to submit to market forces. "It was five dollars when I was ordained twenty years ago," Father Frederick complained, "and it's still five dollars twenty years later. It's ridiculous. Either make it so that I really should be doing this and it's worthwhile, or it's not worthwhile and I shouldn't be doing it." For other classmates, the sleaziness of the stipend-giving ritual exacerbates the insult; as one of them said, "People slip me an envelope; I feel like I'm in a spy novel."

No form of their financial compensation, in fact, has ever been based on evaluations of performance or graduated according to merit. The

1980 "Rationale for the Current Remuneration of Priests of the Archdiocese of Milwaukee" states that "a remuneration is considered just and equitable when priests of the same number of years in the ordained ministry are compensated the same amount regardless of assignment."

In Milwaukee, the first substantial reverberations from the Vatican II changes were felt in 1974 and had nothing directly to do with salary. At that time, the archdiocese, in tandem with a number of dioceses across the country,[5] instituted a policy of "open listing," whereby all priestly positions would be advertised in the *Catholic Herald* (the archdiocesan newspaper) as well as in a periodic bulletin sent to all priests.

Yet it was clear from the beginning—memos from the Priests Senate address this issue repeatedly—that only if priestly terms were limited would open listing contribute to fresh thinking and new leadership: what would be the point of listing jobs if parishes opened up only once every thirty years or so? Several of my classmates, eager to introduce liberal change and, not coincidentally, impatient at the thought of being kept from power by the seniority system ("What the hell is with these guys who have been thirty-five, forty years in a parish?" Father Tod remembers asking), were active in the movement toward limited terms. It is one of the accomplishments they cite often to demonstrate their class's assertiveness.

The policy of fixed term of office was put into place in Milwaukee in 1980, when the archbishop requested the change and Rome granted it by an "indult" (official permission). Accordingly, within the limits set by their own diminishing numbers, parish priests change assignments every six years; the pastor, but not his associates, can renew for one additional six-year term. At present, priests in Milwaukee can also attempt to move by choice, either because they don't like their present assignment or because they want a "better parish," the definitions of which are also in flux now that the big parishes with extensive physical plants often bring with them more headaches than status. Under the procedure of "open listing," they make their wishes known to the personnel board, which considers their requests along with those of other priests and then makes a recommendation to the archbishop.

Many members of my class still strongly endorse the fixed-term policy. They remember the old-time parish monarchs very well; many of them "served" under such pastors in their first assignments and are horrified at the thought of repeating that history; they endorse the notion that "the parish belongs to the people and not to the pastor," as one of them put it. They appreciate the benefits of introducing new ideas to the parish, and in general, they have come to like the idea of moving around, as one of them said, "to keep my juices flowing."

The mobility seemingly offered by the new system has its underside, however. Precisely because the personnel committee elicits requests to move more often and more openly than under the old system, its refusals to honor specific requests often take on an air of rejection, especially for priests who still incline toward a personal view of the church's workings (even as they complain of encroaching impersonality); Father Herbert confessed to feeling "burned and betrayed" by the process. This personalizing bent has made the no longer uncommon experience of being fired particularly harrowing: as one classmate said, "They fired *me! Me!*"

In any case, although they can make all the requests they want before or after their six-year term is up, the *Clergy Manual* reminds them emphatically (under the heading *An Assignment must be accepted*) that "in the final analysis, should there be no position available to the liking of a particular priest, he is not free to reject an assignment, albeit temporary, made by the Archbishop. To do so contrary to obedience to the Archbishop would render the Archbishop's ministry in the Archdiocese ineffective and also render harm to the People of God." Thus the assignment process, underneath it all, is yet one more reminder, as one priest said, that when push comes to shove, "the archbishop still holds all the cards."

As a result, to many of them, mandatory movement after six or twelve years now looks less like an opportunity for them and more like a mechanism of control over them. For those who have been around long enough to have suffered the pains of being moved from parishes where they wanted to stay and where they feel that they were doing their best work, the bitterness of being moved against their will is especially intense; several echo the resentment of one classmate that "over the great protest of the parish, the personnel board in its infinite wisdom decided that I had been there too long."

Furthermore, my classmates are admittedly uneasy at the thought that it is now *their* ideas which are being replaced by the more conservative younger generation of priests; the very system of changes they worked for—changes which they viewed as liberal—now run the risk of facilitating what they see as the church's regression to an authoritarian mode. So although none of them openly espouses a return to the idea of an irremovable pastor, they now feel some of the anger those older men felt when their tenure was destroyed and the world they had built around them crumbled.

Perhaps the archdiocesan change with the greatest repercussions is that, at the age of mandatory retirement (currently 75), pastors in Milwaukee must now move out of the rectory and shift for themselves; the prospects of a graceful, secure retirement at "their" parish are gone. To provide care for retired priests, the old "St. Michael's Fund," a formless, ad hoc mechanism established in 1901 to provide financial aid to infirm or disabled priests and later expanded to cover exceptional hardships and the odd case of indigence under the old system, has been all but replaced by a more systematic, diocesan-wide retirement plan, which provided $690 a month in 1988.

That sum is far from adequate, however, now that parish room and board are no longer provided in retirement. Furthermore, since the government defines priests as self-employed in relation to social security, they are not automatically covered by Medicare. At several points in the last twenty years, the government has opened a "window" to allow priests to enroll in social security voluntarily. Yet I was told by a high diocesan official that in Milwaukee the percentage of uncovered priests is very high, partly because the social security tax is so high that many cannot afford it, and partly because many priests retain the old conviction that the church will somehow take care of them, all evidence to the contrary. Many of my classmates remain unenrolled. So far, the St. Michael's Fund—itself on shaky ground—has been covering the cost of supplemental health insurance for retired priests on Medicare; but for unenrolled priests eligible only for the far more expensive Medicaid, the diocese has been providing merely the same amount. (This is a "justice issue," one diocesan official told me, since priests who chose not to go on Social Security had a good deal more money at their disposal all along.)

Even the retirement plan itself is shaky. The archbishop has made public his commitment to keeping it afloat; but Milwaukee, like many other dioceses, has no history of expertise in such issues, and priests I talked to both inside and outside of official archdiocesan offices are not sure where the necessary money will come from in the long run. Hence, with no guaranteed place to live anymore (the diocese has 31 low-cost retirement units, all full, with a long waiting list), priests in Milwaukee face a bleak retirement, with "Title 19" (county welfare) or bankruptcy a real possibility. Several of my classmates discussed the prospects of "Title 19" matter-of-factly, as part of their current landscape.

Their fears have already produced a folklore about aging priests who suffer heart attacks as the prospects of indigence loom before them; whether factual of not, such stories convey an emotional truth unknown to earlier generations. At one time, my classmates could assume with Father Frederick that the Mother Church was going to take care of them; at present, however, they do not feel like partners in a supportive marriage or like offspring nurtured by their mother; they feel more like middle managers cut adrift from above, with no safety net beneath.

If it was part of my classmates' naiveté not to think initially about needing recognition because they assumed it would be there, it was part of their idealism not to worry about being paid in any sense of the word. "The last thing on my mind when I was twenty-six years old in the late sixties," one priest said, "was money or retirement or anything of that sort." Even to think about making or saving money at that time, another told me, would have been "awful," both a violation of ideals and a betrayal of his trust in Holy Mother the Church.

But over time—this is close to the core of their midlife uneasiness and to that of many in our generation—they have realized that none of these things are automatically provided for them anymore. As with status, they now find themselves wanting money, having to agitate for money, and irritated at the very fact of having to think about money. The whole grubby process makes them wonder whether the Vatican II mandate to "embrace" the world was merely a prelude to being shoved out into it without preparation or protection.

If the priests who want more money represent a mix of practicality and a post–Vatican II embrace of the material realm, those who resist these arguments cling to what they see as the purer, otherworldly view. And although they are in the minority, they are equally as vocal; this is an issue which energizes nearly everyone who engages it. They argue that priests develop their spirituality best by moderating their needs rather than by looking for ways to indulge them. Their insistence that priests are by definition "counterculture" provides them with a 1960s claim of their own for their more traditional, ascetic stance: that priests, current revisionism to the contrary, are essentially not "of this world," should not espouse its values, and must remain suspicious of personalist philosophies which run the risk of putting the self before the other, the "needs" of the individual before the rightful demands of the community or of the church. Of the handful of my classmates who subscribe to this vision, the most vehement was a priest who had served in the military and found the complaints self-indulgent and deceptive. "I have little time for priests who say they are struggling," he told me. "The number of priests with second homes on lakes far surpasses those who are struggling. We're strictly middle-class, too middle-class."

Others purport a greater sympathy with salary agitation but simply take a different stand. Father Herman, for instance—who has held several high diocesan offices and stands at the center of a circle of like-minded priests—acknowledged that "the money issue is real, all right," but still finds that "I'm always wondering, where is the countercultural sign value that suggests that materialism isn't the key issue?" He prefers to drive modest cars, camps out on many of his vacations instead of staying at hotels, often buys seconds and even misshapen goods, and looks forward to the possibility of eventual bankruptcy with relative equanimity; he'd get by with a little help from his friends. Although he is unsure how his ideals work in the practical world, his affinities remain elsewhere:

> There is in me and in some of my priest friends a kind of a Franciscan spirit. I don't know how that stacks up in the real world. I don't. It's easy and poetic and a little bit exciting to talk that way or live that way. . . . It may mean Title 19. I know priests who have gone on that. There's

something in me that says that's not bad. It would not be such an in-
dignity as long as I had friends. There's a certain simplicity of life that,
if you're struggling with it at age forty-five, I think hopefully would
make sense at seventy-five too.

Similarly, Father Eugene feels that seeking money merely for what he
"wants" would not affirm his humanity/spirituality but would simply
infect him with worldly values dangerous to the life of the spirit. He vigorously echoes the 1960s fear of being co-opted:

It's an issue for me, for the reverse side. I think we make more money
than we need. I choose not to take a full salary, because I don't need a
full salary. I have everything that I need; I don't have everything that I
want. I've found that whenever I go after everything I want, that's a
dead end. Our society says you should be rewarded with money. What
am I going to do with the money? I have money now that I don't know
what to do with. I get angry, because what is the image you project if
you've bought into the world's values? I really believe that because I've
found it true in my own life, not because somebody says, "Believe it." I
really believe that it dead-ends us.

At the time of these interviews, this entire debate was taking a new
turn as the archdiocese of Milwaukee moved toward a compensation
plan which would base priests' salaries on those of Protestant ministers
and of CEOs in nonprofit organizations. Under the pilot plan in which
forty priests were then participating and which would eventually extend to the entire diocese, total compensation would range from $26,756
for newly ordained priests to $33,956 for priests with forty or more years
of experience. For my classmates, for instance, that would break down
into $13,712 in salary, $3,600 in "stipend offset"—the money to be provided in lieu of stipends, somewhat in the manner of congressional
raises as a substitute for honoraria—and up to $13,044 for housing and
food, to be used at the priest's discretion should he choose to live away
from the rectory.
Interestingly enough, this proposal does not seem to have affected the
entrenched attitudes either of those priests who agitate for more money
or of those who insist that money is not an issue; both seem to see their
perspectives validated in the new plan. One priest, for instance, whose
notion of a controlling church is central to his way of thinking, suspects
that the archdiocese will never fully implement these changes for fear of
losing its power over priests: "I control your pocketbook, I control you."
Father Malcolm, for whom salaries were a major source of irritation
when I first interviewed him, now resents the fact that the diocese plans
to discount the figures for Protestant clergy and CEOs by 30 percent because, as the pilot project states, "priests are single" and don't need as
much money as their secular equivalents. In his view, this represents "a

continuation of the benefice mentality: *they* decide what *we* need. I don't want anyone deciding that for me; I want to be paid what I'm worth."

To others, the new plan does not go far enough toward the professional model they desire. They feel that in openly refusing to introduce merit into salary considerations—years in service will still be the only criterion for increases; all priests of the same seniority, no matter what their positions or how well they perform in them, will be paid alike—the diocese is refusing to make the distinctions necessary to provide motivation. Others feel that the new salaries, far from signaling the archdiocese's reawakened concern for its priests, are instead the archdiocese's way, as one of them put it, of "writing us off," of openly acknowledging its refusal to take care of priests as the church once did:

> Instead of leaving the money thing alone and saying, "You guys need anything?" the archbishop can now say, "Hey, we gave you enough money. You take care of it yourselves. We're washing ourselves of you. We're not taking any responsibility for you in later years." In fact, he's almost used those words.

By contrast, for instance, Father Herman still feels little need for increased salaries. He remains relatively content in his rejection of what he sees as mainstream materialism because he feels that the church even under the old plan offers him a comfortable and secure refuge from it. He feels, in short, that he still has a personal relationship with a nurturing church: "I value that dependence," he says. "There's a positive side to this commitment within family. Within a Catholic system, if everyone perceives the value, the outcome is security. And you get on with the rest of your agenda. I think I imbibed that in the fifties, and I've carried that through."

Nearly all of us, as far as I can tell, entered the seminary with this traditional view of the church. We expected it to be our home, our "helpmate"; we hoped that it would provide the personal warmth and support which, to a surprising degree, many of us did not find in our family of origin. At the same time, we had been educated to think of "the world" as the dread locus of materialistic forces, a negative force field allied with the flesh and the devil in an age-old conspiracy to drag us under.

In his persistent view of a benign, caring church, however, Father Herman is now a distinct minority. The more typical stance is that of the classmate who says, "We can try to hang on to the teat for life, but it's not going to be there for us"; the Holy Mother lives on in my classmates' imagination only in ironic residue such as this. Most of them now see themselves in an impersonal institution which has shown little gratitude for their efforts and has undercut their security in the process, an institution which is willing to manipulate their loyalty to higher values in order to continue paying them less: "The church is not interested in celibate priests," one of them told me. "The church is interested in unmarried priests. A cheap labor pool."

Meanwhile, if my classmates' view of the church has hardened, their view of the "world" has softened; in many ways, the two forces have changed places, with the former taking on the near-demonic traits once attributed to the latter. Just as others of the 1960s often find ourselves nowadays more comfortably related, though not without lingering uneasiness, to a mainstream society we once dismissed as corrupt, most of my classmates now feel, along with poet Richard Wilbur, that "love calls us to the things of this world," a world which no longer constitutes, in their minds, a suspect realm lower than that of the spirit.

But where, in the world, are they? As we will see in the next chapter, for priests uncertain about where they fit in the scheme of things, questions of class have inevitably become as important as questions of money.

Four years after our original conversations, I mentioned to Father Herman that he was one of a handful of priests who resisted the agitation for more money. He laughed sheepishly and said, "Well, in fact, I may be moving more toward that other position after all. I just bought a new car, cost close to $20,000, and I find myself wondering where the payments are going to come from. It bothers me that I'm thinking that way, but I am."

In that context, he went on to describe the ambiguities of the new diocesan stipend policy. Priests can now choose either to continue receiving stipends—$75 for a wedding, $50 for funerals, still $5 for a regular mass—or a "stipend offset" of $3,600 a year in lieu of specific payment for individual services; they can, in effect, continue to do piecework or go on (professional) salary. And since his current associate has opted for the offset and Herman has not, "I feel torn between assigning the associate a lot of weddings and funerals—since the parish is already paying him the offset—and taking most of them for myself, since I need the money. But it's a lot of work, too: our parish has two funerals a week and about thirty-five weddings a year. And in economic terms, of course, my associate has less incentive to do a lot of weddings and funerals; he gets nothing extra for volunteering. Luckily he has not resisted; but structurally, he could."

Weddings, he went on to point out, often involve a year of meetings with the couple, complicated arrangements and scheduling, etc. So although the $50 for funerals isn't bad compensation, since funerals are more self-contained, $75 doesn't look like much once you start considering it from a financial perspective. "I'd rather not look at it that way," he said. "But then when the young couple pull up to the church in two limousines and you know how much they cost, I find myself saying, 'Hey, I want a piece of that action too.' "

*   *   *

Although it has been my primary purpose throughout this book to describe the situations that my classmates faced in the late 1980s, when I talked with most of them, a modest 1995 update in regard to money is worth providing, since financial insecurity was such a large issue for them. The pilot plan for salaries has indeed been extended to all the priests in the diocese, with yearly, indexed cost-of-living increases. Newly ordained priests in Milwaukee now earn salaries of $12,976; priests with forty years of service or more earn $20,176. All priests may claim a food and housing allowance up to $15,760 and a stipend offset— should they choose it—of $4,350. Mass stipends are still $5.

The retirement plan is now on a sounder basis and provides $850 a month, an amount which still leaves priests eligible only for Medicaid in a highly tenuous condition, needing to provide at least $3,000 to $5,000 a year on their own. The St. Michael's Fund, no longer under the burden of providing retirement funds of any kind, has been redirected specifically toward indigent priests in need of short-term moneys. Priests must submit tax returns to prove need; not all requests are granted.

However one judges archdiocesan efforts to improve the priests' financial situation, the emotional and monetary aspects of retirement remain dire. Most priests in the archdiocese, I was told recently by one classmate, do not want to retire even at seventy-five for fear of loneliness; they dread the thought, he said, of going "from phones ringing all the time to no phone ringing at all." Even now, my classmate said, "most priests in Milwaukee die in nursing homes on county assistance."

The Professional Priest

> I'm managing a million-dollar business here. I manage close to thirty full-time people. I can manage and work with people; I have talents that could be put into something else.
>
> —Father Albert

"I didn't want to be a priest until the end of the eighth grade," Father Malcolm told me over dinner one night; we were at a modest Greek restaurant, but one nonetheless that his parents would not have been able to afford. "I was all set to go to the public school. My goals were to be a baker, to own a bakery shop. But my mom and dad both kept saying to me, 'You know, you'd have to work hard.' And I'd say, 'Well, that's all right, I want to be a baker.'

"Then at the end of the school year, my parents said, Did you ever think about becoming a priest?' And all of a sudden, bang, I had this funny feeling. I can't describe the feeling."

Like Malcolm, like Frederick, most of the members of my class are the second- and third-generation sons of a relatively uneducated immigrant class. Approximately 80 percent of us come from parents without college education; even fewer have parents with claims to professional status. My father, for instance, dropped out of high school and began working to help his parents through the Depression. Typically, our parents were either laborers—glass cutters, assembly-line workers, maintenance men—or marginally white-collar: salesmen, office workers, store managers.

It is not necessarily that the priesthood was our sole escape route from lower-class status, as it had been for the previous generation of seminarians closer to immigrant roots; on the evidence of what our siblings did, many of us, myself included, would have gone to college anyway. Nonetheless, in social and economic terms, the priesthood would be either our particular point of entry to the middle class or a step toward securing a previously tenuous toehold.

My classmates were ordained, however, in the midst of the church's post–Vatican II uncertainty about the role of the priest; and no sooner were they ordained than their sense of themselves was shaken further by the rise of the laity on the one hand and their own concomitant slide into economic insecurity. As a result, they feel something akin to what Barbara Ehrenreich describes in her study of the newly arrived middle class in America over the last three decades: an intense "fear of falling" from a position too new to them to feel secure, a fear fueled by their anxieties about belonging there in the first place.[6] Ehrenreich is particularly interested in what she sees as the professional middle class's "retreat from liberalism" as they came to see themselves as an elite set off from ordinary people and thus dependent for their self-esteem on keeping such people below them on the social scale. The extent to which my classmates feel anxious helps to explain why they have a complicated set of feelings toward the empowering of the once-docile laity, an empowering which they so clearly endorse on the level of social conviction. In class terms, the laity are to priests what blacks have been to white ethnics: the threat from below.

This insecurity, I think, helps explain my classmates' resentment at being treated like "worker bees," in Father Leo's terms, or as "just a bunch of workers," in Father Tod's; it lies behind their resentment at having to pay lay personnel more than they themselves are paid. It also helps to explain their surprising resistance to—and in many cases scorn for—the thought of being, as Father Jeff put it, "just a parish priest." As Father Leo's comments suggest, they no longer embrace the implications of being the church's foot soldiers:

> The archbishop said to me last year, "Why don't priests want to be assigned to parishes?" He completely caught me off guard, but I thought for a while and said, "Maybe part of it is expressed when the archdiocese as well as priests every so often refer to parishes as 'the trenches.' The trenches ain't a nice place to be. It's a dirty place to be. It's where you get fired at, it's where you get a lot of crap thrown at you."

My classmates no longer want to be on the firing line, taking orders, doing the dirty work and getting no credit for it. Instead, a great many of them now want to be seen as men of advanced training and specialized expertise whose very title would suggest status, authority, and control—not directly over the laity, for they resist the "new clericalism" even while sharing some of its impulses—but over their own careers. Like the Protestant clergy at the turn of the century, and under similar circumstance of class anxiety,[7] they want, in short, to be seen as professionals.

As Father Frederick describes it, the urge for professional standing draws not only on the desire for more money ("If you don't have money, what does that do to your self-worth?") but on the underlying need for a strong sense of individual identity not often encouraged (though often achieved) in the traditional priesthood:

> What we are experiencing in the church now is more and more people specializing. That's very healthy, because gradually people are getting to see that we have to treat each person as an individual, and not just rotate them around, like generic pastors. That's still a misconception we have inherited: dress them all alike, they should all wear the collar—so there is no such thing as individual worth. And I think that the more we have people going into specialized ministry, the more we see that to be in specialized ministry you have to be professional.

Similarly, Father Alex links professionalism with personal growth, describing his ability to move into and out of several different "careers"—parish priest, high-school teacher, grade-school principal—as crucial to his conviction that he can "achieve self-actualization within the church, within the priesthood." And for all his emphasis on specialization, Father Frederick insists that "being in a parish is also a form of profession" demanding years of training and highly developed expertise. The church's "general practitioners," the model still proposed by the 1962 seminary self-study, now aspire to a higher status—and to no longer being on call twenty-four hours a day.

The insistence on professional status reflects, I think, both the uncertainties and the possibilities of men newly dislodged from their once-stable position under the wing of the Holy Mother. They are "anxious" in both senses of the word, as eager to move up as they are afraid of slipping down; the fear of falling fuels their desire to rise—and adds energy to their insistence that they *have* arrived. For though they are only two or three generations removed from one old country or another, the church they belong to is no longer an immigrant church, and they no longer limit themselves to immigrant aspirations. They are eager to move from the traditional priesthood's peculiar brand of trade-union socialism to a more independent, self-defined, high-status model of priesthood.

Their uncertainty is reflected in their language, which often expresses a wish to be professional rather than a conviction that they already are. "I'm trying to be professional," Father Frederick asserts, "and I'm trying to keep up my self-esteem that I am professional and I am doing quality work." After volunteering that they were impressed that I was a university professor, several of them reminded me that they have at least four years of graduate education in theology. Many of them emphasized that they have master's degrees or more in various fields (by my count, half of them have done graduate work beyond their seminary training). Others have shifted openly toward a more monetary rationale, seeing themselves as middle managers of considerable financial value to the diocese: they want to be respected as well as paid in a manner befitting that station.

A number of my classmates, primarily those who also reject the call for higher salaries, scorn the professional designation. For some of them, the model of "alter Christus" still locates their chosen frame of reference elsewhere; for others, the more earthly claims are simply unfounded, linked more to insecurity than to achievement. "I don't need to call myself professional," one priest insisted. "I know who I am." When I asked one of our former professors what he made of the claim to priestly professionalism, he snorted in derision:

> Professionals in what? Professionals in spirituality? Professionals in sacramentality? Professionals in calling forth the gifts of the laity? Where is the professional quality of priesthood? We have laity who could give homilies as well as many of our priests, and they've majored in scripture. People go all over the lot for counseling. Support systems are all over. If you lost your child or have a stillborn, you go to a support group. You don't come to Father anymore. All we have left as our realm is the sacraments, and that doesn't constitute us as professionals.

This same priest has his own vision of the future: a pared-down, part-time priesthood with men (or women) making a living at other jobs and performing the sacraments, their last claim to unique power, at night or on weekends:

> The priest is supposed to say mass, okay. But after that, he's left with
> reconciliation, which nobody comes to one on one. They'll come to
> communal penance; I can pack 'em in on that. But I could sit in that
> little area that I have for private reconciliation for days on end and no-
> body would cross the threshold. So there's liturgy and what, admini-
> stration? Get Father to open the school. A light bulb burned out. What
> else is there going to be?

Mandatory celibacy, he suggests, will presumably disappear under
this arrangement; the church could not expect people to give up sexual
intimacy for a part-time job. (How about part-time celibacy, I found myself wondering.) And the way would open for former priests, now em-
ployed elsewhere anyway, to return to priestly work without great cost
to the church, thus alleviating the crisis of diminishing numbers. The
priesthood as it is presently constituted, he feels, is "fast fading"; the
only way to save it is to acknowledge its shrunken role and make the
best of it.

I would not venture to assess the merits of this proposal, nor those of
several other models offered by sociologists such as Andrew Greeley and
Dean Hoge for coping with the shortage of priests.[8] What I am interested
in is how thoroughly this stripped-down vision of priesthood differs
from the enhanced priesthood for which my classmates yearn. For inherent in their desire for more pay and higher status is a desire for a
re-energized priesthood of undiminished if not expanded scope and importance; they do not want to be reduced to changing light bulbs or, in
Tod's terms, to "reading the funnies and taking the CYO out."

Their model, vague though it is in specifics, aims at giving them a
greater sense of independence and status; it would move them closer to
the norms of achievement held by secular society; it would provide them
with a way to think about themselves as successful *men* in the terms they
were raised to respect. At the same time, it would offer a self-definition
commensurate with and supportive of their still-active desire to save the
world and to offer a full range of services in the process; they merely
(if that is the right word) would like to be rewarded more fully and regarded more highly for their efforts. In this respect their idealism and
their newly acknowledged ambition—their 1960s side and their 1980s
side—gesture toward one another, hoping to make a pact.

The professional model would also, ideally, signal the church's increased appreciation of them; for it is their conviction that the church
has come to treat them as "a bunch of workers," to requote Father Tod,
that serves as the thorn under the saddle. Acknowledged professional
status would thus solidify their desire to negotiate "the world" more
comfortably and to remain content inside their own institution at the
same time. Yet the hierarchy, perhaps as anxious about encroachments
from priests as the priests themselves have been about the laity, shows

little inclination to recognize the increased priestly professionalism which the later stages of my classmates' seminary training actively encouraged. As a result, their attempts to follow their own institution's promptings have alienated them from it further—and heightened their resentment at its attempts to keep them in their place.

The Controlled Priest, Priests under Control

> The key concepts in the newer dynamic psychology are spontaneity, release, naturalness, self-choice, self-acceptance, impulse awareness, gratification of basic needs. They used to be control, inhibition, discipline, training, shaping. . . .
> —Abraham Maslow, *Motivation and Personality* (1970)

> The church has got us by the balls.
> —Father Malcolm et al.

Father Leonard and I were sitting in a conference room at the Cousins Center. It was 5:30 in the afternoon on the annual Clergy Day for the Milwaukee archdiocese; Leonard had had a full day of meetings, we had already talked for an hour and a half, he had a seventy-mile drive ahead of him, and he was obviously tired. Before leaving, however, he turned to me and said, "Can I give you a really good story? A really good one? And then I'll go."

In the seminary, I thought of Leonard as one of the mildest of my classmates, conciliatory by nature; it seemed inconceivable that he would ever raise his voice or use it to complain about anything—or that he would ever break a rule. He had grown up in a rural German family, speaking German at home, and had taken its conservatism with him to the seminary, where his docility fit the old seminary very well. "Under the Schneider years," he says, "you weren't supposed to be asking questions. A good priest did what he was supposed to do." Even in the wake of Vatican II, he admits, "my whole concept of theology was extremely conservative. I would hear this new theory and feel that it was being unfaithful to the truth. I have no doubt that this still has a hold on me."

By chance or perverse logic, Leonard's first pastors were extremely domineering, a perfect match—and test—for his docility. One of them, he told me, would barge into the office while Leonard was counseling someone and say, "I don't know why you're talking to him; I'm the boss here." That same pastor loved the theater, so he would fly out to New York on Sunday, come back on Thursday, and fly out again on Sunday. "He'd come home to do the bulletin," Leonard said. "He didn't trust me to do the bulletin." The rule in that rectory was, "He answered the phone and I answered the door. So the phone would ring at night and he'd answer it. Then he'd come upstairs and say, 'Leonard, St. Luke's [hospital] has called. Do you want to take it or do you want me to go?' " Leonard laughed. "Do you want to know the truth? I'd go. I'd go. I just took it."

Summarizing that stage of his priesthood, Leonard said, "It was just me not having the guts. If I could have just once yelled at him or shouted—never did. I don't know that I ever spoke an angry word to him. I remember one time standing in the hallway and just saying, 'Damn it, I quit!' But nobody else was in the house." He smiled. "You know, I saw that man this afternoon and still have trouble acknowledging his presence because he didn't acknowledge mine."

In Leonard's other early parish, the pastor also expected to call all the shots. For a long time, Leonard was willing to listen. One night, however—this is the story he wanted to tell—he received a phone call from Stevens Point, where two of his parishioners, a doctor and his wife, had flown in their private plane. The plane had crashed, the caller said, and both of them had been killed; could Leonard go over and stay with their five grade-school-age children until their grandfather arrived? Leonard told his pastor where he was going and why, and left. When he got to the home, "We did a lot of hugging and holding, and then they went immediately into denial and played games and did some laughing." At 10:30, Leonard called his pastor to let him know that the grandfather had not yet arrived. The pastor replied, "Well, Father, you know eleven o'clock is curfew. You'll be here."

"I was just in shock," Leonard told me, with more agitation in his voice than I could ever remember hearing from him. "Can you believe that? Five orphans, Grandpa's coming, and he says, 'Eleven o'clock is curfew.' " But Leonard replied simply, "No, I won't" and hung up; he did not return to the rectory until the next morning, after an unmarried aunt had finally arrived to take over. "It was never talked about again, that I disobeyed him," Leonard says. "I get goose bumps thinking about it."

Leonard's story is not one of radical transformation; he has not become as vocal in his various discontents or as theologically liberal as most of his classmates. And overall, he is happy that he stuck it out through those hard early years and stayed in the priesthood. "I'm glad I did it," he said. "If I had known what it was going to be, I don't think I would have done it. Would I do it again? I sure would—but it would be a whole different priesthood than I went into."

He does acknowledge some changes in himself, however. Now, at least, on matters such as birth control, he says, "The pope can talk," but "you just bend that when you say to yourself that you cannot in conscience come down on somebody for that." And he no longer believes that the church has the right to act *in loco parentis* toward its own priests.

My classmates' dilemma: having imbibed growth psychologies which prize internal development over external controls, and in the further context of their own heightened desire for the autonomy and respect which (they assume) accompany professional status, they perceive the hierarchy as tightening the screws from above, reasserting the church's parental authority over them—just at the moment that they are letting go of, or losing, their control over the laity.

Money is part of this ("I control your pocketbook, I control you"), but so is the church's control over their movements, in several senses of the word: from one parish to the next, from one kind of assignment to another, from one rectory to another—where, as several of them suggested, they can be watched more closely: "Rectories," says Father Herbert, "save money—and offer sexual control. When I got an apartment in 1987, that was one of the most significant steps toward independence that I was able to achieve as a single male. It gave me independence from other celibates who wanted to control me."

To Herbert, one impulse behind living in apartments is that "you can have a lifestyle—a term that came into popularity among priests in the mid-eighties—and a personal life," a life not dictated wholly by the church. As he tells it, the laity don't like that very much:

> There is no doubt in my mind, certain people are very threatened by this. Recently, a suburban woman said to me, "Oh, I understand you're at a new assignment. *Do you live there?*" I said, "No." She said, "Can they get hold of you?" I said, "You know, many of us are living in alternative residences." She said, "Oh, but we have to pay you for that. Can we afford that?" I told her, "I can live the way you and your husband do." She looked startled.

According to Father Brent, the archdiocesan authorities don't like this assertion of freedom very much either, for similar reasons; "They are afraid we'll get out of control":

> The archdiocese didn't make it easy for us to have alternative residences. Ten years ago you had to negotiate the amount for one. He told me, "This is the most anyone has ever requested." I said, "I can name four others who are higher." He said, "You're not supposed to know that." I said, "And you're not supposed to lie to me."

Even when my classmates see a rationale behind the church's restrictions on their movements, they resent and resist in the interests of their own development. Father Tracy, for instance, who teaches political science at Marquette University and has a sophisticated sense of how and why the church works, acknowledged that the shortage of clergy has driven the archdiocese to welcome priests from other dioceses and at the same time to make it difficult for its own priests to leave. He is indignant nonetheless:

> The temptation is to fill the church's needs, namely to keep all the par-
> ishes filled. And you've got this pool of talent that might not really grow
> by putting them in those slots. There isn't much mobility in the priest-
> hood. Basically, I can't leave the ten colonies of this diocese. And none
> of the other priests can. The institutional church has such a hold on its
> clergy. I'm much too liberal in my thinking to think that's the way it's
> to be. Institutional needs are not the needs of the personnel.

The exercise of such control once reflected the church's paramilitary
view of the priesthood as the "Army of Christ" ready to go anywhere on
command; placing the needs of the church over the desires of individual
priests was seen as a reflection of a proper set of priorities. It was all part
of the package.

But to my classmates, such priorities now constitute institutional sins
against their legitimate needs. By their lights, an assignment which goes
against the individual grain is no longer the voice of God demanding
assent but, as Father Leo sees it, simply "bad management. It's as if the
university forced you to teach chemistry instead of literature and insisted that you would be violating your contract and undermining the
university if you refused."

If my classmates resent the church's restrictions on their movements
within the priesthood, they are particularly appalled by its renewed
threats of moral and social sanction if they try to move out of the priesthood. From 1965 through 1978, under the reign of Pope Paul VI—from
their last years in the seminary through their first decade in the priesthood—priests were allowed to laicize without great difficulty. Essentially, they had to do little more than write a letter to Rome saying that
they wanted to leave the active ministry for reasons of their own. Six of
the seven members of my class who have left the priesthood (an eighth
was in the process during these interviews) left during this period; and
even though only two of those six went through the laicization process,
the others benefited as well from the general atmosphere of acceptance
which characterized such actions at that time.

Furthermore, my classmates tell me, rumors were rife during the brief,
thirty-four-day reign of Pope John Paul I in late 1978 that he was about
to loosen the celibacy laws. His death put an emphatic end to that hope,
however, as it did to their overall vision of an easy, continuing, liberaliz-
ing process. The option to laicize all but disappeared under Pope John
Paul II, who suspended the "norms for laicization" within a month of
taking office in 1978. Now it is necessary for priests wishing to laicize
with permission to marry to undergo something akin to an annulment
process—their own comparison—which means, in effect, claiming that
the ordination never really took hold in the first place, that they were
somehow incapacitated, misled, or pressured into an incomplete and
thus not-quite-binding commitment. "This is tantamount to lying," as
one priest put it; and even for priests willing to do so, the application

has almost no chance of succeeding. Between 1967 and 1979, 134 priests resigned in Milwaukee, an average of about 12 a year. From 1980 on, they have resigned at a rate of 4 a year; the last successful application for laicization, I was told, took eight years.

Laicization was especially widespread in the late 1960s; the peak year was 1969, the year my classmates were ordained, when 22 priests resigned. The shift between then and now is dramatic: the current attitude of the church, according to Father Leo, is that "you will be betraying Jesus Christ if you leave." Of course it remains possible simply to walk; but within the present church structure, according to another classmate, "there is no way out for a priest."

Consistent with their view of priesthood as a career, however, my classmates see this locking of the exit doors not as theology or as the necessary effect of commitment but as a form of entrapment; in the developmental terms which they have embraced, such restrictions are inhuman. The effect is to distance them further from their own institution even as they comply. Like someone in a troubled marriage, one classmate made it clear that he can remain committed to the church only by believing that somehow, all current evidence to the contrary, his spouse will change:

> I think the church will eventually have to get over the notion of ordination for life. We just have to change our legalism on that point because we structure that decision with all kinds of guilt terms. We're living with an incredible situation now where a man is told that he cannot make that decision, that if he does make that decision he is in sin and cannot be accepted.

To make matters worse, my classmates feel that their lifetime tenure is now held against them by an increasingly ambitious laity who equate permanence in one job not with loyalty or commitment but with lack of sufficient talent or gumption to move on and up. "That's the unkindest cut of all," admits Father Herman, "the implication that people level at clerics: what else would you be doing, what else *could* you do?"

And precisely because of their long-term dedication to activities geared to the church's needs rather than to their particular talents, priests who do consider leaving the priesthood often find themselves in the position of marginalized laborers with no recognized skills to draw on. One of the central reasons for Father Edmund's remaining a priest instead of leaving to marry Anna Maria, for instance, is that he fears radical underemployment: "I'm a professional now; what would I be if I left?" "You find," says one former priest who moved from the priesthood to driving a bus, "that you've got a tremendous education and no salable talent." Like the traditional housewife, my classmates find that long-term dedication to their spouse's agenda leaves them with few options.

Midlife timing also contributes to their frustration. According to a recent study,[9] the satisfaction of business executives—the archdiocese's own pilot plan recognizes one group of businessmen, CEOs of nonprofit organizations, as comparable to priests—tends to drop off after nine to eleven years in a given job; at that point, they either change jobs, redefine the job they have, or else suffer discontent and decline. Pope John Paul II's tightening of the reins in 1978 came nine years after my classmates had been ordained; and it came during their mid- to late thirties, a period in which, according to Daniel Levinson, 80 percent of American males, feeling the accumulated frustrations of their current paths and the renewed lure of roads not taken, experience moderate to severe dissatisfaction with their lives.[10] To feel locked in at exactly the point when the majority of men in our culture express a keen need for freedom and flexibility has done little to deepen my classmates' loyalty to the church.

Some of my classmates feel that the fixed-term policy allows them enough room for change, even though that policy mandates movement and controls its terms. Others have, in the words of one admiring classmate describing another, "tailor-made the priesthood" to fit their needs. These initiatives, however, are exceptions. For most of my classmates, the feeling of restriction continues; in direct contrast to their expressed wish for a more elastic and varied priesthood, they see themselves fenced in on all sides. They now have earlier access to the pastorate but feel blocked once they get there: "Upward movement?" asks Father Alex. "Where have we got to go?" The diocese no longer confers the honorific title of monsignor, another gesture toward dismantling the old status system which my classmates originally welcomed but now view with at least partial regret. Becoming a bishop is roughly as likely as making the major leagues. And even the satisfaction of getting and keeping a "better" parish, whatever that might currently be, is mitigated by the pastor's limited term.

Just at a time, then, when "career" has replaced "vocation" as their own predominant term to describe the priesthood, the most they have available to them is a series of lateral moves, completely subject to the church's approval in its own interests. If they stay permanently in one "place"—within the priesthood itself, at least as presently defined—they run the risk of feeling devalued by outsiders and personally inert, a particularly frightening prospect in the context of their theologies of growth. If they consider leaving anyway, they face social ostracism by the church and the threat of moral sanction. Meanwhile, as priests, they are still subject to the traditional pressure (though many of them resist it) to live in parish rectories and to be on call twenty-four hours a day. "I'm a kept person," Father Tod lamented, overtly linking the church's sexual and economic control over him. "All in all," Father Malcolm told me in a phrase I heard from other classmates as well, "the church has got us by the balls."

A few of my classmates, like Father Herman, still speak the traditional language of acceptance: "I have spent my priesthood," he says, "doing what has been asked of me instead of doing the asking myself." They are still inclined, on balance, to equate putting themselves in God's hands with putting themselves at the church's disposal. But for the most part, that stance was conspicuously missing from the interviews. More typical are the angry comments of Father Frank to the personnel board when it asked him to leave an early parish, in which he was doing what he still considers the best work of his priesthood, in order to live at the seminary for a year without official portfolio:

> I remember saying to the guy at the personnel board, "You've already got a guy slated to take my place here, haven't you? You bastards, I haven't even said I'm going to do this and you're already replacing me." I looked him right in the eye and I said, "This is my life we're talking about here. I'll be damned if I'm gonna move until I have a place to go. I'm gonna sit there for a year at the seminary and not do anything? That would drive me crazy. I can't do it." I thought to myself, "This is so typical of the problem that a lot of priests experience, that you're controlled so much by the institution. Unless you can be somewhat assertive, they're gonna nail you to the wall. Half the time they make you feel guilty for it." But I thought, "I'm not gonna do that."

In today's culture, in today's church—far closer terms than they used to be—self-abnegation is more likely to elicit assent to its seeming premise (that the self is worth little) than it is to win respect; and my classmates feel that they have lost enough respect already.

Thus the final blow: without the status they had expected, without the money they feel they need, and without greater control over their careers, they fear that they will become in their own eyes what they feel they have become in the eyes of the institutional church—in effect, what the nuns once were: the church's bottom rung, its exploited housewives, those women who were simultaneously praised and condescended to because of their total dependence upon the church and their ready acquiescence to orders from above; women whose work carried no overt financial tag and who thus ran the risk in our culture of being denigrated as without "value"—until they agitated for lay equivalency in salaries and, at least in Milwaukee, got it, to my classmates' simultaneous applause and bemusement: good for them, and why not us too? In a follow-up to his comments on professionalism, Father Frederick makes explicit the equation between the status of today's "generic" priests and that of the traditional nuns:

> We have to treat priests as individuals, not rotate them around. You know—they should always be wearing the collar, so there is no such thing as individual worth. Just generic priest. Treat them all alike. Treat

them like they do the sisters. That was great. They didn't have to pay them. Generic sisters. Now we are struggling with that.

In the seminary, we were trained to see money and position as false gods, distractions from more important things. Now, however, my classmates are wondering whether money and position might not be genuine "goods" which can enhance the self in a legitimate way and contribute to the pursuit of higher values. At the very least, they have learned that the lack of these satisfactions is an irritating distraction, a drain on their attention which undercuts their priesthood instead of ennobling it; what Father Frederick postulates about the unwillingly celibate priest—"I'm not productive at all because all my energy goes into coping with this"— holds true for the underpaid and undervalued priest as well. At its worst, the combination of an imposed celibacy and lack of institutional reward can unman them. As Father Frederick says, "It all goes together: you don't need a woman and you don't need money."

As Frederick's comments suggest, there is another, gender-related way to look at all this. In the seminary, we made an unspoken pact. We would aspire to be exemplars of traditional, self-abnegating Christianity; we accepted a diminished sense of individual ego in return for an exaggerated sense of collective "specialness." As a result, we avoided, for the most part, extremes of individual vanity or arrogance. We were nice guys; we gave the American virtue of being unassuming a theological twist ("Catholics have no presence," a woman friend once told me).

As part of the bargain, we assumed that as a reward for not giving ourselves over wholly to the pleasures of this world, we would not be subject to its pains and insecurities. As long as we stayed meek, we would inherit a modest portion of the earth without suffering its burdens. Nor would we be subject to its judgments; by staying above it all, we would remain protected, different, a category of being unto ourselves—as different from the rest of men as traditional wives were thought to be different from their husbands, and in similar ways.

Now, however, the priests in my class feel that the church and the world have colluded to violate that immunity. They are no longer exempt from having to pay the bills, from competition for jobs, from having to provide for retirement, from having to please clients or risk losing them. At the same time, they are granted less rather than more respect from the culture at large as well as from their own people for not receiving a salary proportionate to these responsibilities and anxieties. So if they are not going to enjoy the fruits of meekness, why be meek?

In their eyes, an institution indifferent to their personal needs has abdicated its right to be intrusive: if you aren't going to watch over me, don't look over my shoulder either. Don't expect me to be on call twenty-four hours a day at a marginal wage. And if I am going to have to make my own way—to act as "men" are expected to act—then treat me like a man: give me the responsibilities and uncertainties of a career, let me cope with its stresses—and pay me accordingly. "One of the central impulses behind the committee I was on to agitate for alternative residences," Father Herbert told me, "was that we would be responsible for our own lives, making decisions and taking the consequences—part of being a man."

My classmates feel, in effect, that the church is still treating them like housewives while simultaneously stripping away from them the traditional economic supports once granted to housewives (or "kept men"); they feel that the church is diminishing their sense of masculinity at the very moment that it is forcing them toward that traditional realm of men, the hard world of the wage earner. On top of everything else, in short, my classmates are struggling with a beleaguered sense of their own masculinity.

The Gender Bind: New Men, Non-Men, Whole Men, (Holy) Mother's Boys, or What?

The way the old-time pastors could move us out without our being consulted—the crucial point was their own insecurities and lack of maleness. I remember in 1984, I had a pastor who was highly dependent on the system; he himself was emasculated by his dependence on it. The spin-off was his attempts to control me. I was ready to kill him for trying to move me out. When he heard about my anger, he hit the ceiling. He cornered me in the parking lot outside the office and said, "I am in a powerful position in the diocese, I can ruin your career, I can ruin your life. You're making me look like a fool, and I'll do anything I can to make your life miserable." Co-dependent and emasculated—it worked together in him. He was emasculated and he was going to do it to someone else. Sexuality and authority are very similar dynamics. How co-dependent does a person become and therefore become emasculated?

—Father Herbert

In terms of traditionally defined masculinity, the church has long sent priests a confusing array of signals. It once gave back to priests in the area of power and status what it took away in the area of sexuality. It trained priests to be exemplars of traditional maleness—the emphasis on reason and will power, for instance; the notion that their job was to be the primary source of their self-definition and status, that it was to be all-consuming, a vocation to which all else, including the merely emotional, would be secondary—while at the same time it rendered them less traditionally masculine by virtue of celibacy.[11]

Yet to a certain extent, as I have suggested earlier, even the denial of sexual expression could be subsumed under the traditional male rubric of superhuman control: the priest as John Wayne, the semi-celibate totally dedicated to his vocation, not easily distracted by mere flesh, all but immune from emotional needs.

The putative femaleness of the church was part of the confusion. (I am using "male" and "female" in their traditional—and traditionally opposed—senses not because I endorse that division, but because the terminology fits church history and the forms of thinking that still persist within the institution and to a significant degree within my classmates, even as they stretch for "something more." I prefer to approach their gender issues as I have approached their other issues, from the inside out.) As either Holy Mother or spouse—an intriguingly disturbing mix of metaphors in itself—the church would be the nurturing female partner, and priests were free to be the rational, "dominant" males who would run the institution at every level. The female church thus supplied a metaphoric rationale for a literally all-male priesthood.

The nuns had their own metaphoric role, of course; they were "brides of Christ." This predominantly personal metaphor, however, did not imply a broader institutional role, except one of subservience. The nuns had the perfect husband—every woman's wish, it was assumed; hence the unreconstructed church's bemusement at their current desire for more. The femaleness of the church, on the other hand, gave its priests a metaphoric mandate for power.

Or rather, priests gave that mandate to themselves. For on the level of organization, of course, priests *were* the church: the decision-making levels of the church consisted of priests. They had married themselves, they were their own mothers/spouses in a self-enclosed, semi-incestuous union, a union shop barring outsiders; hence they were required to supply as well some of the church's female nature—conceived of as its receptive, sympathetic side—because the church in all its facets was supposed to "nurture" its clientele, after all. Thus priests were to be, alternately, male and female: wielders of power and comforters of the vulnerable and powerless; active, authoritative preachers of the definitive word and receptive, compassionate channels of forgiveness.[12]

Because these roles were seen as distinct rather than interrelated, they tended to flip-flop instead of merging; the alternation, far from inviting psychological "wholeness" in the terms my classmates have come to embrace, induced instead a low-level schizophrenia. The resulting confusion gave rise to the genre of confessional horror stories, in which, to the terror of the penitent, the priest as anticipated comforter transforms into the priest as raging judge. I remember hearing my own pastor scream,

"You filthy pig! Are you going to do it again?" to an eighth-grade penitent who then had to face the giggling horde as he left the confessional.
I don't think I have ever met a Catholic over forty without at least one
such story in his or her repertoire.

Today, however, this gender confusion has been complicated in a new
way deriving from the old. For my classmates are now actively struggling to restore a healthier balance in themselves and in the church. Well
aware that they have been shaped by twelve years of all-male training
for an all-male priesthood, they now feel the need to unify their internal
genders. To requote Father Edmund, "We can't say that humanity is just
composed of Adam and it's not composed of Eve. It's a matter of integrating the feminine and the masculine. . . . I'm really struggling with
that—to say, 'Well, what is the feminine part of me and how can I draw
on that?' " Similarly, Father Tod:

> There is a complementarity in the ministry. I find now, when I experi-
> ence only women running something, I don't feel comfortable there.
> The same thing when I experience only men. Clergy gatherings—it's
> good to see the brothers, but damn it, it feels strange not to have women
> in the group. It's like stew when you've left out an ingredient you've
> become used to.

It is one thing, however, to seek a balance between traditionally
defined "male" and "female" traits; this is the midlife agenda which,
according to Daniel Levinson and other psychologists, often surfaces in
men who have persistently denied their emotions in order to make their
way in the hard world of work.[13] Such integration is hard enough for
priests who were steeped in the church's male tradition long before they
converted to integrative psychologies; as Edmund himself recognizes
and regrets, "Unless I concentrate on it, I tend to believe that I'm complete without that female side."

It is something else, however, for my classmates to internalize the
value of the female when there is precious little of the traditional male—
in terms of sexual expression, financial achievement, social status, or
power—left in them to balance it against or to integrate it with; their
sense of themselves as male is already so beleaguered that they risk being completely overwhelmed if they embrace their female side fully. Ad-
ditions to maleness, lamentably or not, are much easier to achieve than
the replacement of maleness.[14]

Consider the various ways in which my classmates' traditionally defined masculinity is under siege. For starters, a mandated celibacy takes
away their most culturally certifiable male activity. All other strains
aside, a publicly declared life of celibacy produces an all but inevitable
degree of defensiveness in men who know full well that in our day, those
who relinquish sexual activity become more suspect than revered, less

than human instead of superhuman. "Anybody who denies that I'm a man is going to be in for a fight," Father Alex insists, painfully aware of that denial. "The thing I find about Anna Maria," Father Edmund says, "is that whether people know it or not, I know I'm not a homosexual."

Of course, priests have traditionally waived their claim to sexual expression not because they didn't want it or need it, but because their jealous Mother/Spouse demanded it of them. But in my classmates' present view, instead of empowering them in return for their self-denial, the church has turned her power against them, making them feel shut out from her decision-making processes. To some, the church has become so emasculating and domineering as to verge on a sex change. "The relationship between bishop and priest," to Father Leo, "is essentially a master-slave type of relationship."

It is this once-nurturing/female church turning impersonal/male who is revealing her less attractive side more fully now that my classmates are well into the middle years of their relationship; it is this church which demands their total allegiance without offering warmth in return, still insisting that they serve her exclusively and until death without promising a comparable fidelity to them. Older priests may yet "love the church" (I heard that phrase from two of our former teachers), but my classmates find it hard to love a woman/man/institution who/which has them "by the balls." It is hard for them to retain a full sense of commitment to someone who "keeps" them under control without keeping them secure and without showing much appreciation for what their commitment costs them.

In such a relationship, even their own nurturing behavior becomes problematic for them. For even though they value the wholeness such behavior engenders in them and in the church, many of them are outraged at being *required* to play the receptive, sensitive "new man" to their parishioners while the institution plays aggressively and indifferently male with them. They are acutely aware of this irony: to requote Father Alex, "We have the hierarchical church. The hierarchy acts like hierarchy. They dictate. They dictate that on the lower level we need to be collaborative. They don't model for us what to do, they tell us."

In this context, increased public perception that a large percentage of today's priests are gay puts an additional burden on heterosexual (even if inactive) priests, who, on top of everything else, now run a heightened risk of being thought "effeminate"—an unfortunate elision with homosexuality which persists culturally nonetheless—at a time when their masculinity is undermined in every traditional area. I have met very few heterosexual males who, no matter how sincerely they accept the homosexuality of others, can remain entirely comfortable when they themselves are labeled gay; the same is true, I think, of women "accused" of being lesbian. Yet by many current and highly public estimates, approximately half of American priests are gay in their orientation.[15] Who can tell which half a priest belongs to?

These estimates strike me as high, if my classmates are representative; but then I did not press them beyond what they were willing to offer. Yet at least in regard to men now entering the priesthood, these figures gain support from Father Thurman, a classmate who has taught for several years at a seminary in the Milwaukee area for what is now called, interestingly enough, "second career" vocations; he ventures that the majority of the men in his seminary are gay.

The issue here, however, is not the accuracy of these accounts but their psychological effect within a culture still hesitant to accept homosexuality and in a church still officially censorious. So today, the "straight" priest is likely to feel caught between two unstated, discomforting questions: Is he sexless or is he gay? (The current issue of whether priests are sexually abusive rose to the fore after my interviews were completed; no one brought that subject up at the time.)

My classmates' sense of beleaguered masculinity in turn provides a context for weighing their efforts to integrate women as fully as possible into the institutional church. For, widespread perceptions to the contrary, they are not operating anymore from a traditional, paternalistic position of strength. Instead, their position in the church is typical of what Sam Keen, in his extended reflection on contemporary masculinity, *Fire in the Belly*, sees as the dilemma of the great majority of men in America: they are in an organization whose power structure is indeed all male; but they themselves are more the objects of that power than its wielders.[16] Most power, that is, is indeed held by men, but most men, including priests, hold less power than it might seem; at the very least, they do not perceive themselves as holding power.

In fact, my classmates share the resentment of Catholic women against the all-male church hierarchy partly because they now feel that the hierarchy's power is turned against them as well. So when they work for more equal treatment of women, they are not reaching down comfortably or condescendingly in order to invite women to share their own elevated platform of power; they are rather trying to make the position of women in the church more prominent even though they perceive that their own psychological and institutional position has eroded severely.

In that context, I think that their efforts on behalf of women have been impressive. In spite of the fact that professionals in general, according to Barbara Ehrenreich, tend to create protective barriers below them—their claim to professionalism *is* the barrier[17]—most of my classmates want to remove those barriers which block women in the church from access to power and from the priesthood itself. "If you're missing that one chromosome, 'Sorry'; that bothers me a lot," Father Tod says. Several priests echoed the insistence of one that "if the church would start ordaining women, the shortage of priests would disappear. The seminary programs are over 90 percent women. These are the people today who are sensing a call to develop themselves theologically."

The fact that my classmates would welcome what could be seen as competition from a large pool of potential invaders of their turf is a testimony that their empathy with women is strong and that in this area their concern for the future of the church overrides their sense of threat from "below." Overall, it is a healthy reminder that men who have come to think in this world's terms in many areas have not by any means been taken over wholly by those terms.

Their preference for collaborative styles of parish leadership—"I bend over backwards making sure that we arrive at a consensus," as one priest said—thus emerges out of the most difficult kind of commitment: they *want* to collaborate even though they are also *told* to collaborate, even though they have less of a power base now from which to shape the collaboration. For, as they see it, mandated or not, collaboration is inherently a rejection of the autocratic, authoritarian (male) model which they resent in the church hierarchy; it is a good worth paying a considerable price for.

They have also incorporated nonsexist language into their liturgies, often beyond what the church officially endorses; "I cannot imagine someone today not automatically changing the words of the liturgy as he goes along to make it more inclusive," says Father Herman, who is in most areas more conservative than his classmates. And most important, they have integrated women far more fully than they were trained for into the running of their parishes and into their diocesan organizations, often finding themselves, as Father Albert did when he hired a woman as pastoral associate, caught in a complex cross-fire as a result.

The full inclusion of women is one of the central items on a list of changes which my classmates long for in the church; but the recurring phrase which they use to describe the absence of those changes—"I don't see it happening"—suggests a sense of helplessness akin to that of a trapped housewife with a dominating spouse: they see themselves as passive observers to processes and decisions of which they expected to be part in the post–Vatican II church.

Because they do identify so strongly with women while acknowledging that they still have in themselves a good deal of the traditional, self-enclosed male, my classmates cannot lightly dismiss the charges which women level against the institution and against them. When a woman religious said to Father Herbert, "You as men are not really liberated yet," he could only agree with her. In the voice of such women, my classmates hear their own, best voice accusing them of their institutional affiliation. Priests are not liberated, to requote Herbert, "because our structure has not liberated us yet as men. That's what we're fighting for."

Their uneasiness gives them yet one more reason to bristle at their own "belonging" to the church.

Hence they feel whipsawed: in relation to the institutional church, they feel all but emasculated; yet in the eyes of many Catholic women, they remain the arrogant male oppressor. They wince at this designation. Sometimes, especially in informal comments, not for attribution, I have heard them lash back at it and at the women who criticize them. And sometimes it was hard for me to tell if their anger at being treated "like women" was a statement of solidarity among the oppressed or a wish to be treated "like men"—i.e., as better than women.

On the whole, however, after listening to everything they said and the heat with which they said it, I became convinced that when they flare out, as they do when they demonstrate a desire for more status in relation to the laity, they do so less from a desire to reaffirm the old church and their lost position of supremacy than to express their frustrated need for a new, less divided church, a church in which newly valued women and newly revalued priests would have no reason to snipe at one another. In the meantime, the bind in which they find themselves does little to help them figure out what kind of men they are, or can be, inside the church.

In *Iron John,* his controversial meditation on the confused state of contemporary American males, Robert Bly suggests that there has been loss as well as evident gain in the last two decades for men who, responding to feminist insights (and pressure), have worked hard to develop their long-suppressed gentler side. Many men have become more sensitive, more receptive, more caring; all to the good. But in the process of accepting a female concept of maleness, he suggests, men have unfortunately lost touch with the discredited "Wild Man" in themselves, that reservoir of assertive energy which civilization prefers to keep caged or at least very carefully channeled. Using the Grimms' tale "Iron John" as his developmental model, Bly argues that for its male protagonist to become whole, he must reconnect with that "Wild Man," from which his mother in particular, as (traditionally conceived) civilizing force or agent of control, wants to "protect" him.

Bly has been attacked from many fronts. Why take a nineteenth-century German folktale as the model of a contemporary gender issue, for instance? Do we want to reassert aspects of traditional maleness or purge them even further? On the issue of the Wild Man, however, he has been misunderstood—although his own mythic language doesn't always contribute to clarity. His Wild Man is neither the savage nor the violent, macho male for whom life is conquest and women are objects; he is, rather, the male who embraces an energy which "leads to forceful action undertaken, not with cruelty, but with resolve."[18] From women, he says, men have learned to empathize more fully, to comfort, to take care, to admit vulnerability; but in the face of continuing pressures to cage their energy, they have not yet regained the ability to seek what is necessary to them in other areas. For this, they will need positive male mentors often lacking in a culture of the absent—or destructively present—father.

Women are not to blame for this suppression of energy, Bly is careful to insist (although he does implicate them peripherally). In his view, the primary enemies of assertive maleness of a positive sort have been the business world and institutional Christianity, both of which have promoted models of male sublimation in the interests of institutional gain.

The jury is still out on whether the men's movement Bly has inspired will concentrate on positive forms of maleness or turn regressive—or, indeed, whether it will last beyond its initial burst of energy. Whatever his long-range effect, however, his comments offer a useful way to focus pervasive yet otherwise disparate issues of identity and self-esteem which beset my classmates in their relationship to the church. And the pertinence of his comments provides yet more evidence of the ways in which the dilemmas of contemporary priests dovetail with those of American males of their generation in general.

First, one of the recurring laments I heard from my classmates is that they have found few mentors and models within the male structure of the church; the only claims I heard about effective spiritual direction, the church's term for mentoring, referred to the women—sometimes nuns and sometimes laity—from whom many of them seek advice. On the whole, accurately or not, they see the older generation of priests as too benighted, too locked into a culture of control—or else so beaten down for so long themselves that they tend to strike back at anyone in their range—to show them how to negotiate the difficult task of being a priest and a man inside the church today. This twinned lack of models and mentoring is one of the central sources of my classmates' isolation. Correspondingly, their seeming hesitancy in mentoring the next generation of priests reflects not only their disdain for its conservatism but their own uncertainty about what wisdom they might have to pass on: uncertain males, uneasy mentors.

Second, because my classmates feel they have no control over the celibacy laws whatever—thus compulsory celibacy unmans them twice over—they agitate for more money and higher status partly because these are the only areas of traditional masculinity in which they *can* assert their needs, the only areas in which they can openly try to regain some of the sexual identity and self-esteem which they feel they have lost.

So if there appears to be awkwardness, contradiction, or excess in my classmates' sometimes strident insistence on being rewarded in social and material terms for their "immaterial" (a revealing term, I now realize) endeavors, on being granted earthly status for conveying a spiritual message, that should not be surprising. In Jungian terms—the terms on which Bly and most of the gurus of the men's movement draw as well[19]—the church has traditionally asked priests to transcend their egos before their egos were developed. In the seminary, we were asked to transcend our sexual needs before we knew what they were, to abdicate the overt quest for status and money before we had a chance to find out through experience what role they might play in the development of our self-esteem. Or more accurately, in regard to money and status, at least, the church promised to take care of these matters for us, so that we would not have to soil ourselves in their pursuit.

In the absence of financial security and ensured position, however, my classmates are all but forced to consider what they might genuinely need in these areas. As a result, they are playing catch-up; and catch-up is not a smooth, graceful process. Moreover, since catch-up in relation to sexuality remains highly problematic for priests, all the more reason for them to put great energy—even a degree of wildness—into less freighted, less overtly forbidden areas. They are trying to become the church's "new men," but in gender as in job definition, they are caught between old patterns not quite left behind and new patterns not wholly established.

Finally, whether in relation to personal relationships, money, or status—in relation to everything they told me, in fact—the openness of the priests with whom I talked highlights a pervasive male dilemma today. Priests who do not express their feelings run the risk of perpetuating the stereotype of superhuman control for which they have long been admired but from which they themselves have suffered. Yet priests who do express their feelings run the risk of having those feelings labeled inadequate, unattractive, not properly evolved, not what the culture ordered. As a culture, do we really want priests—or men in general—to let us know finally what they think and feel? Or are we like those members of the laity who want human priests but only in terms attractive and undisturbing to them?

Father Edmund and I had just had dinner on the near north side of Milwaukee. We had talked for four hours about a number of things evidently on his mind. He told me a good deal about his personal life, about his relationship with Anna Maria; but especially he talked about his continuing commitment to the priesthood and the various personal and institutional frustrations which made that commitment difficult. On the way back to the car, close to midnight, I broke into the voice of a carnival barker:

"Step right up, gentlemen—not you, ladies. Join the priesthood! Low wages! No sex! Low status! Terrible retirement plan! Now is your chance!"

Frederick laughed. I went on:

"Aggressive clientele! No job security! Lifetime loneliness! No time off from the job! Step right up! A few openings still left!"

Frederick laughed again. So did I.

"That's it, all right," he said. "That's really it. The chance of a life-time."

7

Divorced,
Still Married

$\mathcal{M}$y conversation with Roy Winston had been uneasy for the most part; he was particularly busy at this time of year in his position as a welfare administrator in southern Wisconsin, he and his wife were expecting company any minute, and our talk had taken on a hurried quality, accentuated by the clipped, rapid manner that characterized Roy's speech now, as it had twenty years earlier.

We had already discussed Roy's reasons for leaving the priesthood two years after ordination. He had found relationships with the laity "phenomenally satisfying" but also "unsatisfying in that those relationships ended at ten o'clock and I went home to the rectory empty, alone by myself." But "the root of the problem," he told me, was "my extreme discomfort at having to be official spokesman for the Roman Catholic Church on some basic moral questions I just couldn't agree with—birth control, divorce, remarriage." Laughing as he spoke—as he did throughout when we ventured onto uncomfortable turf—Roy told me how he would rattle off the church's official position on these issues to young couples and then tell them what he really thought; he had been pained, he said, at the inconsistency.

Just as his wife arrived with another married couple and it was clear that Roy wanted to extricate himself for the evening, he nonetheless took the time to tell me of an incident that had not involved him directly but that had played a central role in his decision to leave. It was an incident that had evoked in him an intense guilt by association, a sense of moral shame at being linked with an organization whose members could act so corruptly. This was in 1970 or 1971; Milwaukee was in the midst of yet another outbreak of severe racial tension between the white ethnic southside and the black central city to the north, and it was time for the annual diocesan collection. Roy glanced at the kitchen, but then his voice slowed for the first time and took on a different timbre; he did not accompany this brief account with laughter:

> The southside pastors, a sizable group of men, probably a hundred people, got together and agreed that they would make the pitch that none of this money would go to help people on the north side of Milwaukee. It was absolutely a racial code. Sure enough, my pastor got up with a black family sitting in the third row who had been coming to the parish for many years. That was the last time we ever saw a black family in the parish.

Seven of my classmates who were ordained in 1969 have left the priesthood, and an eighth was in the process at the time of these interviews. Their satisfactions and frustrations were not different in kind from those experienced by the men who have remained priests; yet they left, while the others have stayed. I can't pretend that I understand fully what tips some people—but only some—past a point of no return on what looks like much the same continuum. Furthermore, issues of leaving or staying in a primary relationship are perhaps the least susceptible to clarity, even in hindsight: is there any question less likely to elicit a reliable answer than "Why don't you want to be with me anymore?"— or, for that matter, "Why do you want to be with me?"

Nonetheless, a few patterns do emerge, however tentative; and in this area, my own divorce, the ongoing uncertainties of my marriage, and my long-term discontent with the university proved to be a useful point of connection: these men did not have to feel that they were talking on a subject I knew nothing about or toward which I was likely to be judgmental. So looking briefly at what some of my classmates say about leaving the priesthood—and how they have fared since leaving—can help to clarify the related issue of why and under what terms other members of the class have managed to make their ongoing marriage to the church livable.

Several of my classmates left the priesthood primarily because they were dissatisfied with the institutional church. "There were a number of things that I didn't believe in," says Eliot Grayson, who left in 1974 and is now a human resources officer for a large national corporation: "birth control, abortion, homosexuality, a host of issues that I was not in concert with." What turned private disagreement into a crisis of conscience for these men, however, was their unavoidably "representative" status within the church, the profound distress they experienced at feeling compelled to link themselves to official church positions they found repugnant.

Such uneasiness is rife among the continuing priests as well; but the men who left seemed particularly disturbed by the threat it posed to their own moral state. Rick Johnson, a family therapist who left the priesthood but stayed in the church, nonetheless confirms the nature of this tension. As an individual layman, he is now able to dissent without qualm from church policies; but as a priest, he felt that the necessity of articulating publicly what he did not believe privately was endangering his own spiritual welfare:

> I didn't feel that I could be true to myself and get up on Sunday and preach about birth control and a lot of other bullshit and be perceived as something that I wasn't. That inconsistency was really working on me. I felt it was just a matter of time before I would start acting out drugwise or with alcohol.

The norm of *integrity* is central here—a traditional norm, to be sure (and characterized by the traditional assumption that integrity is an original state of intactness to be defended at all costs), but now intensified by my classmates' personalist theologies. Consistent with that norm, for instance, what bothered Eliot Grayson most about his extensive sexual activity in the early years of his priesthood was not the activity itself, which was compatible with his personal code of "love and freedom" and with his conviction that "you don't become better by locking yourself alone," but the fact that "I couldn't handle the dishonesty of saying one thing—even if it was institutional—and then doing another."

For anyone who suspects that the standards of these men were too high and that their concern for their own moral purity was excessive, it is important to remember that our generation was trained to believe that the church we were to "represent" was a church we could and should identify with fully; we could represent the church enthusiastically because the church—the Holy Mother, after all—was no mere institution in our eyes, it was the very embodiment of our ideals. From Roy Winston's present perspective, it was precisely the church's superhuman image of itself which sowed the seeds of later disillusionment:

> The problem with our training was that we were somehow led to believe that the church was different, that it wasn't a human institution. And it is. It is no different from the U.S. government in the way it works. It's no different from General Motors in the way it works, or the uni-

versity. It's a human institution and needs to be understood and dealt
with in that same way. And we were not given the tools to do that.

Thus my classmates' bind. They were still traditional enough (more
so, in this regard, than many of the men who stayed) to feel that they
had to say what the church expected them to say. Yet they became convinced that to promote positions with which they fundamentally dis-
agreed, or to be associated with actions that appalled them, would destroy their personal integrity, their moral fit with themselves. And yet
again—because they identified with the church—to stand apart, to dis-
sociate themselves from church positions and actions while remaining
priests, would be to embrace a fissure in their very personality.

Members of the Vietnam generation, they became the church's conscientious objectors; and in their eyes, they faced the dissenter's dilemma, a dilemma usually articulated by those in authority but in their
case more internalized than imposed: love it or leave it. For as they saw
it, either they had to agree with the church—or rather, the church had
to agree with them—or they had to get out; the motherland had to be
worthy of their identification with it, or they would flee. They could not,
they would not, compromise. Compromise was not a necessary accom-
modation to earthly realities; it was a moral failing, a threat to themselves. Leaving, by contrast, was both an act of principle and an act of
(moral, spiritual) self-interest.

To put it differently: on the whole, the men from my class who left the
priesthood were wedded to the church in a particularly strong way, akin
in some ways to what psychologists now call co-dependency; they had
fused with the church. They cared deeply about what their spouse did
and said; they took the institution's behavior personally, they felt implicated in it. When the church disappointed them, when they realized that
they couldn't control their spouse's behavior, they came to the point
where they could not bear the connection any longer, lest they be borne
down with it. As they saw it, theirs was a principled refusal to "work
within the system" and thereby risk moral taint. Their Vietnam-era attitudes echoed in the demands they made upon their relationship to the
church: they would not live with a flawed marriage to an imperfect
spouse. For them, the choice was marriage as it should be, or divorce.

For the men who left the priesthood, that is, when the church's flawed
side surfaced, that side became for them its characteristic side, its dominant side—for some, its only side. In the position of a committed husband who sees his spouse's infidelities as utter betrayal, they transformed their devotion into scorn, and the once-beloved into a bitch—in
Eliot Grayson's terms, a corrupt institution out only for itself. "I saw that
the church is essentially caught up in maintaining organizational values," he says. "It's a kind of shibboleth: they have the message of Christ.

Well, the real message is, 'This organization will survive over Christ's dead body.' "

I felt much the same way when I left the seminary: the church had become in my mind a retrograde institution oblivious to social concerns and on the wrong side of the issues it chose to engage. I could think of nothing good to say about it—a stance which made leaving relatively easy at the time. Now, in retrospect, I wonder whether my classmates and I were acting as admirably principled idealists demanding that our central relationships be what they should be or as rigid absolutists whose insistence that our partner be perfect isolated us from the support we continue to need, from the very relationships which need our commitment the most, and from a part of us which still has a hold on us.

This last question is relevant precisely because for those who left in anger, the church and priesthood remain potent psychic forces in a manner which confirms the emotional intensity of their original marriage to the church. In *Second Chances*,[1] their recent study of the long-term effects of divorce, Judith Wallerstein and Sandra Blakeslee argue against the optimistic, adaptive view of divorce promulgated in the 1960s and 1970s. Their research has shown that men and women who divorced ten, even fifteen years ago have often found it impossible simply to slough one another off and "grow in different directions," as we liked to say. To the contrary, divorced couples remain married in complex, deeply felt ways long after the documents of dissolution are signed.

Wallerstein and Blakeslee suggest that a combination of factors makes it particularly hard for divorced people to put their old marriages behind them. First of all, almost by definition, divorce is usually the result of unfinished business between the partners; it results from festering issues which led to the choice of separation rather than to the choice of ongoing negotiation and adjustment. Secondly, it is very difficult to complete that unfinished business even years later, precisely because the severed spouse remains firmly lodged in the former partner's emotions—in either anger or longing, or both —without being in his or her actual presence to negotiate with. Those who are nominally severed from their former partners—divorced and ex-Catholic, I feel the double force of their analysis—are often paradoxically locked in their intense emotions, with no clear way to turn down the heat.

This description accurately describes most of the former priests in my class, whose anger remains strong and undiminished. The church continues to enrage Eliot Grayson, for instance, even though he has no direct involvement with it anymore—or rather, *because* he does not. Hence he is still in what he acknowledges as "a reactive state":

> I have a lot of hate feelings about God and religion, priests and nuns and ministers. I have a lot of anger at the pope and at the church. Weird

little things. You know, if Notre Dame loses, I'm happy. Another parochial school closes, or the church has trouble collecting money from
Americans. When I see the pope in the newspaper, in my gut I say,
"Fuck you, fucker." I have an active rage in me about the whole fucking
shit. I could really stomp on them. I'm not interested enough to lead an
active schism, but I'd like to see someone do it.

"I know I need to explore these feelings," Eliot acknowledges; he insists that "at some point I'm going to take the time to do it." But in the
absence of the once-beloved spouse to fight it out with, the only way he
can imagine being free of his hatred is never to have entered the marriage in the first place:

If I were left to my own designs right now, and I didn't have a lot of
fears, I think I'd like to be an atheist. I'd like to deal with life right now,
planning that I'm going to live seventy-five years and that's going to be
it. I almost wish that I didn't go through all that Christianity stuff, that
my dad was a scientist and had said, "Eliot, that stuff's bullshit. Deal
with life on a day-to-day basis. There's certain things you've got to do
to make it worthwhile that are somewhat painful, but take the joys with
the sorrows."

Roy Winston, by contrast, seems to have moderated his earlier anger.
Roy's marriage to a previously divorced woman with two children of
her own and his work inside government bureaucracies for the last fifteen years have led him to realize more than notionally that all relationships are complicated, that all institutions are flawed, and that willingness to live with the implications of such awareness, though full of risks,
is the key to getting the benefits which affiliation can still bring. Roy
has thus earned a perspective which few of Wallerstein's subjects have
achieved. His comments suggest that his marriage to the church might
have worked out if he had known then what he knows now:

I know some who stayed did it because they were able to reject the institution and still work with the people. At age twenty-six I was not able
to do that. I probably could do it at age forty-six. At forty-six you've
more experience and a little more wisdom, hopefully. You don't take
official positions as seriously as you did when you were twenty. For
good or bad you can tolerate hypocrisy a little more. You're willing to
go, "Okay, we'll say this publicly," knowing that you don't really mean
that. But what we mean ain't all that bad. (*laughs*)

Most of the men who left because of institutional discomfort have
sought out and found professions which engage at least some of their
idealistic energy: Rick Johnson as a family therapist; Eliot Grayson first
as an administrator of programs for mentally disturbed adolescents and
now as a human resources officer with the goal of "helping supervisors
and managers make the most of their people"; Roy Winston first through

government affirmative action programs and eventually as a welfare administrator drawn to government not only because of its "upward mobility," but also for its "public contact . . . and community building." In a basic sense, the priesthood has remained the implicit norm for these men: something like it, or at least what it tapped in them, is what they want, what they have actively looked for. I feel that same impulse myself.

Yet it is also true that none who left the priesthood largely in search of a better "fit" between themselves and their institution or profession have been particularly successful in finding it, any more than I have. Eliot Grayson complains that in his company, he can be "about 60 percent myself—the rest is a mask" to satisfy corporate expectations. He also admits that the dependency which the church encouraged in him is "an ongoing struggle that I still have to deal with"—especially since his company encourages dependency just as much as the church did. Rick Johnson is now the head of a consortium of therapists; with the increased "expectations and responsibilities" which accompany that position, it feels to him as if "all these things keep me locked in. It's almost as if I'm getting the same feeling now that I had in the priesthood: I don't need to do this." And Roy Winston, as we have seen, has not so much found an ideal place for himself as he has accepted the fact that there are no ideal places.

Years later, a good deal of experience later, and too late, as he sees it, to draw him back to an active relationship, Roy has come to a kind of critical yet tolerant view of the church very similar to that of those priests who have made relative peace with it. He also suggests, however, the dangers inherent in such tolerance:

> There's a good and bad side to that. It does show adjustability and flexibility. On the other hand it also shows flexibility of ethics sometimes too. You end up misleading people. Those who stay in the priesthood and distance themselves from the institution run the risk of hypocrisy.

*   *   *

No one in my class brings the paradoxes of priestly discontent with the institutional church into focus more clearly than Father Leo, who was in the process of leaving the priesthood during the two-year period in which I talked with him several times. On leave from his priestly duties, living with his parents while considering his options, Leo had no rectory or apartment to invite me to; with no space of his own and in full awareness that "I don't actually know where I'm going," he conveyed a pervasive sense of uprootedness.

Leo, like many of the priests who engaged me in the most intense conversations, was someone I had barely known in the seminary. He had been a "day dog" in high school, a serious, highly focused student not much engaged in school activities; he took the bus to school, then took it home and studied. In the major seminary, he maintained an equally low profile which previewed the marginal position he has felt throughout his priesthood; he sees himself as an outsider, a man who has consistently done the "trench work" and has gained only the reputation and the meager rewards of a foot soldier.

Leo came very willingly to the seminary dorm at Marquette where I was staying, sat upright in a chair opposite me, and with little instigation began talking excitedly, hammering his points across with repeated karate chops. On later trips, when I phoned him first for another interview and then for clarifications, he expanded eagerly. He struck me as someone who needed to express his distress but had not found many audiences he could safely open up with.

Leo is widely read, highly articulate, and occasionally intimidating in his intensity. Yet he was as receptive to my story as I was to his—no doubt priests, like therapists, are trained to listen, but I was impressed with this trait—and he would break periodically into one of the most boyish grins I have seen in a long time. And in spite of his bitterness, his continuing connection to the ideals of the priesthood was evident; the divorce he was contemplating was not going to be easy.

Nineteen years after ordination, Leo continues to hold the church to a very high standard of behavior: "The purpose of the institutional church," he insists, "is to adequately represent God." Yet his experience as a priest—which he describes as a series of confrontations with remote, authoritarian pastors, self-serving and manipulative diocesan administrators, and, overall, a church structure characterized from the top down by its preference for appearance over spiritual substance ("The church is concerned with looking *good*")—has convinced him that the church, far from meeting that standard, has degenerated into a "dysfunctional system" engendering negative energy rather than "helping people become the people they were meant to be"; it has become a barrier to growth rather than its agent. Thus for Leo, the institutional church has rendered itself obsolete:

> You're dealing with a structure that's adverse; and at least for the time being, that structure is better off dying. God does not rely on the Roman Catholic Church as it is presently structured, and He's not shackled to it. Right now the Spirit is more effective outside the church than in it. The best thing that could happen would be for the Vatican to go bankrupt.

Leo echoes Roy Winston's complaint not only that the church is flawed but that it continues to claim not to be. "The church," he says, "has never come to grips with its own institutionality." To make matters worse, the church denies its own earthliness not to promote higher ideals but in order to manipulate its priests; the church becomes a highly controlling, all but irresistibly coercive boss by claiming not to be operating on the earthly level at all:

> Ray, you have a job which is recognized as a job. The university doesn't claim to possess you, so that you would be betraying Jesus Christ if you left. The priesthood is a job, too, but it's not recognized as a job—and the way we are treated or what we are expected to do is not recognized as mismanagement. They claim to be guided by God, so you have no way of arguing with them. They come on to you with "You're a priest of God." And therefore, their second come-on is "You have to accept and do whatever I tell you, and I'm going to manipulate you and put you into this slot."

To Leo, the image of a purely spiritual church is used against the priest twice: first to force him to "do his job" and then to deny him rewards for doing it well—because, after all, spiritual activity is beyond earthly calculation. "Well, how do you gauge spirituality?" one of Milwaukee's auxiliary bishops replied rhetorically to Leo's complaints, as if the question were its own answer. "How do you measure how well a priest is doing in his parish?"

In Leo's eyes, priests who accept this argument are not idealists rising above the material plane; they are simply deceiving themselves to their own spiritual detriment: "They sublimate, saying, 'Well, we're doing this for Christ.' What they are really doing is destroying their humanity in the process. They become nonpersons, walking zombies." Drawing on Adlerian psychology, he argues, as Herbert does, that the subservient priest inevitably turns authoritarian:

> The priest is very often dominated for a long period of time so that he is led to believe that whatever authority says is the voice of God. Consequently, when he finally reaches authority, he becomes very domineering and uncompromising himself. His life has been filled with so many frustrations for so many years that he better damn well get his way because this is his last chance.

And since "the manipulated priest tends to manipulate," he becomes a source of negative energy in his own right. As a result, "the more thinking the laity become—they are so educated now—the more they are inclined to reject that kind of system." Thus the "system"—Leo's 1960s perspective now directs his energy against the church instead of toward it—perpetuates itself, serves no one except those who are in power, and in spiritual terms does not even serve them; it merely sucks them into the vortex. They become part of the system, identified with it in the worst way, and inevitably malformed by it as the former priests I interviewed feared they would be if they stayed. No wonder that "the best thing would be for the Vatican to go bankrupt" and for the institutional church to fade from sight.

By attributing to the church the ability to "squash," to "possess," to "destroy the humanity" of anyone who ventures too close to its center, Leo expresses a vision of the church as perverted but all-powerful: the bitch supreme. It is a vision characteristic of the former priests in my class, men who saw themselves living, by definition, too close to their spouse to be immune from her destructive force. And if the church is (negatively) so powerful, if fusion with the church is the ultimate threat to the self, and if there are no boundaries available to protect them from its force field, no distance available within its borders, then what else can they do but sever themselves? For men who view their spouse that way, the only safe place is out.

A month after our last interview, Leo sent me a copy of the letter he had mailed to friends and parishioners. Citing "nineteen years of too many aggravations, frustrations and discouragements with the system," he announced, "I could no longer continue living in futility, and so, like Abraham, I had to go forth in a new direction." He expressed "confidence and peace in knowing that the Lord is pleased with the way I had served him in the past, and that he will direct me to serve him in the future, only in another way."

By his own admission, however, that way "remains unfocused with ambiguity and uncertainty." For as he looks to enter the world on its own terms, he has found so far that his considerable education and experience as a priest are discounted in the marketplace. In our last conversation, he said that he has finally decided to return to school at the University of Wisconsin–Milwaukee in counseling.

But if the men who left only a few years after ordination have had a hard time moving beyond their priesthood, how difficult will it be for Leo, with nineteen years as a priest behind him—or rather, inside him? He insists, "I won't miss it, because of the stresses I've been under," that although he had been intensely involved with his ministry, he was too fed up to harbor regret. I found myself wishing him well, but I wonder nonetheless: he may not miss the church, but I would be surprised if he did not miss what the priesthood enabled him to do.

It was Leo's own evident, continuing engagement with priestly issues which raised this question for me. In a touching story about attending his aunt's funeral soon after taking official leave from his duties, he told of sitting in the back of the church, trying to remain detached, yet still feeling outraged at the presiding priest's slipshod performance, still imagining ways in which the service could be improved to reach its listeners, still lamenting the missed opportunity to reach people, the blown save:

His heart wasn't in it. His homily was mediocre, very blah, very abstract. He was talking about the difference between faith and reason, that "reason can't explain this but faith can." And I can't believe this. Most of these people don't have a college education; they're just normal, average, blue-collar, everyday people. I thought, "God, this guy is not speaking on their level at all." I thought, "Shit! No wonder so many of my cousins are no longer in the church."

And although during our conversations Leo did not stray often from his highly detailed sense of grievance with the church, when I began describing my analogous distress with the university and the uncertainties of my marriage, Leo's focus shifted, his voice softened, he began to draw on a different kind of energy, and he gave me, unselfconsciously and without condescension, what I can only call a sermon about productive uncertainty and the authentic spirituality of the search. He reminded me that whatever I might undertake at this point would involve risks, and held up Abraham as someone I too should think about. Abraham was a gutsy man, he said, for "in the ancient world, to go into an unknown land was a risk. You lost your civil rights, you lost whatever protection you had from your family, you were not defended by the government. Abraham didn't know where he was going, he didn't know how to get there. My point," he said, "is that 'God was with him.' What you need to do is to recognize in your life how God is with you, how He helps you." I was touched by Leo's interest; I felt I was in the presence of a priest at his best.

Such comments made it clear to me that even now, Leo would still reaffirm his marriage—if the church would change, if it would meet his own, still-uncompromising terms.

Out of Place, Locked in Place

If their relationship to the church remains unfinished business for those men in my class who left the priesthood in anger, it remains unfinished in different ways for the two men who left to get married. For both of these men—Hans Ziegler, who left in 1974 and has been a policeman ever since; and Mark Klugman, who left in 1977 and is at present a part-time hospital worker—adhere even now to a traditional faith which, precisely because it remains "finished" in one sense (i.e., relatively unchanged from their early days as priests), makes it difficult for them to address fully, and thus finish in that sense, the present issues which beset them.

On one level, Mark and Hans have lived through a curve now widely recognized in many former priests: both found significant chunks of the priesthood deeply satisfying, both left to get married immediately, and neither has found either personal or professional satisfaction equal to what they had enjoyed as priests. Whatever else they suggest, their disappointments serve as a cautionary tale for the men who have remained in the priesthood: those who leave a satisfying calling in search of even greater personal fulfillment may end up with less rather than more.

But there is more to Mark's and Hans's stories than a frustrated sense of purpose, however important that is. For in spite of everything that has changed in their lives—or because of it—both of them remain set in basic ways of thinking deriving from, or at least confirmed by, their lives as priests. Looking at how they have *not* changed in the midst of the evident disruptions in their lives will help to clarify how the continuing priests *have* changed in the midst of their seemingly stable position inside the priesthood.

Hans Ziegler lives in a modest duplex at the end of a cul-de-sac on the southwest side of Milwaukee; he would like more space for his wife and especially for his two sons, he said, but the money just isn't there. Hans had been a friend of mine in the seminary, a basketball teammate who played, in the currency of that period, like a Russian; when he drove for the basket, the rest of us slid discreetly out of the way. He is square-jawed, intense, and unrelenting about whatever he does; those traits have served him well and sometimes not so well.

Hans invited me out to the house for dinner the first time I called him, and invited me there again on a subsequent trip; yet he was more eager to see an old friend than he was to talk about his current life. After dinner we went over to his parish; his home did not offer the privacy he wanted. He showed me around the church with evident pride; he is still an active Catholic. We ended up taping our conversation in the comfortably appointed "reconciliation room," my first exposure to the more therapeutic version of the confessional. Hans had obviously been in this room many times, but I felt spooked, back in the heart of the heart of the country.

In our conversation, Hans began slowly, choosing his words carefully and breaking into his own sentences to clarify his thoughts. He eventually talked with considerable openness about the frustrations of his life; but his revelations came hard, for he was still in the midst of the tensions he was describing. He looked drained as we finished. "You have to understand," he told me, "I don't allow myself to think about these things on a day-to-day basis."

We returned to the church a year later for a follow-up talk, and met again on one later occasion in a Big Boy restaurant. The next time I came to Milwaukee, he told me he just couldn't bear the thought of talking again; it cost him too much to dredge up things he was trying not to think about.

Hans is emphatic in asserting that he loved priestly work: "Giving homilies, counseling people, saying mass—I loved it all. I thought that one of the most wonderful things you could do was to give your life to God, to serve God and His people in the priesthood." Eight years into his priesthood, however, partly as the result of his immersion in a charismatic renewal group—and, he admits, in response to his feelings for a woman in that group—he felt "freed up" to look "deep down at the core" and admit that although he had felt called to be a priest, he had never felt called to be celibate. He became convinced that "I would be happier and a better person if I were married." But this realization "scared the hell out of me," he said, "because I thought I knew what I was doing was what God wanted me to do. My God, my stomach was turning at this point."

But when he asked himself, "Am I going to live and die, and deep down not be at peace for twenty, twenty-five years?" his own answer was, "No, that's not the God I know. I don't think he would expect that from me. Once I came to realize that I would be happier and that I would be a better person if I were married, what to do about it? It looked more and more like I was called to move in the direction of marriage."

Because he is by his own description a "structured person," he knew that the only way he could leave the priesthood would he to go through all the proper channels: he told the archbishop, talked with his parents, applied for laicization, and within a year married the woman he had met earlier. "If you talk to our classmates," he said, "they could give a shit [about going through channels]. But I can't; that's not me." Even so, leaving was "absolutely hard, because here's the key to the whole thing: I enjoyed doing what I was doing. The work of the priesthood I enjoyed immensely." His continuing involvement in the church was evident as he showed me around his parish, describing its energetic liturgy and strong sense of community. "The Catholic Church is part of my fiber," he says. "I have not repudiated it."

By his own description, Hans has always done what he was told. When he felt called by God "to do heroic things," he answered by entering the seminary. When he was told there to "keep your mouth shut and your shoes shined," he did so, because "the purpose was to become a priest, and I was going to do everything that it took to become a priest." After ordination, he was "good at the things that were expected of me." Leaving the priesthood to which he had felt called, therefore, would have been all but impossible had he not felt equally "*called* to move in the direction of marriage" (my emphasis). And he sought laicization because "for me to live with myself and to be at peace, I had to go about this in a structured way."

In his responsiveness to whatever authorities asked him to do, Hans was an ideal candidate, he now says ruefully, "for life prior to Vatican II." The God Hans believes in is traditional: He is the providential God who always takes care of those who follow His will, and thus takes particular care of His priests. When, in each of the central decisions of his life, Hans did his part by acting in accord with what he saw as God's will, God did His in return, bestowing blessings which confirmed Hans's initial decision.

In his view, the most dramatic example of God's providence came when, on the brink of leaving the active ministry without any career plans at all, he was offered a job as a police social worker without seeking it, without even knowing it was there; the police chief simply called him one day and asked if he knew anyone about to leave the active ministry who might be interested in a job just opening up. This timing—"I get teary-eyed when I think about it"—confirmed his conviction that it was "the spirit of God" moving him to marry rather than a merely selfish impulse: "That made me feel that God was with me in this decision. I still see that as God saying, 'Don't worry about that. That has been taken care of.' "

The same pattern recurred seven years later, when the chief warned Hans that his job was in danger of being phased out and recommended him for the police academy. After twenty-one weeks of training, Hans found himself sixth on the eligibility list. Once again he seemed charmed; the five who were ahead of him either were hired elsewhere or chose not to come: "I was the next one on the list, and the opening happened at that moment."

In short, what Hans describes as an effortless, "natural progression" from priesthood to the secular world and from one job to the next reconfirmed his ingrained conviction, to which we were all bred in the seminary, that he was an object of God's particular favor and protection. Even today, he continues to believe that "this specialness never left me, it's still a part of me." During one of our talks, he admitted that although he did not consider himself better than me, he could not shake the thought that he was still set apart, above me in effect, by the permanent mark of ordination.

Hans acknowledges that he has had a hard time adapting to the uncertainties of a post–Vatican II world and his post-priesthood status. Nowhere is this more evident than in his attempts to square his present discontent with his continuing sense that he is being cared for, that he is entitled to be cared for. "I still see the spirit of God working through all of this, leading me to where I am today," he insists. Yet he also admits, "There isn't a lot of satisfaction at this stage of my life."

Indeed: the marriage to which he felt called has proven no more fulfilling than his job, which is simply "what I do to make money." Although he said nothing critical about his wife and considers her "the right person" for him, he has not found with her the intimacy he sought; his conviction that the problem originates primarily in him—seminary prohibitions against intimacy still have their effect, he says—does not in itself resolve the issue. Meanwhile, his fond memories of the "transcendent moments" he had as a priest make it all the harder for him to accept the mundane responsibilities of family life. "I get so bogged down," he laments, in mowing lawns, fixing doorknobs, coping with distraught children; these necessary activities become merely a "pain in the ass," largely because "I never had to do those things as a priest."

Overall, instead of the better person he anticipated becoming through marriage, he finds that "I am not the man I was" ten years ago. He feels, rather, that he is in danger of becoming a "couch potato" addicted to Clint Eastwood movies; his wife, gently rather than critically, confirmed that judgment when the three of us had dinner together. "At this stage of my life," he says, "I feel like I'm just going through the daily motions: sleeping, eating, going to the bathroom."

Hans is well aware of the irony of this situation:

> Now anyone listening to this would say, "Look, you had these transcendent moments and you really got a lot of satisfaction out of working with the people, but you hadn't come to terms with whether you should lead the celibate life. Now you're married, and you're not getting any satisfaction out of your work or your marriage. What the hell's wrong?" (*laughs*)

Hans does not know where to turn to find a better job, partly because "I have such high expectations. Anything less than the transcendent becomes boring rather quickly." He would love to function again as a priest, but knows that his own "call" to marriage has made that impossible. In short, he is profoundly confused: "I don't understand everything that's happening in my life. I wish I could accelerate this process."

Hans is perplexed not simply by the unhappiness he feels, but by the underlying questions it raises: How could a lifetime of following God's will lead him to this? If God is providential, where is His care now? Concretely, where are the clear "calls" now that he really needs them? And in the absence of any such "calls," what is he to do? Discontented when he expected to be happy, wanting change but not accustomed to having to produce it on his own, Hans expresses no realistic hope for movement in his life. Instead, he is left wondering, "How long is it really going to take me to be comfortable with the life I'm leading?"

Hans's dilemma suggests an ironic, psychological version of the church's traditional, moralistic assertion: "once a priest, always a priest." As a husband, father, and police officer, he would seem on the face of it to have entered "the world" and its complexities more emphatically than those who have remained priests. And yet, instead of entering that world on its own terms and making his way in it, he remains in a state of passive expectation, which characterized many of us in the seminary. This is his version of the dependency to which Eliot Grayson alluded: a temperamental bent toward acquiescence nurtured by the seminary ideal of docility and buttressed by the theology of providential care. "God's will, not mine, be done" can easily become "God will act, and so I don't have to."

Hans still feels that since he has done his best, God will—at least, God should—begin again to nudge things his way. His abiding sense of specialness is his principal consolation, and his providential faith is his principal source of hope; yet together, they are also the source of the inertia which locks him into his discontent.

A similar curve reveals itself in the life of Mark Klugman, who left the priesthood in 1975. In the seminary, Mark had been known as "Potatoes" because of his enormous appetite for the food he had come to love on the family farm in southern Wisconsin; in refectory, he would beg, borrow, and cajole for extra portions. He ate more than most of us and studied less than many—though he was still a talented student— and yet always played by the seminary rules. Unlike most of his classmates, he describes himself as a "moderate conservative"; and everything he said in our conversation suggested his continuing devotion to the values which his parents instilled in him and to the traditional faith which they exemplified for him.

Like Hans, Mark loved the personal side of the priesthood: "Contact with people—absolutely. To me that's what the priesthood is all about. The pastoral things—if somebody had a problem and wanted to talk, geez, you lived for that." Yet he found little such contact in most of his parishes. One was in a rural area populated with immigrant laborers whom, he admits, "I just didn't grasp"; another was a railroad community settled by "outcasts from the neighboring town" who remained aloof from him as well as from one another. Even when he finally found a congenial parish, his satisfaction was quickly undermined, he says, when his pastor "stabbed me in the back" by publicly questioning his choice of reading material for an adult education class.

His characteristic stance as a priest, he admits, had been passive and docile: "I basically said, 'What am I supposed to do?' I never did take a lot of initiative in things." When the pastor undercut what Mark saw as "one of the first things I had done on my own," he withdrew: "After that, I felt like, fine, if that's the way you want to play this game, then I'll be in my room. I'll say mass, I'll go over to school and talk to the kids in the classrooms and do my sermon on Sunday. Don't bother me."

Soon after this incident, Mark met a woman named Karen in the sort of counseling situation which he enjoyed so much—a situation whose more complicated emotions he, like so many of his classmates, did not know how to contain. Nor did he necessarily want to, in his state of anger and withdrawal from his pastor. And so, under cover of the kind of protective naiveté which so often facilitates the erotic involvement of idealists, he became involved with her:

> There was a problem that needed dealing with, and I helped her with that. One thing just seemed to lead to another. It can sneak up on you. We didn't really have as much background as we should have in the ethics of counseling. We had some sensitivity training, so you weren't afraid to put your arms around somebody and give 'em a hug when they needed it. But then that can lead to other things too. So maybe I didn't act entirely professionally.

Once his relationship with Karen developed, Mark's traditional values reasserted themselves; it became clear him that "I was going to have to make a choice in one direction or the other, 'cause I wasn't gonna try and get cute and do both. You can't stand up at the altar and say you're one thing, and then go off in the evening and be something else. I said, 'This is not going to work. You'd better make up your mind which way you're going.' " After a month's leave of absence, "I finally reached that decision [to leave] and I lay on my bed and cried." Going through the proper channels was as important for him as it was for Hans: "If I hadn't gotten a dispensation, that would have thrown up a roadblock for me, because I had no quarrel with the church as such."

Since leaving the priesthood, Mark has experienced adversity on many levels. He and Karen have three children. When the youngest two, twins, were only eight months old, Karen was in a car accident which left her physically incapable of taking care of them; she has been chronically ill ever since then. As a result, with Mark working, they had to leave the children with a nanny during the week and were reduced to seeing them only on weekends.

During this period, their oldest son manifested a mysterious developmental disability akin to autism—"He's very much to himself; it's hard to get him interacting"—which, according to Mark, "we're still trying to fathom." In Mark's mind, this disability stems from the time his son spent at the sitter's, when he was left largely on his own. "Whether he'll ever fit into a normal educational system, I don't know. Whether he's ever going to be independent, I don't know." Providing care for their son has been especially difficult on Mark's salary. He has moved through a series of low-level jobs, ranging from bus driver in his own parish after he left the priesthood (how must that have felt, I wondered, but did not ask him) to stock boy to insurance salesman; Mark was working part-time on the night shift in a local hospital when I talked with him.

"There's been some rough spots," Mark admits. "Everybody has 'em, everybody gets 'em." Yet in spite of all these hardships, Mark considers himself "a lucky, lucky man" and remains "grateful for the fact that overall things have been easy for me." He doesn't go to church every Sunday and admits that "I don't pray as much as I probably should," yet he also insists that "faith is a central point in my life. It's a quiet center that says, Yes, I do believe in God."

The nature of that faith is reflected in a story which he told with great feeling about his contact, just before he left the priesthood, with a dying sixteen-year-old boy. When Mark entered the hospital room, the doctor had just told the boy that he had cancer of the spine, and that there was nothing they could do.

> I talked to him for a good hour, and he said, "Why?" I said, "I don't know. I wish I had an answer for you but I don't. I don't know why you—I don't know why not you. But you it is and let's go from there." He was angry, and I said, "Fine, be angry. You want to tell God off, tell Him off. Tell Him it isn't fair. Tell Him whatever you like. I don't think it's fair either, but my vote doesn't count." I just let him get it off his chest.
>
> I said, "Jim, I don't know. I don't have an answer but I believe there is an answer. I believe that we just have to accept what's given to us and do the best we can with it." He got settled down and I left. I couldn't tell him that in a week I was gonna be gone; I wasn't gonna see him again.
>
> A year later, I noticed in the paper that this young man had died. I said, "I gotta go over there." I felt a little funny, after not seeing this kid. When I walked into the funeral home, I could have been a long-lost member of the family—they almost literally ran up to me, saying, "Hey, Father Mark, good to see you." The father said to me, "Jim always talked about that talk you had with him and how good he felt about that."

"You talk to a sixteen-year-old who is dying of cancer," Mark reiterated later in our conversation, "and you say, 'I don't have an answer. I have faith.' I guess God wouldn't be God if you could figure Him out." That straightforward acceptance of a divine wisdom behind human suffering—and beyond human understanding—expresses in capsule form the faith to which Mark still adheres, a faith which leaves room for doubt on the local level but remains firm in its ultimate certainty. It is a faith beyond analysis, or before analysis; it is the starting point from which Mark views his life, not a tentative conclusion or working stance vulnerable to changing circumstances.

It is also a brand of faith which, along with Hans's, helped me to clarify some of the differences between those men who left the priesthood and those who have stayed. The faith that Mark retains, to be sure, is different from Hans's in its emphasis. Hans continues to believe in a God who will give him a guiding hand and a pat on the back, while Mark's God does not necessarily show His hand so readily. Hans believes that God is manifest in His care, whereas Mark believes that God is present and at work whether we immediately see the signs of His care or not. Yet both brands of faith were familiar to me, both are reminiscent of an earlier church, and—more to the point—both are unlike anything I heard articulated by the priests in our class.

The priests I interviewed have not lost their faith. But theirs is a more adaptive, reformulated faith than Hans's and Mark's. It is as if Mark and Hans, having left a priesthood which was important to them, continue to demonstrate a stable set of values and a continuous, secure identity by affirming their original vision of the world, a vision which they might otherwise seem to have abandoned by the act of leaving the priesthood. Yes, of course, I have entered "the world," they both imply; but I have not converted to its worldly wisdom, nor do I endorse its cynicism. I am less changed than I appear to be.

(I have my own version of this: the God I no longer believe in is still the traditional, anthropomorphic God. I cling to Him—and to His capitalized pronoun—in an act of disbelief. In place of God's photograph, I now carry around the negative; to abandon the image itself would be too painful a break. I too affirm my continuity with my old self.)

By contrast, the priests who every day proclaim their ongoing commitment to the church and to the realm of belief by the very act of continuing to function as priests can afford to modify the old-time religion without calling their faith into question; they can reformulate their beliefs—redefine their marriage—without fearing a loss of self or identity in the process.

Given their predominantly liberal convictions, in fact, *not* to redefine themselves or their faith in the face of a retrenched institution would threaten their sense of themselves far more than passive acceptance of the current church would; they *need* an ongoing stance of relative independence to avoid the pitfall of self-destructive acquiescence which Father Leo feared. Of course I believe, their status as priests announces; but don't think for a minute that I do so in a simple, unthinking way. I am less docile than my continuing affiliation might suggest, I am more critical and skeptical than you might suspect. Granted that I am in some sense still married to the church; but I have not fused with it. I am more of a piece with my (converted) liberal self than with my old self; I expect change.

There are other reasons for these differences as well. For the continuing priests are, in effect, keeping up with their field when they rethink or redefine their faith and their priesthood. They are, as they insist, professionals; and hence there is a professional as well as a personal impulse behind their reformulations and negotiations which those of us who have left do not feel. Furthermore, the very act of staying in the priesthood has prodded their continual engagement with—and against—the church's teachings and structures. The friction they feel within the institution forces them to ask themselves continually why they stay, what they believe, how to deal; it all but forces them to be flexible, mentally active.

Mark, by contrast, precisely because he is not deeply engaged in church affairs, can afford to take a long-term view which is both providential and passive: he can look patiently at the slow changes of the church, can regard with equanimity what he sees as its very gradual, not yet realized maturation:

> The church is two thousand years old. I think it got trapped in childhood at the Counter-Reformation. And the Second Vatican Council was sort of a breakout time, not into maturity, into adolescence at best. A lot of weird stuff went on in the sixties and seventies, and even today in the eighties. Not just the Catholic Church, but a lot of Christian churches are suffering through a time when communications have exploded, ideas are everywhere. You have theologians who are speculating in the middle of their classes to young Catholic students at colleges all over. And it's hard to deal with these ideas and maintain your background and a sense of what's real and important in the church. The church has suffered through this and is suffering through this. So I think we're moving toward a more mature church. But you've got to look at this through almost geological time.

The priests I talked with also draw on the long view. "Part of me is just beginning to say, 'So?' " Father Tod acknowledged; "We're looking at thousands of years. So, there are difficulties." But for them, this is an edgy, reluctant perspective, not characterized by Mark's passive patience; enmeshed in the church by definition and affected by it on a day-to-day basis, they do not have the luxury of "geological time." What they see as the church's present, ongoing, institutional indifference to them has all but compelled them to seek antidotes, to think in new ways, to create an integrated life instead of defending their original integrity, to devise new ways to salve their discontent, new ways to find satisfaction—or old ways not yet sanctioned. Reluctantly convinced that the church is no longer going to take care of them, many have decided that it is up to them, within the limits of their continued affiliation, to take care of themselves. Thus they remain within the institution, within their marriage, but no longer depend on it or on its traditional definitions as completely as earlier generations of priests were encouraged to.

8

A Livable
Priesthood

The statements that come out of Rome are remote
enough from me that they aren't a real crucial factor. The
great issues of the church today, the statements that make
the news, just don't have a great deal of effect on us locally. There is a great deal of freedom within the parish
to set the overall tone; I don't sense that people are looking over my shoulder directly.

—Father Albert

S itting in his chaplain's office at one of the largest hospitals in
the Milwaukee area, Father Eric poured out his resentments
soon after we began talking. He bitterly resents the "infinite wisdom" of the diocesan personnel board for forcing him to move from two
successive parishes against the expressed will of the parishioners and
his own conviction that he was "having very good influence." To him,
the fixed-term policy reflects the worst aspects of the church's institu-
tionalism in deadly conjunction—remoteness and the urge to control: it
is a policy "written by people who have never been in a parish" driven
by the impulse "to fix what works instead of what's broken." In general,
he feels, doing good work doesn't get a parish priest anywhere. "Today,"
he says, "the reward system is based on the color of your nose."

Yet he resisted my suggestion that he sounded alienated. As he sees it, his response has been "to stay out of parishes from now on," to avoid contact with diocesan officials as much as possible (he had chosen not to attend the recent Clergy Day), and to concentrate on his work as chaplain, which he can largely define for himself and which he enjoys immensely. He feels content with his stance of internal independence:

> I've resolved it for myself. I do not cooperate. I do not participate in the larger entity. I have a lot more control over my life ever since I've decided they can go to hell. I never realized the truth of this until the last couple of years. A friend of mine is an accountant for a large pharmaceutical firm. He says, "What you do is, when you start working, you save up so that you've got six months' salary in the bank and you never touch it. You call it your 'Go to Hell Fund,' and the first thing you do is let your boss know you've got one." Well, in relation to the institution, I've got an emotional "Go to Hell Fund." All of a sudden, one day, literally, I woke up and decided, "What do I need them for?"

*   *   *

If the frustrations that I have described thus far constituted the whole picture, the priests in my class would appear an alienated, dispirited lot. But if that were the whole picture, it is unlikely that twenty-two of their original twenty-nine would still remain in the active ministry. Nor is it likely that I would have found myself looking forward to talking to them every time I made a trip to Milwaukee.

For after four years of conversations with them, my overall sense is that although they feel lonely, underpaid, undervalued by the laity, and unacknowledged by the hierarchy, most of them still remain relatively happy to be doing the work which *they* define as central to the priesthood. Twenty years after ordination, that work has not lost its meaning or become stale; they describe it, in most cases, with great enthusiasm. For men at midlife—most of whom, in Levinson's study, had lost their enthusiasm for their work—this is no small triumph.

What they consider central to their priesthood, however, has changed considerably from the traditional definitions of priestly work. The liturgy is less important to most of them than I would have expected. Few of them emphasize prayer or contemplation in their descriptions of what they do, except to lament its relative absence in their lives and to puzzle over why this has turned out to be so. Not very many of them mentioned God, for that matter, in describing their motivation. God tends to be the indirect object of their attention; they reach Him by tapping their own best energies, primarily in moments of intense, nurturing contact with other people, through those acts which blend—to the point of submersion—the pastoral impulse encouraged by the church with their own deep need for human relationships. These moments—counseling, visiting the sick, one-on-one relationships of various kinds, homilies which evoke an immediate sense of connection—define their priesthood as "personal" and bring them alive in the process. My classmates are, in their own way, members of the turned-on generation; they like their highs.

We Catholics once knew, because the Baltimore Catechism told us in very clear terms, that we were made "to know God, to love God, to serve Him in this world and to be happy with Him forever in Heaven." If I were to paraphrase my classmates' present sense of mission, however, it would go something like this: "We have been made to know men, to serve men, to help as many of them as possible to grow, and to develop our own potential to the fullest in the process. The next world, if there is one, will take care of itself, because the God or force who probably reigns will surely approve of such efforts and will, perhaps—although it is not central to us—reward us later as well." The region in which pastoral activity and personal growth merge, where they help themselves and others at the same time, is the zone of their most cherished activity, the heart of their ministry. Indeed, as the institutional church distances itself from them, or vice versa, these interpersonal satisfactions become all the more crucial to them.

In the context of a spirituality in which service to others and personal growth are inseparable, "mere" service—the grunt work not conducive to growth—has little appeal to them; hence, for instance, their reluctance to be on call twenty-four hours a day. And although they describe their most spiritual moments in the traditional language of "transcendence," what they seek to transcend (i.e., ignore) at such times is not the earth as a realm but their own usual limits—or, more often, those abrasive reminders of the institutional church (such as its hierarchical structure) which block genuine contact with others and thus impede mutual growth.

Most of them do not regard the church as an end in itself or as an inherent source of meaning. Instead, the people are their goal and rationale; the institutional church is reduced to being the available medium—murky at worst, fluid at best, but something to move through rather than to imbibe. "It isn't the church that has a mission," Father Brent insists; "it's the other way around, that the mission of Jesus has a church." In short, for them the church seems to be shifting from the primary, definitive, foregrounded presence it once was ("Lord, to whom shall we go?" St. Peter said when things got sticky. "You have the words of eternal life") to a usable but secondary institution. They are no longer married to the church in the traditional ways.

Yet because their priestly work remains important to them, because they have been within the church and priesthood for a long time, and because they still give weight to the longevity of the relationship—rather than because of a felt moral imperative to stick with it at all costs—they are willing to put considerable effort into finding ways to work things out. They have not written the relationship off; they struggle not only to survive within it but to keep it viable somehow. They are now married in a looser, more contemporary, semi-independent way.

The question of relative distance is therefore crucial to them. In effect, they have taken the painful gap between their own needs and what the church provides and discovered there not the prelude to divorce but room to maneuver, an area of autonomy where they can exercise a considerable degree of independence. In the arms of the Holy Mother, after all, there may have been warmth and security, but there was not much leeway. Distance within the marriage, by contrast, may be initially painful, but it also provides "space" within which they can no longer be so easily constrained by their spouse's dictates. Insofar as they can define that space as positively charged, they can feel energized instead of cut off, free instead of abandoned.

To the extent that the institution is no longer a supportive partner, they will refuse to depend on it for their satisfaction. "We can't allow the institution to have power over our happiness," one of them declares. "I was much more married to the church in the past than I am now. Growing into fullness has to do with our own self-sufficiency." Or as another insists, "I don't need the church to provide me with my self-actualization."

The church they are willing to pledge their allegiance to, the partner they are still willing to embrace, is in fact not the entire church at all: "Many people," said Father Eric, in a description which included himself, "are turned off to the church in the larger sense. The church has become the local church, the church in terms of where you are." This church is coterminous with their own space instead of a threat to it; it is the place where they *can* get things done, where, in Father Albert's phrase, "I don't sense people looking over my shoulder."

They define the local church in a wide variety of ways. For Ralph, it is "the parish I'm in"; for Eric, it is "the people I work with, the people I work for. Doing a day of recollection or visiting someone who's in the hospital or holding a father whose son has just been killed in a motorcycle accident. That's church." For another, it is the genuine "personal relationships" he has been able to establish in his work, relationships contrasted by him to the "generic relationships of the church"—a distinction which turns the seminary's traditional caveat about the dangers of "particular friendships" on its head. *Their* church is built from the inside out, not from the top down.

Carrying this localization process to its logical conclusion, many of them find the church real only in those "transcendent moments" in which, through their ministry, they feel most alive, most in touch with other people and with their own powers. Theirs is not the universal, omnipresent, intractable church; it is a church they can conjure and dismiss (nearly) at will. "I never think of church as 'what goes on in church,' " says Father Frank. "Call it church only if something happens there."

Whether my classmates describe their church geographically, interpersonally, or experientially, its two constant elements are their insistence on the right to define it for themselves and their repudiation of whatever elements of the institutional church they find offensive, intrusive, or irrelevant. "It's not pumping religion down people's throats or insisting on vestments," Father Eric maintains. "And it ain't got nothin' to do with bishops." *Their* church is in fact barely institutional at all; it is a movable feast, an enterprise zone of the spirit, a magic circle, a place/space which cannot be willed into existence but which appears when the moment is right.

Their emphatic refusal to "belong" to the other, institutional church while also choosing not to abandon it—or, more to the point, their declaring psychic independence from the other church so as not to have to defect from it formally—defines their characteristic midway stance: they dissent without rebellion, they keep just enough distance to avoid needing more. This is their own particular twist on the strategy once proposed by an older generation: the notion of working "within the system"—not directly to affect it or change it, however, but to remain alive and functioning within its borders. Like other members of our generation who find ourselves unwilling to "marry" our institutions till death and yet need them to do what we care about (can't live with them, can't live without them), they now look for the balancing point between a stifling intimacy and a debilitating alienation.

This stance is a long way from "loving the church," the traditional definition of wholehearted affiliation conjured for me by a former seminary professor as the essence of the priestly stance. But it is also a long way from the radical alienation which drove several of their classmates from the priesthood and out of the entire institution. For men such as Leo, the "system" was harmful, pervasive, and inescapable; thus working within it meant the ever-present risk of being ground up by it, of having their integrity destroyed, their humanity squashed. Those who have stayed, for the most part, also see the institutional church as destructive; but they believe that it is possible to keep far enough away from its negative energy that they can breathe their own clean air. For them, "working within the system" is not only compatible with maintaining their integrity; the creation of positive space is in fact the very way they shape their identity.

Their degree of distance from the institution and their stance toward that distance vary considerably, ranging from the wry conviction that the church semi-intentionally colludes in their modest deviations from its norms ("If I understand my privileges correctly," Father Ralph asserts,

"I can tailor a number of things locally even though they may be questionable in terms of anything official") to angrier assertions such as Eric's that they have had to seize every one of their freedoms from the clutches of a grasping institution. Yet not even the most critical priests in my class have given up all hope for the "larger church" or all desire for a closer relationship with it. Even Eric, who asserts on the one hand that "the hierarchical part is damn near dead," concedes on the other that "the hierarchy is resuscitable," however unlikely it is to him that a regeneration will take place "in my lifetime."

"Not in my lifetime" is a phrase I heard often—along with "I don't see it happening"—in relation to desired institutional change of various kinds: a liberal pope, a married clergy, the ordination of women. Such phrases capture my classmates' blend of immediate pessimism and lingering, long-term hope—or perhaps even faith—that things might eventually be different. What each of them seeks consequently is a stance which keeps him in touch with the institution without feeling bound by it, independent but not irrevocably estranged. Several said that the radical changes in Eastern Europe have been an inspiration to them. They don't know how to bring about the church's new day; but in case that day should miraculously come and the walls of the Vatican start to crumble, they haven't sold their tickets to the dance.

There are risks as well as advantages to this strategy, I think. In some ways, despite their laments over a retrenched church, their personalized space suggests a retrenchment of their own, a spiritual version of the bureaucratic niche: find a place where you can be comfortable, a place where you can do your work, a place that buffers you from irritation, and—once again—let the world go by. At its worst, this approach to institutional frustration, like my tendency to retreat to the classroom, inclines toward "operating" within the system without affecting it, however spiritual or noble the ends of that operation may be. Concentration on what they can do with satisfaction—but without broader effect— might be seen as a socially conservative form of self-indulgence.

Yet the work they do is, of course, *ministry.* They aim at a hassle-free zone, all right, a place where they can do their own thing; but their goal is a psychic region in which a semi-independent and therefore healthy self can continue to help others without interference. Furthermore, the one-to-one relationships they foreground are not easily reducible to the "merely" personal; for the personal, feminists have reminded us repeatedly, is always political. My classmates within the church, like many women in a male-dominated society (analogous situations, I have already suggested), have insisted that change can and must originate from the most local actions and attitudes and then move outward. Personal or local space is—or so I too hope from inside my classroom—by no means a social vacuum.

Interestingly, my classmates' revised notions of what they can best do as priests provide yet one more tie with current trends in therapy, hence one more hint that they have moved closer to secular culture as they pull back from the institutional church. At first glance, their local emphasis would seem to reflect that prominent, current therapeutic tendency—derived from Freudian analysis, though the linkage is rarely acknowledged by therapists—according to which distressed people are encouraged to concentrate on what they can change (themselves, their own thinking) rather than on what they cannot (anything or anyone else). I have heard this advice many times.

But at closer range, their priesthood more closely resembles an equally current but non-Freudian school of therapy, the family systems model to which I referred in chapter 5. According to this model, which has affinities with contemporary physics as well, *any* pattern within any system (the self, a family, a relationship, and beyond) tends to replicate itself; but precisely because of that tendency, changes introduced within the system inevitably ripple out to change the entire system.[1] Hence change which occurs even in a small space is never confined to that space; the enclave becomes an inherently active force. The family systems approach, like personally oriented feminism, thus embraces on the level of theory what my classmates aim at in practice: a blending of the 1960s with the 1980s and beyond, a (down)shifting of the still-powerful reformist urge to the interpersonal realm without abandoning its outgoing, socially oriented core.

Compliance on Their Own Terms: A Celibacy of Their Own

The right to define for themselves an otherwise unacceptable church has a direct corollary in my classmates' insistence on controlling the *terms* they use to describe what they are willing to do inside that church. They can reconcile a considerable degree of compliance with institutional requirements, but only insofar as they can translate their compliance into their own chosen language. For articulate members of a verbal generation which believes in the importance of what is consciously stated ("Let's be clear about this relationship from the start"), what they do is in some ways less important to their sense of themselves than the reasons they give for doing it.

Thus they repeatedly insist on having their own grounds for actions which the church itself encourages or requires; the gap between official rationale and private motive constitutes one of the spaces where they can breathe. They insist, for instance, on the primacy of a "personalized priesthood" (in contrast to the church's impersonality) while underplaying its considerable overlap with the pastoral emphasis of the post–Vatican II church itself; they fling their "professionalism" in the face of what they pose as a resistant church, without drawing attention to its source in the heightened emphasis on professional training in the latter years of their own seminary education; they consider themselves priests so long as they can refuse to call themselves churchmen; they label themselves spiritual but not religious. Religion belongs to the institution; by thinking in their own terms, they do not.

Nowhere is this blend of independent thinking and behavioral adherence more evident than in their desire to redefine mandatory celibacy in terms they can accept. As we have seen, they are emphatic in rejecting the church's traditional grounds for celibacy. Yet as far as I can tell, for most of my classmates, these scornful dismissals are not the prelude to pervasive sexual activity but the necessary psychological groundwork for celibate behavior. For if my classmates are going to have to live a celibate life as one of the "tradeoffs" the church demands, if celibacy is, as Father Eric says, an "occupational hazard, the price of admission" to a priesthood they still desire (of course, such phrases are themselves a denial of the church's grander terms), then it is all the more important for them not to acquiesce in the church's institutional rationale for it. Eric's formula for a psychological freedom to balance the force of external controls ("They can jerk me around geographically but they can't touch me internally") has its analogue here in this most personal area of behavior: if my classmates cannot act independently of certain church requirements, they can—they must—at least think independently. Their heads—the ultimate "space" for children of the 1960s, after all—are, as we used to say, in a different place.

In regard to mandatory celibacy in particular, they have developed a conceptual tactic which, in its combination of self-defense and activism, makes clear how enmeshed with one another these notionally distinct strategies are. First of all, protectively, they analogize celibacy to the very state it denies them, marriage—not, however, to marriage as they imagine it when they speak enthusiastically of the potential wholeness it offers, but to marriage as a source of frustration and loneliness rather than their antidote. By conjuring marriage after the fall rather than marriage in its first flush of intimacy and hope, they can assert that celibacy, with all its problems, is like rather than unlike marriage. "The struggle I go through," says Father Spencer, "is trying to be present to people, and finding that [as a celibate] you can be only *so* present in a male/female relationship. But then you have the same struggle; you have a wife." "I've never had an affair with a woman," another classmate said. "Thought about it? Sure. Married people think about it too." They live in a restricted arrangement, my classmates admit; but then, they continually asked, don't you?

On the day-to-day level, in fact, they suggest that celibacy may be less frustrating than marriage. "There is never an argument in this apartment about who gets to watch what on TV," Father Alex said. "I never have to explain where I've been or with whom." For Father Tracy, the thwarted promise of marriage may be worse than the predictable loneliness of celibacy: "Sometimes," he says, "I think the marriage relationship is more devastating than celibacy, if both partners aren't on the same plane and aren't giving each other the kind of love and support that are absolutely necessary." "I would find the companionship of marriage very good," Father Ralph says, allowing himself the language of desire, but only for a moment. "Then I look at some of the people I have to deal with, and I say, 'Well, look at the crap they're going through. Gee, I'm kind of glad I'm not married.' " "The grass is not greener on the other side of the fence," insists Father Alex, raising this grim comparative strategy to the status of folk wisdom, "it just has different brown spots."

Whether or not these statements represent a realist view of marriage earned through a lifetime of counseling or a negative fantasy rooted in a longstanding seminary tradition of disparaging marriage (a little of both, I suspect), they constitute a functional strategy, one of the oldest on record: take down a peg or two those you might otherwise be tempted to envy. As my mother used to say when we drove past the rich houses in town, "Don't worry, son; those people aren't happy."

Characteristically, this defensive, negative strategy is not enough for them, however; for at the same time, my classmates reveal an equally strong desire to see celibacy as a source of Jungian/Rogerian integration, to translate the traditional (and for them discredited) self-abnegation of celibacy into the very terms of personal growth by which they question the necessity of celibacy in the first place. They struggle with this translation, to be sure—I heard a good deal about the need to "integrate loneliness," for instance, from lonely men unsure of what this term might mean—and they achieve only partial success. Yet the struggle is important to them, for it represents a crucial attempt to render legitimate in their own eyes an inescapable policy which would otherwise remain repugnantly coercive to them.

One representative model for their thinking is the humanistic psychology of Donald Goergen, a Dominican priest whose 1974 book, *The Sexual Celibate*,[2] enjoyed wide currency among them and was recommended to me by several of them. Goergen's basic strategy was to extend Abraham Maslow's theories of self-actualization into the realm of celibacy. To Maslow, humans need intimacy more than they need genital satisfaction, and the two should not be confused. Genuinely self-actualizing people, insofar as they are already taking care of their intimacy needs, are able to be sexually abstinent without harming their overall psychic health. Therefore abstinence, although by no means necessary for self-actualization, is compatible with it.

But Goergen goes further, and this is the particular move which I see reflected in my classmates' language: for he insists that celibacy is itself an expression of sexuality rather than its denial or suppression. He makes this claim by appropriating the whole sphere of emotional warmth to the realm of sexuality. For him, the affections are "the nongenital aspect of sexuality" (71); and though the affections bypass the genital realm when they assume a social rather than a sensuous aim, they remain connected to their root and source, sexuality itself. So when we are expressing "affectivity and all that it implies," we are in fact being sexual, because "gentleness and tenderness are rooted in human sexuality" (26).

Goergen, no doubt reluctant to endorse the old models associated with now-discredited seminary training, works hard to distinguish his theory from Freudian sublimation. To Freud, he emphasizes, the expression of nongenital affection remains a form of "aim-inhibited sexuality," a second-class, derivative, partially blocked form of sexuality rather than a fully legitimate version of the real thing. To Goergen, however, the affections are as fully sexual as genital expression is; hence the warm, loving person (genitally active or not) has integrated his sexuality fully into his personality rather than repressing it or settling for less (71–72).

The most enthusiastic proponent of sexual celibacy in my class is Father Lawrence, a highly articulate man who has earned his present convictions the hard way. In the first years of his priesthood, Lawrence began to feel the truth of what a seminary professor had told him, that "the day after you're ordained, your prick isn't going to know that you're celibate." Consequently, "without the psychological equipment to be able to deal with sexuality in a mature way," he found himself going through "a delayed adolescence in my late twenties." For three years he experimented with every variety of sexual activity he could muster: homosexual as well as heterosexual, with friends, strangers, bar mates, prostitutes. Uncertain at that point about who he was or whether he could or should remain a priest, he apprenticed himself to a wise older priest, went on an extended retreat, and eventually learned "to embrace the warts as well as the good aspects of my life, the things I liked and the things I didn't like about myself, to accept myself more holistically."

Feeling freed from the burden of a lifelong perfectionism and able finally to accept his sexuality as a positive trait, he was also able to recommit to the priesthood—and to a version of celibacy closely akin to Goergen's model. For he had come to feel that "intimacy and sexual expression are not necessarily identical, that I can be a warm, caring individual, that I can love people and be committed to individuals and to groups of people like the parish. And I can really love them in nongenital ways. I came to the conclusion that I could be celibate. And I have done this to my own satisfaction."

As Lawrence's comments suggest, it is indicative of my classmates' pastoral impulses that the integration they try to see in celibacy does not stay in the realm of mere self-actualization. They won't endorse celibacy unless it is compatible with wholeness—they won't accept sublimation equated with denial—but they won't define it as wholeness in the first place unless it moves them outward to affect positively the people they serve.

Lawrence's version of celibacy is the result of a developmental process which raises questions of its own, not the least of which is the issue of how his various partners fared during his process of experimentation; I admit I did not ask him this. But more directly pertinent to my classmates: insofar as Lawrence has adopted a stance of sexual celibacy, it is also true that he expressed his genital sexuality extensively before arriving there—perhaps in order to arrive there. The question for most of my classmates, then, is whether it is possible, within their preferred paradigm of growth, to move genuinely beyond the need for sexual/genital expression without first moving through it.

They certainly try hard; and their conceptual strategies, if not their behavior, resemble Lawrence's. Father Ralph, for instance, finds that tradeoffs and negative comparisons to marriage can carry him only so far; he ultimately insists, "I have had to find positive reasons for being celibate." His chosen rationale has to do with directing his energies back to other people, but not in a way which emphasizes self-abnegation or loss to himself. Rather, he insists that although he could indeed grow through marriage, he can also grow by helping other people grow. On those grounds, he has found it possible to affirm that "it is not incompatible being a human being and choosing to be single":

> I realize it was a decision forced on me and it bothers me—maybe more so now than at the time we were ordained—that I didn't have any choice in the matter at all. I couldn't say I choose not to marry. I had to say I want to be a priest, therefore I know I cannot get married. [Yet] I believe I'm being creative by being with other people, seeing them maybe go through bad times, and just being an instrumental person to help guide them or be with them as they're changing their lives to something more successful, something more at peace with themselves. I do get satisfaction out of that. I do see it as creative energy. Giving new life in this sense has meant a lot to me. And as long as I can keep thinking positively about being creative in this way, I find it very fulfilling. It doesn't have to mean making babies. That's where I'm translating it.

The similar efforts of Father Alex make even clearer the complex, positive interplay between an enclosed, personal space and an outward-oriented, pastoral ministry. What makes celibacy occasionally joyful for

Alex is not merely its freedom from marital strife. Nor is it (not immediately, at least, or solely) the channeling of his energy to others. Rather,
he is one of a significant handful of priests in his class who, while acknowledging that "celibacy can be damn hard," also cherish the benefits
of solitude: positive time alone, time for creativity, for the development
of the self, for pursuits often denied to those whose attention is constantly directed to fulfilling duties or maintaining personal relationships. Solitude constitutes private space.

Alex paints—he showed me several of his landscape watercolors—lis-
tens to classical music, reads popular fiction, collects western movies: "I
love the unreality of it all, the free lifestyle." He travels as often as he
can to dude ranches and to Disney World, where he responds with much
greater enthusiasm to the childlike qualities of the Magic Kingdom than
to the more rational appeal of Epcot Center. "It's all part of the kid
in me," he says, evoking more of the language of humanist psychology,
"and I'm going to let the kid out." And although he does not see any
concrete threat to these activities from the church, he makes it clear that
he would defend them if necessary, that "they would not take that away
from me."

Yet ultimately, Alex is not merely personal in his uses of his own time.
When he goes to Disney World each year, he makes it a point to take
a child from his parish who could not otherwise afford to go. Furthermore, "I've found that since I've done this kind of reading [popular
fiction] and that kind of escaping, that I have great material to draw
upon for my homilies. To me it is just as important to read Robert Lud-
lum as it is to read the scriptures. It stimulates me to bring some stuff
which is pretty intellectual into common, ordinary words." Thus he is
ultimately able to integrate his expanding inner life with his priestly activities; he can direct the energy available through celibacy to others—
but only by directing it first to himself. Given no choice in terms of behavior, most of my classmates are still willing to move through celibacy
toward the "other"—so long as they do not have to sidestep themselves
completely in the process.

Of course, these strategies are far from definitive. My classmates have
not resolved their problems in relation to the institutional church once
and for all; how would one go about that in any complex relationship?
Especially in the transitional state in which they find themselves, their
attempts to order their lives and seek satisfaction are inevitably partial,
tentative, and often problematic in their own terms.

For the same reasons, their tactics, suggestive though they are of
broad, evolving trends, are also, as one of them acknowledged, "highly
idiosyncratic," rooted as much in each priest's particular temperament
and history as they are in a new but uncertain priestly culture. The dis-

creteness of their strategies reflects the highly personal nature of their worldview: the priesthood, even the church, is what each of them chooses to make of it. On the other hand, it also reflects one of the problems they suffer, the unwillingness to share their anxieties with one another. In any case, each of them struggles in a somewhat different way. In many instances, their entire lives as priests have been attempts at learning how to live with and make the most of the inherent problems of affiliation with the church.

So both to honor the extended, ongoing nature of their engagement with their central issues and to convey the energy with which they engage them, I have chosen to look in greater detail at a few of these men and how they lead their lives. For in the long run, what drew me were the men themselves, their commitment to keep on looking—at times confusedly, at times ingeniously—for ways to *make* sense of a way of life whose sense was once a given.

Six Priests

The "Underdeveloped Priest": Anxieties of Searching for a New Priesthood

Father Herbert and I had not been close in the seminary; yet he responded warmly to my initial phone call and was eager to talk when I arrived at his apartment on the near north side of Milwaukee. The apartment is modest but well situated, a few blocks from Lake Michigan, near the coffee shops, health-food restaurants, bookstores, and bars which constitute this area, he told me, as the yuppie part of town.

Herbert, whose struggles with money we have already seen, lamented the sparseness of his furnishings and alluded to having to buy a new wardrobe soon because "I like to have nice clothes." His father, he told me, is "very influenced by money" and makes it clear that he would like to see his son in a position of power. Herbert has resisted this pressure, but feels some of its marks; he is as aware of the increasingly tenuous material side of his life and of his current uncertain social status as he is of the pastoral center of his ministry.

"Herbert," a classmate had told me, "is a great priest, but has really been shat on by the diocese. I don't know why the hell he stays in." I found myself interested both in what bothered Herbert and in what, indeed, kept him in. I was also struck by his intense memory of his theology years at the seminary in the late 1960s. He recalls a good many nights of post-exam drinking with "tremendous friends"; for him it was "a wonderful time, a time of bonding, of togetherness, with a tremendous sense of humor and dialogue about politics and church and society issues, people-oriented issues. I really sensed community in that experience." He feels, however, that we no longer live in "a high people world," and he laments the fact that "the peak moments are not that many now." I was more than a little curious about how he was dealing with the absence of that intensity.

Herbert and I ate and drank our way across many of the north-side restaurants he recommended. At each extended stop, he was good company: unstinting with his time, quick to laugh, eager to hear whatever I could tell him about common issues among our classmates, forthcoming and unguarded in his own comments, and intensely interested in mine. He would often interrupt his own narrative, lean forward, and ask, "What do you think about that, Ray?" His open admission that he is still in the process of sorting out "all the negative midlife things you hear about" appealed to me. We matched one another well, uncertainty for uncertainty, and I made a point of getting together with him on each of my subsequent trips to Milwaukee.

The first time I talked to him, he mentioned his weight gain and his need to work out more often. He had also just lost his position in campus ministry. It was, he said, "a decision made on a bureaucratic level. I had no input into it." Worried in every way about the shape he was in, faced with the necessity of finding another job and yet no longer interested in "just parish work," Herbert was in a thoughtful and troubled frame of mind.

Perhaps more than any priest I interviewed, Herbert has been disoriented by the changes in the priesthood, in the church, and in American culture in the last twenty years. A reflective man, he sees himself as part of a generation of what he calls, using Eugene Kennedy's term, "underdeveloped priests."[3] Such priests were trained in a protective atmosphere, imbued with a traditional mythology of priesthood, and then forced to function in a changing priesthood for which they have no emotional preparation; they have, Herbert feels, little readiness for emotional complexity of any kind. A demythologized priesthood requires them to do things they were not trained to do, does not offer them the rewards they anticipated, taxes them far beyond their initial expectations, and leaves them fundamentally uncertain about whether to remain in the priesthood and about how to function there if they do. They are a generation, he feels, in desperate need of new ways to be a priest, yet radically unsure of what those ways might be.

For Herbert, the seminary's insularity dovetailed all too well with a sheltered, rural upbringing; the result was a form of culture shock when he entered the priesthood:

> My parents smothered me with all this protectiveness. That was reinforced in the seminary: you couldn't leave at certain times, etc. That

retards the growth process all the way to your mid-twenties. Your feelings in terms of sexuality are really delayed. You get out and you're in another protective environment under the senior pastor who has control over the parish setting. But then, all of a sudden, the church really starts changing. . . . You can't continue in that adolescent behavior and be credible. I just wonder in terms of psychology where I really am. I notice that the other priests I can relate to well are thirty-five, thirty-six, thirty-seven—almost ten years younger. Maybe that's where I'm at psychologically.

"In the 1950s and 1960s," Herbert remembers, "we were given an image from teachers that the priesthood would be quite fulfilling in terms of the people we served. And I found that to be true during the first five or six years." Even now, Herbert asserts that the most satisfying things about the priesthood have been "the people I've known, the people I've been intimate with." He seeks, above all, to nurture and be nurtured, to support and be supported.

Precisely because Herbert sees the priesthood in relational terms rather than in theological or doctrinal terms, his personal frustrations have hit him where it hurts the most. As with many of his classmates, "getting along with authority" is difficult for him; he has had a nearly unbroken string of conflicts with his pastors. The worst of these, a dispute eight years ago over whether he should concentrate his energies on parish teaching or turn that function over to the laity, led to extended litigation, a lasting sense of "tremendous anger, tremendous betrayal," and an enduring alienation from diocesan authorities because "I was not listened to by the central office. My person was violated immeasurably. As a result I became more distrustful of people in general."

Herbert cannot find much relief from his institutional alienation in his own generation of priests. In his early years, he enjoyed a more leisurely intimacy with some of them; but now, he feels, many have assimilated both the competitiveness of this era ("Sometimes they have to step over another priest in order to get a position they want") and its workaholic tendencies. As a result, they have little time for the extensive, unstructured contact which makes genuine connection and support possible. "They say, 'Let me see if I can work it into my schedule.' It's hard to get peak experiences out of that stuff."

Perhaps most poignant, the changes in the church which Herbert welcomed in the 1960s have had the unanticipated effect of distancing him from the laity, with whom he had expected to find closeness and fulfillment. Like Tod, he found himself instead in parishes whose newly emerging and often divided constituencies he found impossible to please. The most disappointing thing about being a priest, he told me, had been "lay people you felt you could trust but who were really not with you, who questioned you and spoke ill of you." He was too liberal for some parishioners, not radical enough for others, and found both groups vocal in their discontent. He welcomed the rise of lay ministers ("They can do our jobs very effectively, if not better"), yet found himself the object of their rising anti-clericalism. He found himself agreeing with Catholic women resentful of the patriarchal church ("I think they're right. Because our structure has not liberated us yet as men. That's what we're fighting for"), yet discovered that he got no credit from them for the admission. He embraced the new notion of collaboration with the laity, but found that under that model "our role was not as clear" and that the lack of clarity "took its toll psychologically."

In short, like many of his classmates, Herbert finds that the church's paradigm shift has registered its fault lines on his own psyche. As a result, he is more acquainted with the personal costs of institutional change than with its benefits: "You are trying to nurture the change. And as a result you get the spin-offs. . . . In the process, you feel very alone. With what I know now, I would probably not have gone through with this. It's the rare fellow from our time who comes out ahead on this thing."

Herbert has fallen in love twice. The first relationship lasted only a few months; it was "very uncomfortable" for him, because "we were trained in the seminary that if this happens, you are going to leave the priesthood." The second one, however, lasted for seven years, and remains "very special" in his memory. "It made me a better human being. I had very good feelings about it." He was not embarrassed to discuss this relationship; the intense terms in which he describes it reveal regret and pain, but not guilt:

> The second relationship started when I saw this very, very beautiful lady on a winter evening when I was giving a tour for a group of adolescents at a church of another denomination. I found Joanne very attractive. Later, through a parish committee, she caught my eye again. She and her husband invited me to come over, and we went out for dinner as friends. Later on, her husband had to work nights. It just evolved. We fell in love.
>
> We were very honest about it. We did not have sexual relations. We both wanted that, of course. She would invite me to her house to go swimming when her husband was out of town. It was gut-wrenching for me; it made me sick to my stomach not to make love to her. But I had tremendous difficulty with church expectations, with all that seminary formation toward celibacy. Besides, she loved her husband, and on principle I could never take her away from her husband. We had a beautiful relationship, but we didn't know how we were going to lessen it.
>
> I justified it in that I was lonely in my parish experiences and I didn't get the support always of my parishioners and my pastor. I felt that I needed more support than a family of origin could provide at that point. I felt that a contemporary I could be close to, as I was set up by

nature to be, was justified. I didn't feel as guilty as Joanne did. I come from this very traditional background, but I was more of the liberal than this woman. (*laughs*)

The cleavage, when it came, was not done smoothly. It wasn't so catastrophic that we wouldn't talk to each other, but it still was very awkward. But I think the parting was easier for her than it was for me. She has her husband, she has her children. Once my parents die, who do I have? I have my nephews and nieces, but my sister runs that boat, I don't. I have parishioners, I have priests that I get along with. They would not mind having dinner with me. But it isn't the same. It has been a tremendous loss for me, and I'm still reeling.

Now we're dealing with sexuality, we're dealing with reproduction. You see colleagues, especially our age, who have gotten married, and their children. Then younger people you had as students, they have their little children in the parish. We're dealing with the whole thing of what legacy I can leave. It's just a horrendous issue. If anything, it's the most haunting of the issues.

Herbert is one of several classmates, including Malcolm, who insist that the pain of not having children is, at this point, the worst price of celibacy; the urge to leave something of oneself behind, Daniel Levinson suggests, often becomes particularly acute at midlife, amid thoughts of one's own death and decline.[4] The fact that most of my classmates are men with a particularly strong sense of values exacerbates the need. Their desire to incarnate those values, to make their words flesh, is often intensified, as it is in Herbert's case, both by their conviction that they have less influence on the laity than they had anticipated and by the fact that their revised theologies no longer offer them the certainty of an afterlife. Priests were once seen as the embodiment of permanent, enduring values; by contrast, Herbert and others like him are now beset by fears of their own transience.

Joanne eventually moved south with her husband, just at the time when Herbert's disagreements with his pastor erupted into legal battles. Two more parish assignments followed rapidly, both torn by conflicts among the pastor, the associates, and the parish staff. The fact that such strife has not been uncommon as parishes attempt to restructure according to Vatican II guidelines ("Many parishes went through so much turmoil in that day") offered Herbert little consolation; where could he go for relief? "I could see myself rapidly declining," he says. I was not as friendly, I was more irascible, I put on weight." To make matters worse, he could not forget Joanne: "Those feelings are never gone. They just don't die." His unhappiness raised what he calls with a laugh "the ultimate question: is this all that there is?"

I had to confront my workaholism, deal with my burn-out experience, and being burnt. That was too much for me to handle. I said, "Is this where it's all at? I go to another parish and I gotta produce again?

That's what's expected of me; I have to be like a slave to the system.
That's all this is for me. And that's all it's gonna be for me." That's
when I really got into the vocational questions.

Herbert came close to leaving the priesthood at that point; but at the
archbishop's suggestion, he took a sabbatical instead. He enrolled in
business courses at the University of Wisconsin, looking for "something
where I could start with a new career" either inside or outside the priesthood. In the process, he came to realize the limits of his own energy: "I
was so exhausted. The body is not the same as it was at twenty-five." He
also felt the differences between the "hard, sterile world" of business and
the "high-people world" which he felt he still carried over from the
1960s. This "eye-awakening experience" led him back toward the priesthood: "Why not go back to where I've come from and see how I can re-
enter and look at things in a new way?"

Herbert returned to Milwaukee and moved into an apartment; "It
takes so much of your person to be in a rectory situation, unless you really know how to sort that out: this is your personal life, this is your
professional life." Since then he has turned down a number of full-time
positions, including clinical pastoral work in a large urban hospital, because they would be too draining: "I could not deal with death and dying, that kind of intense emotion. I didn't want to take on seeing five
people die in front of me every day."

For now, he has been working in campus ministry and helping out in
a number of parishes, a piecemeal approach that has intensified his characteristic financial anxieties. "Money is a real pressure point at middle
age particularly, because you find out all of a sudden that you haven't
saved too much. There isn't much there."

Herbert is convinced that "the church is a declining environment, no
doubt about it," and he does not feel morally bound to remain a priest:
"I know that a person can leave the priesthood and find his life." Yet, as
it does with other classmates such as Tod, the church as heritage accom-
plishes for him what the church as law does not; the "larger church"
which still appeals to him is the church with a history. "At this moment," he says, "I should stay ordained. Our training says something
good about the church and something good about the priesthood. It represents a long tradition." Moreover, he still clings to his core values of
preaching—"They can't take that away from me. I can still preach, and
I will preach the big issues. There is some meaning to that"—and counseling: "Because I've been so broken, I have empathy for people going
through divorce or remarriage." The priesthood, stripped to its basics,
thus turns out to be an area where he can put to good use the very experiences which disoriented him in the first place.

Nonetheless, he is uncertain how to use concretely the sense of purpose he still feels. Because he is convinced that "role expectations are still the same for pastors; you live where you work," and because he husbands his energies nowadays and knows he doesn't handle conflict well, Herbert doesn't want to be a pastor, where he would inevitably be "caught in the middle of school arguments, political realities"—i.e., in situations which would exhaust him and undercut the relationships he still places at the center of his priesthood. "I want to make a difference in society," and for him, that difference is personal: "I would like to get into some kind of work where I can deal one on one with people. I would like to remain in ministry with another job." In effect, he wants to do what he considers priestly without stepping into the currently defined "jobs" which make it hard to do those things. He feels that other priests share that need: "A lot of these areas need tremendous change, just for the humanity of the priest, so the priest survives emotionally and can go the whole gamut."

Perhaps the highest price Herbert has paid by functioning in a priesthood which he has found to be more draining than supportive is that he feels that his own capacity to nurture has diminished: he trusts less than he used to and acknowledges in himself some of the unwillingness to "commit, to pay the price" which he laments in others. He finds that lately, because of his own personal problems, "I haven't been able to free people from a lot of their bondage" as readily as he once felt he could. He feels regret over Joanne—"I really wish I could have been married for these years"—and acknowledges that he has been suffering from recurrent depression, that "I've really gone into a tailspin."

Because Herbert now defines morality less in abstract terms of good and evil and more in terms of human growth or its absence, his professional and personal frustration elide into spiritual stagnancy; for him to assert, "I'm in decline," to feel that he has not been able to "actualize the potential" he was given at birth, is tantamount to an admission of moral failure. When he looks forward, he sees no clear way out of this slide; instead, he thinks a good deal about future loneliness and death:

> I just think about being put in that casket, closing the door, put underneath six feet of ground. This is really nightmarish. I have a plot with my mother and father. I know where that spot is. I think that is a very threatening thing. What is the death experience like? I want to die a happy death. We've heard about that from the old-time priests. Now I'm saying it. I don't want to be the fatalist, the Jewish notion that there's nothing after this. I hope there's something, I hope there is.
>
> I saw Archbishop Cousins in the casket last week. He was such a vibrant man when he was fifty-seven years of age, when he came to Milwaukee in '59. And I saw how the body looked in the casket. Boy, the body looked old. You could see in the pictures how he got older, how

he gradually disintegrated. I'm thinking, "What about myself as I get older? Can I keep the spirit I have alive like Archbishop Cousins did, to be a source of life when you know that you're facing your own death?" I find that very haunting. I have no answer to that, outside of what I shared with you.

God gives us these gifts, and we are asked from infancy to actualize the potential. In our careers—celibate, married—to take these gifts and to bring them into this society. So at least, if there is the possibility of another life, you can say, "God, I've done something with what you've given me."

But all of a sudden, you get bumped out of a job, and you feel like you can't actualize your potential. You get down on yourself, you feel like you're not productive anymore. You're supposed to be in your prime; why aren't you getting off your rear end and doing something to improve our society? If I work off that vision, if I'm not using all my gifts for the "greater honor and glory of God," building the kingdom, now I've been a failure.

For Herbert, the prospects of old age and death become even grimmer when he looks at the "lean and mean yuppies" who inhabit his apartment building. He chooses to live in that building because he rejects the traditional expectation that the priest will be constantly on call. But because he is also unwilling to embrace "the extreme individualism I find in the young generation today—I don't feel that comfortable with it," his apartment brings him loneliness more than independence, emptiness as well as space. In the eyes of his young neighbors, he sees no sense of community to take the place of what he once had in the seminary, no promise of warm future care to comfort his old age. In general, he sees in the impersonal culture around him no happy alternative to the frustration he has felt within the church and within the priesthood:

Let's say I try to break into a conversation with a young person I meet on the elevator going down. I have one hell of a job. I'm the one who initiates about 98 percent of the time. I've got to be persistent enough to want to break the isolation. They have a right to that isolation, but I find that to be some scary business.

This is a fear that I have, okay? I am worried as a middle-aged man, from our background now, looking toward the future. I'm afraid we're going to have to deal with a very cold, calculating young generation that comes behind us. When I'm an old guy in a nursing home—now this deals with the death question again in terms of euthanasia. I am scared crapless, I really mean that. I do not look forward to the day when I'm sitting in the nursing home—now granted there are young people who are compassionate—when those lean and mean administrators are making the decisions.

Because regardless of the pros and cons of the seminary, I think we came out of a communal, compassionate environment. Our community has already been so broken up, our community feeling. I hate to see that happen, but it's happening more. I can see life becoming very unhappy.

Herbert's admission that his upbringing and his seminary training left him radically unprepared for the complexities of adult life was not uncommon in the interviews. Many of us tend to hold the church or the seminary accountable for being precisely the safe environment we sought; at the time, we were thinking of how good it would feel to be protected, not of how uncomfortable the contrast would be later. The moments of entry—into a changing priesthood, into sexual passions whose force and implication we had no inkling of, into complicated marriages, into a realm of professional uncertainties and personal ambivalence where scholastic logic had no application—were our versions of the fall from innocence. Since we were more naive than most and expected a smoother ride because of our special status, the fall has often been hard.

Of all the priests I talked with, Herbert seemed the most defenseless. On the one hand, he has found no local space of his own, no way to protect himself from what he sees as the invasions and abuses of the church and its churchmen; on the other hand, he has not found in a changing church any attractive or acceptable channels for his still-active priestly idealism. Without a place to which to retreat or a specific priestly job to which to dedicate himself, he is unmoored, without harbor or definition.

The priests who follow in this section have gone further toward finding workable strategies for moving past these uncertainties than Herbert has. And although they are not as close to one another as they had anticipated, they do keep track; hence the depression Herbert acknowledges, like the stories of former priests now adrift, functions for them as a cautionary tale, a fate into which they too could fall. Herbert's story reveals just how urgent the need is for my classmates to find new ways to make the priesthood livable.

Nonetheless, I developed great respect for Herbert. His uneasy but determined attempts to find a place for his vocational drive somewhere in a priesthood whose outlines are still unclear, and to remain energized in the meantime, struck a chord with me. He retains his sense of humor at the very time he needs it most, when nothing seems very funny. And above all, Herbert remains in the hunt; he sees himself as down and knows that it could get worse, but he has not counted himself out.

In the process, he offers an interesting alternative to the strategy of protective retreat; for although he does not relish the exposure of his nerve endings, Herbert is nonetheless willing to "feel the pain," as the therapists say, instead of buffering himself from it. In the long run, that may be his best chance to move through it.

Since our initial interviews, Herbert has flown to Florida three times to see Joanne. She was reluctant to talk to him at first, but eventually warmed to his efforts to "heal the relationship." In their latest, three-hour conversation, she told him, "If I had that part to live over, I would not be as loyal to my husband." "My hunch," Herbert told me, "is that this was a present-tense statement too," a possibility which he finds "tantalizing, yes. But I haven't seen her since. I would like to have another close relationship, but I'm not a stalker. And at my age, I'm not all that certain that another one will just happen."

"Representative" Priest: Is There Breathing Room "at the Center of the Diocese"?

I ran into Father Frank outside the residence hall on the first morning of my extended stay at the major seminary in the fall of 1988. I had my touring bicycle with me; Milwaukee has a seventy-six-mile bicentennial circuit along the lake and through the park system, and I knew I was going to need to sweat. Frank stopped, recognized me immediately after twenty-five years, as I did him, and we compared notes. He is an experienced transcontinental cyclist, and I felt a slight competitive edge to our conversation: he was a better cyclist with a better bike. He laughed readily, as he always had, and his voice sounded authoritative, as it always had. His voice had the same quality later, during our talks, even as he described the burdens of unsought authority.

When Frank was still a seminarian, he and I would argue politics; he was part of what I then saw as the radical left-wing caucus in our class. In retrospect, I see that he was merely an ardent Democrat, the son of a working-class family and an avid supporter of JFK, LBJ, and liberal social policy in general. Meanwhile, I was still my parents' Republican child, one of the understandably few Nixon supporters in our class and later the only seminarian in the school with a Barry Goldwater poster on his door. Frank and I did not see eye to eye, and that left us often mouth to ear—his mouth, my ear.

At the time I found Frank offensively certain about his positions; he would stare at me with his deep-set eyes, steamroller me with his bass voice and long, articulate pronouncements, and in general make me feel like the ill-informed naif that in fact I was. He didn't make compromises, and he didn't suffer even semi-fools gladly.

Twenty-five years later, although my politics have changed, his have not; nor has his tendency to intense anger with whatever he sees as foolish—now, however, not so much inside American society as within the structure of the church. Since we now agreed much more often than not, our conversations tended toward crescendo rather than antiphony, with both of us gesticulating wildly with our hands as we fed into and off one another's statements. Over dinner one night in an otherwise quiet restaurant, we came close—so I felt, at least—to getting tossed out for disruptive behavior.

If Herbert suffers from a feeling of marginality, of floating undefined at the edges of a changing church, Frank suffers from the converse problem. He is a professor of theology who teaches at the seminary and lives there as well; thus he resides, in his words, "at the center of the diocese"—and finds these close institutional ties very discomforting. In a class of predominantly liberal priests suspicious of ecclesiastical authority, Frank feels a characteristic tension between his scorn for many of the church's policies and practices and his public role as representative of the church—a tension, as we have seen, which has driven several of his classmates from the priesthood: "I don't like being identified with the institution in that way," he lamented, in full knowledge that everything he says, on campus and off, inevitably carries "institutional weight." If Herbert is "out of shape" and would like more definition, Frank is wary of being so defined by his position that he cannot retain his own profile.

Our first conversation took place in his seminary apartment, where Frank is constantly on call to counsel both the seminarians who reside in the same building and the considerable number of Catholic women who now study theology at the seminary but who remain barred from ordination. That setting was a reminder to us both that Frank lives within the institution in the most literal of ways and must confront his uneasiness with it on a daily basis, in class and out. In that context, and because the discomfort he feels within his institution dovetailed with my uneasiness within my own, it is not surprising that our conversation kept circling back to the sources of meaning and frustration which he finds within his institution.

Like many of his classmates, Frank has traveled a long way from the 1950s church and his initial stance as "very straight, very conservative." An excellent student, he was sent to Europe by the archdiocese to study theology just after the Vatican Council had ended. As a result, like Frederick, he was exposed to many of the prominent theologians who had formulated the council's most liberal documents. He speaks passionately of this formative experience; the atmosphere of "change and newness and fresh breath" which he found there enabled him to move "from a more exterior, authority perspective to an 'interiorizing your faith' perspective. It came at the right time in my life. I didn't need more control, because I was too controlled to begin with." Although Frank describes himself as having been rigid when he first entered St. Francis, he also remembers that even then the church he cherished was a church not of exclusion, nor of self-referential rewards and punishment, but a church of "relationships," of "community," of "people caring for other people"; the priesthood he was drawn to was a priesthood of "touching people's lives":

> I remember sitting on the porch in the rectory when I was in first-year college. The pastor was an old-school guy. He had all of the seminarians over for an evening, and he was asking all of us, "Why do you want to be priests"? I said, "Well, I'm doing it because this is a way of helping people." He said, "Oh, no, you're doing it to save your soul." I remember thinking, "No. No, that's not why I'm doing it. That may be why you do it, but I can't live with that. That doesn't make any sense to me." Already by that point, I had framed it in a more communal sense. I never could deal with that language. I didn't know what the hell it meant. Certainly today I don't. I can't understand what that means.

Frank's conviction that his greatest strength as a priest would be pastoral rather than doctrinal was strengthened in his second assignment after ordination, which he looks back on as "the best years of my priesthood" primarily because of his extensive work with young parishioners. In the mid-seventies, just as Pope Paul VI was making it relatively easy for priests to laicize, Frank's contacts with these young people made concrete to him the attractions of a personalized priesthood and gave him some of the warmth other priests were seeking in marriage. "They helped me by accepting me," he remembers, "and I in turn helped them by showing that you can be caring and sensitive." He feels that he worked hard during that period "to give them an experience of church and community." Above all, with them he felt that sense of creativity common to all those classmates who have been able to find satisfaction within a celibate priesthood:

> I spent a hell of a lot of time with those kids. I directed two plays with them, took them on campouts for a week every summer. I took them on retreats, I witnessed their marriages, I baptized their babies. Even more so than with the guys I have in class here, or the women that I have in class here, I feel I was most generative with these people. That gave me strength to do all kinds of other things in the parish. It was a powerful experience. Those eight years I was in my element. There were certainly times that I felt frustrated and angry; a lot of my friends were leaving the priesthood. It makes you think, "Maybe I should leave." Part of the reason that I didn't was this youth group and the way they drew the best out of me and allowed me to develop. They let me see that I was doing something that I felt was really worthwhile. Touching their lives. And they in turn touched mine.

While stationed in that parish, he began teaching one course a year in the seminary; he found that the conjunction of active theology and parish work provided a way to integrate otherwise disparate elements of his life: "I was able to use the insights from the theology with my youth group and the insights from the youth group and parish work with my students here. This is the way you do theology: being creative and reflecting on what is going on."

We have already seen Frank's vehement resistance to the personnel board's attempt to move him out of the parish to the seminary, especially since there was as yet no full-time faculty position open there. His defiance is one of many indications that my classmates no longer operate wholly inside the traditional model of quasi-military obedience to ecclesiastical authority. On the other hand, few in my class are outright rebels; Frank eventually consented to going east to earn a doctorate in theology. He had been teaching at the seminary for nine years at the time I interviewed him.

He enjoys his seminary work: "In some ways, I am just as pastoral here as I was in the parish. I end up giving a lot of spiritual direction and counseling, especially to the lay students." Yet his position as authorized spokesman is inherently difficult for someone who disagrees with so many of the church's official stands—most notably its teachings on birth control, its continued insistence on an all-male priesthood, and, overall, what he sees as its unconscionable treatment of women.

For his close and continual contact with the women now enrolled in seminary theology programs has convinced him that they are the church's most serious Christians—"One of the things that make this whole thing with women so hard is that basically they have taken the gospel seriously"—and potentially the church's most committed priests: "The last woman I listened to, I thought to myself, 'If I've ever heard a story of a person who wants to minister in the time I've been here, this is the story. This is the woman.'"

Thus his counseling of women—the very kind of personalized priestly activity he cherishes most—makes their frustration an immediate and intense source of grief for him: "The more you hear the stories," he admits, "the more the pain really eats at you. The students I've taught, the women whose stories I've heard, are—Jesus—such bright, honest, caring people. And you say, why? Just because of their gender, they can't . . . ?" As a result, the natural interplay between theological insight and pastoral work which he savored in parish work—the integration he seeks—is no longer there. The church's practices drive a wedge between them, and Frank feels less of a piece than he once did.

Frank's conviction that the church is causing pain where it should be alleviating it means that, at least in this area, the institutional church is nothing less than an agent of evil:

> I had a student a couple of years ago in class. She's a good woman, and was very vocal about a lot of things. She said she felt *Humanae Vitae* was evil. It certainly wouldn't have come to my mind to say that it was evil;

I might say it was wrong. After my class, I went back to my room and thought, "You know, she's probably right. What's evil about it is what it does to people, its effect. It really is a choice of authority over care. And you say, "Shit, that's evil."

And so—this is the greatest source of his personal discomfort—Frank finds himself giving women extensive theological training while at the same time, as both professor and priest, he remains a central part of the very institutional structure which refuses them the chance to use it fully:

> Women in the church are suffering so much—to hear their pain is just agonizing. It makes you question whether you want to be part of an institution that is really so blind. Do you want to continue educating these women and creating the problem for them? On the other hand, what's the alternative? Not give them any kind of sophisticated perspective for thinking about what's going on in their lives? It's a real painful thing. I don't have it worked out. I'm thoroughly convinced that women have to be dealt with honestly; they have to be ordained. This is ridiculous; it's very much like the blacks are treated in South Africa. Most recently, I saw the movie *Cry Freedom,* and the next day I had one of these women coming in and telling me her story. It was the same kind of thing. You like to think of yourself as not being part of an institution that would do that to people. You don't see yourself as that kind of a person. Boy, that's very painful.

Frank has several strategies for easing his discomfort. He makes known in class his liberal positions on a wide range of church issues, including birth control and the ordination of women: "People certainly know where I stand on everything in the church; that's part of why I continue to teach. Maybe it's whistling in the dark or a rationalization. But teaching here, you have a hell of a lot of influence." He challenges his students—"I question them, I push them hard to think"—and is "very vocal" on issues in faculty meetings. He speaks out in forums outside the seminary as well, in sermons and in programs for engaged couples, not so much to advertise his stance as to develop a sensitivity in his listeners which he finds lacking in official church positions.

Overall, he tries to subsume his frustration within the post–Vatican II conviction that the church community is "bigger than the pope and the bishops. We're part of something that has an integrity about it, and a vision, even though particular institutional ramifications can be very distorted and highly dysfunctional." In this regard, at least, he expands rather than localizes his sense of church in order to survive in it.

The larger church he is willing to belong to is a church *somehow* still anchored in and validated by the ideals of pastoral care and community even when it often violates those ideals in its concrete behavior. The "somehow" by which spiritual ideals and institutional practice are felt to conjoin in spite of all appearances is precisely the point where his faith is called into play; consistent with their horizontal spirituality, the mystery which perplexes my classmates is not the existence or nature of God but the workings of His church. That "somehow" is also the point where outsiders like myself are most likely to affirm their skepticism— unless they admit, as Frank forced me to, that I make the same leap of faith in regard to my own institution.

Perhaps most important, although the church as institution is a constant source of grief to him, his ideal of "church" remains very much alive. It becomes real in those fleeting but intense experiences of personal closeness and communal sharing which so many of my classmates place at the center of their ministry. Frank was able to remember one such moment the two of us, political differences notwithstanding, had shared in the seminary; I remembered it too:

> The other day, when I saw you outside the building, I couldn't help but think of a crazy Saturday night—we were setting tables, we were waiters—when we had to do the dishes real quickly. You and I were singing all the songs from one of the musicals [*Music Man,* as I recall] as we were setting up tables. We were running from table to table singing at the top of our lungs. I saw you and I thought, "My God, that was twenty-five or thirty years ago." It was as clear to me as if it happened last week.
>
> There's something about that. It's very adolescent, but there's a certain free spirit about it that's the best of the boarding school. That kind of experience where you can feel a closeness to people: you studied with these guys, you spent time with them, you know them, and you can have that kind of fun with them. I feel that if anybody in the class came to me and needed help, I would do whatever I could. And not feel "Well, this is an obligation," but feel like "Damn it, gotta help the guy if you can."
>
> I would say, that's experience of church at its best. Church is that kind of community where that's fostered, where people can live with that kind of trust. Now there was a lot of it that I think was shit. But it was almost incidental—even the rules and the ridiculous education—to what really happened. The relationships: that was church.

The evident contrast, in the seminary, between the positive experience of one another and the negative experience of the rules—the genuine sense of community in the face of pervasive institutional obstacles to any form of intimacy—sowed the seed, for him and for many others, of an operating distinction between institution and spirit, institution and genuine church. That distinction continues to depress many in our class when they focus on "institution" and its tendencies; but it buoys them up when they focus on the semi-independent possibilities of spirit.

When I described to Frank my own most satisfying moments in the classroom, when, occasionally, immersion in the here and now of the material connects me to the students and them to one another in a way that makes everyone in the room feel intensely alive—and when, not coincidentally, for a time all my reservations about the university evaporate—I told him that these were the closest things I knew to spiritual experience. He went further: these too were "church," he felt.

His comments gratified me. It was while talking to Frank that I realized just how much my classmates' judgments mattered to me; they came to represent the church's standards to me, standards I thought I had dismissed long ago as irrelevant. It also became clear that mine mattered to them: I think I embodied the standards of secular society to them, the standards to which they are now more responsive than they once expected to be. Our conversations, highly personal though they often were, thus took on a slightly allegorical quality: the spiritual realm meets the worldly realm (me?), the embodiments of the church meet the (tenured) embodiment of the state, the two now looking for confirmation—and "integration"—rather than confrontation. Quite apart from our lingering personal ties, the fact that we so often were able to find common ground had a resonance of its own.

When I asked Frank if he ever had such experiences of church *in* church, he said yes; but the baptism he then chose to describe did not in fact take place in church and had less to do with the official ceremony than with a moment of intense personal connection:

> Yeah. With one of my CYO kids, this is two or three years ago now. She married a Jewish man, so they were married under a canopy. But she wanted her babies baptized. He agreed to it because he was really more Jewish by culture than by practice. I came to his house; I didn't want him to feel that we were imposing this on him without respecting him and seeing what he felt. The baby was a month old. I knew the mother when she was in second grade, and she's now twenty-five years old.
>
> She gave me her baby and she had me feed her. I was holding this little gal. After she drank, I thought, "Wow, I have to burp her." I put the diaper on my shoulder and I patted her on the bottom, and she started trying to burp, but of course she fell asleep. I felt the breath of her, her breath on my neck, and that was a transcendent moment. I really felt the presence of God as Creator, and how precious life was. I felt very connected to them and to their life. Here's a kid that I feel I've known for a long time. I know her family, have been part of their life in some good times and some shitty times, struggling with a lot of stuff. Just to be there and to hold that baby felt like a precious thing, because I don't get a chance to do that very often. It was a transcendent moment.

By promoting such moments to the status of pure or real "church," Frank implicitly relegates "merely" institutional events or characteristics to secondary status; such events have, in the scholastic terms which still lurk in our memory, less "act"—less being, less reality. It is this accomplishment, I think, which sets him and many other continuing priests apart, however narrowly, from those former priests for whom the institution constituted the unavoidably real, the unavoidably oppressive. Within Frank's immediate pastoral sphere, he can have effect. There, only his people are real; the institution is but a shadowy presence:

> I really do believe in community, but in a very concrete way. That means *these* people at *this* time. So on one level, the tension over women or certain teachings of the church—if you asked me about them I would tell you I don't agree with them and give you a rationale for dissent in the church. But it doesn't always affect me in the day-to-day, because I'm concerned with this person in the here and now. How can I help her? Or how can I help him? What can I do? That's true in parish ministry, and even here—although it's more difficult here because it's a more public situation. I don't give a damn what the big shots are saying, because I ignore it. When push comes to shove, that's not really what I'm dealing with. I'm dealing with these people now. That's the way I live with it. Now maybe that's . . . it's not a highly congruent way of doing it.

The incongruity to which Frank alludes is indeed implicit in my classmates' characteristic reduction of the church to their own enclave of activity within it; for in one sense, this refusal to acknowledge connection with the church "out there" violates their cherished value of integrating on as many levels as possible. And Frank's pastoral antidotes to institutional control have the further disadvantage of intensifying his anger at such control, just as the antidotes to personal loneliness taken by classmates such as Tod (close friendships with the laity, for instance, especially with women) often end up intensifying their alienation from the institutional church. For it is precisely in those direct, personal encounters that he sees the abstractions of power-based theology and insensitive policy becoming immediate burdens and sources of intense pain for the people to whom he ministers.

And yet this strategy is integrative in the most basic and difficult of ways: for just as Herbert draws on his own pain to motivate his search for new ways to be a priest, Frank draws willingly on his own distress as a priest to motivate his central activities as a priest: he is trying to be the kind of priest who does not "represent" the church at its worst, but the church as he would like it to be.

In the midst of all his ambivalence, Frank remains honest about a fundamental paradox of his priesthood: that in spite of his distress at the institutional church, he continues to need it. For it is the church which provides him with the authority to preach, to teach, and to counsel; it is because he is a priest that he was invited to baptize his close friend's baby. In effect, the institution enables him to do the things which he feels are essential to counteracting institutional insensitivity. It is a paradox, he reminded me, that I also experience inside the university:

> Yeah—you're part of the institution. On the other hand, how the hell are you going to teach American literature? You're not going to sit on the street corner and say, "Let me tell you about black literature in America." There's no forum there. So it's really a difficult thing. I think it's true of the gospel too. So you say, "Well, I have to do it." The problem is not to compromise so much that the ideal is lost, but not to be so removed from the institution that you can't use it. That's a real sticky thing.

Frank's awareness that the church blocks what it facilitates and facilitates what it blocks constitutes the abiding dilemma of his priesthood. In his final assessment, he was willing to pose what seems to me the central issue for him, for his priest classmates, and for many of us who are uncomfortable in our various institutions: "Does it come to the point where you say that what you believe the church is and what it means to be a Christian is incongruent with the actions of the institution? And you have to say that you can no longer be part of or identify with it?" The answer for some of the former priests in our class has been yes, it does come to that point. At the time I talked with him, the answer for Frank was—no, not quite, not yet. He is walking a fine line, but hasn't lost his balance yet.

Listening to Frank, I found myself wondering, however, whether he and I have not demonstrated a lack of imagination: are we really as dependent on our institutions—as locked inside of them in order to act on what we value—as we tend to think, or do we continue to *think* that we need them as a way of avoiding the leap into a less structured world? I began to wonder: aren't there forms of preaching and teaching out there somewhere, perhaps not called by those names, which we will never discover until we start actively looking for them? It is one thing to acknowledge the need for institutions; it is another, I fear, to accept their versions of our central activities as the only versions available. I left the church for the university, a relatively small leap in terms of structure; leaving the university for something less defined would be for me a much larger, much more terrifying leap—and perhaps more exhilarating.

The Flexible Priest: Self and Church, Self and Other

Father Ralph greeted me at the rectory door in the same soft-spoken voice I remembered from the seminary. There he had been all but invisible. He was quiet and gentle, seemed to obey the rules without murmur, hung around with similarly unobtrusive classmates, wasn't very involved with school activities; as far as I was concerned, man about campus that I was, he didn't take up space. The only things I remember clearly about him were that he tended to walk, monklike, with his hands folded in front of his stomach—he seemed devout even in the classroom—and that he had an enigmatic smile. Until I interviewed him, I could never figure out how the smile, which he still has, fitted.

For our conversation made it clear that all his life—in his family, as the youngest of six children with parents who cared, he insists, but did not pay much evident attention; in the seminary; and now in the priesthood—Ralph has worked to carve out a satisfying if unobtrusive psychic realm for himself. In fact, no one in my class inhabits a "separate space" more self-consciously and consistently than he does. Precisely because he has done so without many people noticing, no one raises more suggestively than he the issue of just what kind of relationship to the church such a space represents. And by extension, no one reveals more characteristically than he the issues of self and institution, self and other which lie at the heart of my classmates' desire to find a livable priesthood.

Ralph, it turns out, is less docile than he seemed; he has simply developed the ability to get around things without disturbing them or being disturbed by them. In the seminary, he says, he "broke rules but nobody knew it. A lot of little junk, sneaky quiet—listening to my radio, having visitors on a Sunday without permission." In his first parish, "my little revolt" against a pastor whom he describes as "mentally retired" involved small gestures such as "not wearing the cassock, not putting the veil over the chalice." Such actions were "my own way of trying to react to authority" without declaring open warfare. In his present parish, he will alter phrases in the liturgy from one day to the next even though official policy mandates against it. He does such things, he says, "not in defiance," but simply because "with this English liturgy you just can't do the same thing all the time and expect it to have any interest."

In relation to many of the church's central stands—divorce, abortion, birth control—he says, "I don't know if there would be any advantage to saying something from the pulpit which would be a radical deviation from the official [position]." Yet he also says, "I will definitely say something in a different light when I talk one on one; the compassion side is there more so when you have one on one."

With the exception of his current agitation for higher salaries, Ralph's acts of assertion were not and are not intended to transform an institution which seems beyond his reach, but rather to provide him and his parishioners with a relative degree of personal dignity and psychological independence. And because he does not define himself as a reformer, much less a rebel, he suffers neither alienation nor frustration from agitating in vain. If his small acts of independence are not going to change the church, neither is the church going to change him.

He chooses to remain a priest, even though—or rather because—he is convinced that he does not have to; he defines himself as free to leave in order to make peace with his decision to stay. He, for one, is "working within the system": he takes what the church allows him and then goes a little further with it, all the while secure in the conviction that, in his words, "flexibility is the name of the game" that both he and the church are engaged in.

I found myself particularly fascinated—and troubled—by Ralph's conviction that getting around things, within limits, is sanctioned behavior within the church. My uneasiness is probably the reason I did something that puzzled me at the time. Over lunch, after Ralph and I had talked all morning, one of his young associates asked about my findings; without further provocation, I said that yes indeed, a good number of my classmates were leading less than celibate lives. I would not have said that if Ralph had been among that number; but something in me enjoyed his discomfort.

For Ralph has carried from the seminary into the priesthood an institutional message which I never picked up but which has been the key to survival for many in his class: The institutional church can be strict, he suggests, it can be rigid—but don't take these strictures too seriously; the institution is the bad cop in part so that you can be the good cop. But where was I when that message was sent? Who sent it? Was "how to get around things," in the words of Father Rupert, really the crucial institutional subtext to which my own obsession with the text itself blinded me? How was it that I attended a legalistic seminary while my classmates were getting secret messages from a more tolerant church? Did I miss the real story by being tone-deaf? Are these guys really involved, for all their ostensible distance, in a subtle and satisfying dance with the church—sometimes together, sometimes apart, but all in tune with the same music which I never heard?

Or is this "getting around things" a new, unsanctioned story they are writing on their own against the grain of an institution which has no intention of tolerating, much less encouraging, their independence or their creativity? If so, aren't they fooling themselves, defining the church as collusive to avoid confronting the fact that they and their partner are incompatible? And how does flexible behavior, the willingness, for instance, to say a repugnant thing in public—even if in order to be able to say something else in private—avoid becoming, as Roy Winston put it, "flexibility of ethics"?

On the other hand, isn't it also true, as Saul Alinsky said somewhere, that "he who fears corruption fears life"? Even if flexibility is a moral risk, isn't it perhaps a useful risk, preferable at least to the purer but potentially rigid, absolutist stance of flat-out rejection of the offending organization, a rejection which runs its own risk of abandoning satisfying, worthwhile work in the interests of avoiding the moral complexities of affiliation?

Even if the territory Ralph has staked out has its ambiguities, one particular facet of his tendency toward the middle ground reveals his characteristic balance in its best light. I am referring to his ongoing mediation between the traditional, service-oriented definition of priesthood and my classmates' more contemporary focus on self-fulfillment.

Typical of Ralph's local focus, when he reached a point ten years into his priesthood where he was not sure he wanted to continue, he found himself tormented not by the large issue of celibacy, a policy of the "universal" church about which he recognizes that he could do nothing, but by the cumulative drain of attending to others so consistently that he had little energy left for his own needs. These demands constituted an area which he *could* allow himself to reconsider "within the system":

> I was asking myself, "Is this all worth it?" You run. You run. You listen. You listen. I was living through expectations and starting to fight them. Father should always be in the rectory. Father should always answer the phone. I was a slave to the phone. It's like you're getting fed up with taking care of other people's problems. I wasn't letting anybody take care of mine. I was supposed to be a priest all the time.

Ralph came close to leaving; he even want to the bank to have "Reverend" removed from his checks. Yet he managed to get through this period—not by trying to ascertain the will of God, however, that traditional, elusive touchstone to which few of my classmates now claim or seek direct access, but by a form of emotional cost/benefit analysis: he balanced his personal frustrations against the human satisfactions of the priesthood:

> I saw the quality of things that had happened and I said, "Hey, I've been a part of that"—the development of programs and individuals. Then I started to say, "I don't know that I could be happy working from nine to five. I'm so used to—not a complex life—but the variety. No two days are the same. I don't know if I could handle myself in a routine: punch in a clock no matter what time it might be."

Partly as a result of advice from a few priest friends—Ralph has been fortunate enough to find several and has worked hard to stay in contact with them—he began at this time to factor in his own desires more openly, giving himself permission, as the therapists say, to weigh his needs against the demands of the laity, allowing himself to insist, in hard-won language acquired from a younger generation: "I deserve it." He came to accept—to embrace, even—a working distinction between his person and his role as priest. "You're first a human being. I've come to live with that. Never mind perfection. I'll never satisfy everybody's needs." Now, he says, at the end of the day, "I just leave. Generally. I don't worry about there not being someone in the rectory if we're gone."

> You get reasonable. We have this call-forwarding business here. I found that evenings are very little to worry about. In the past church I think I said, "What if somebody says they're dying?" What am I going to do? I'm not a doctor. You can be in the house twenty-three hours and forty-five minutes and you took a fifteen-minute walk—three people could die. And they call during that time. Big deal. So am I a bad priest because of it? That may have concerned me in early years, but it doesn't anymore.

To Ralph's present perspective, priests deserve more money and have a right to agitate for it; he deserves his days off and he will take them. "You don't give me this," he told one of his pastors, "I have a right to it." His unprovoked insistence on these rights during our conversation, however, suggests that he is conducting an ongoing argument, not so much with external authority but with the part of himself which, by his own description, originated in the "old church."

Or to put it differently: for Ralph, the self has fought its way out from hiding—no small accomplishment for those of us with strong roots in the church's long tradition of self-abnegation. Yet the self has by no means taken over. Ralph is now willing to seek what he "deserves"—or more precisely, to articulate needs and rights which he once fought for more covertly, less self-consciously. Yet he just as emphatically rejects the self-absorption of the "me generation"; he often describes his own assertive actions without using the first-person pronoun—"went to the personnel board, argued with them"—and, with a defensive energy suggesting his awareness that even relative selflessness now cuts against the cultural grain, he insists, withal, on the continuing centrality of service:

> I don't want to say that my life is just my own. I believe that, even in the days of "I've got to be me." I think I was there for a while. But I much more believe that my life is not just for myself. That others have an interest in it, have a responsibility to it just as I have a responsibility to their lives.

Ralph invoked the Jonah story more than once in our conversation: "Good old Jonah. 'No way!' he says. And yet he ends up going through all these things even as he was resisting." His fondness for that story is suggestive of his basic stance: he sympathizes with Jonah's defiance, his bristling at God's "control"; yet at the same time he has come to see the wisdom of accepting the existence of a bigger picture than he has access to at any one moment. For Ralph, the Jonah story has been played out through a series of conflicts with the diocesan personnel board, which has consistently assigned him to parishes he had specifically asked to avoid. His retrospective awareness that these assignments have turned out surprisingly well has led him to the reluctant conviction that sometimes he should just "shut up and listen a little more."

That conviction is constantly at odds, however, with his hard-won, now-cherished sense that his own needs are valid, his own instincts reliable. He will not give up his right to speak—if only, at times, to himself; he chooses to continue in the priesthood while insisting that he is free to leave it without guilt; he continues his affiliation with the church while refusing to feel totally defined by it. Like Jonah's, his life is an ongoing, often tense negotiation with a "higher" authority which is sometimes external, sometimes internalized. It is also—for much of our generation, well beyond my class—an ongoing negotiation between the newly validated "self" and the still-valid "other."

When I told Ralph that one of his classmates had called him a "model priest," he laughed and said, "Do you know what a model is? A small imitation of the real thing." I am not quite sure what my classmate meant—his was a casual reference by way of urging that I interview a good priest—but I know how I would use the term in regard to him: Ralph offers a working model for living with the tension—a tension increasingly acknowledged in other areas as well, especially marriage—between service and self-fulfillment.

It also struck me in talking to him that this is not a bad tension to have to negotiate. For Ralph makes it clear that both service/duty and self-fulfillment can be positive forces, especially when they do balance one another, keeping service from becoming self-denial and fulfillment from becoming indulgence. The two ideals, in tandem and yet distinct—like Ralph's duet with the church itself—form the particular space within which he can, and does, operate admirably "within the system."

* * *

Finding ways to work—genuinely to work—within awkward, often uncongenial institutions is, of course, a more modest success than my classmates aimed at when they saw themselves as "an army of youth flying the standards of truth, fighting for Christ the Lord"; when they flew their kites during their final retreat before ordination; when they marched to ordination singing, "Give God your glory, glory"; when they drove into their first parishes and said, as Hans Ziegler did, "I'm going to save all these people." My classmates have not saved the world, and I cannot help but share some of the sadness that mutes their satisfaction at finding ways to keep on keeping on.

Who sets out to be a minor regional novelist, a middle manager, or a utility infielder, after all? Who aims at a workable marriage? And what newly ordained priest—especially what 1960s priest—would be content with the modest prospect of influencing a few people here and there, of carving out a space where he can experience occasional moments of transcendence, of negotiating tolerable tradeoffs among personal need, localized activity, and institutional demands?

Not that there is anything inherently wrong with that achievement. Daniel Levinson argues that in our middle years, it is often necessary and healthy to go through a process of "de-illusionment" whereby we let go of the unrealistic goals we had set for ourselves in our youth, reassess our abilities and aims, and learn to enjoy what we can do—or to turn to what we can do—instead of becoming permanently depressed over what we cannot do. At the same time, he reminds us that our earlier, (usually) illusory goals were often useful: without an exaggerated sense of what we might become or what we might attain, most of us would not achieve even the limited goals we do reach.[5]

Yet if, as Levinson suggests, living with the gap between exaggerated expectations and attainable achievements defines the normal course of events, it may also be true that our generation of self-defined saviors has to work especially hard to maintain the distinction between letting go of illusion and losing sight of ideals.

Enclave as Model: The Team Parish, a Marriage of Choice

Although most of my classmates have opted to marshal their forces inside a semi-enclosed space, hoping for a ripple effect but not concentrating on it, a few of them are more overtly activist, more inclined to envision and shape their local efforts as a model of and prod to larger changes. They too have sought refuge, but they end up less protected than their classmates, for their reformist actions, instead of buffering them, inevitably bring them into direct, abrasive contact with institutional irritations. Yet overall, they struck me as among the most energized priests in the class, for their approach also keeps them more directly connected to their original vision of a church that can be moved and to their 1960s sense of themselves as men who would contribute to its movement.

Father Spencer is one of the most gregarious priests in my class. I remember him from the seminary as a witty, engaging talker who could usually be found in a card game or in an animated conversation outside the dining hall, jabbing with a cigarette that had little chance to reach his mouth. Spencer liked contact; he liked to get along with people, and he was good at it. I once went on a week's vacation to northern Wisconsin with him and several other classmates; it was Spencer who told the most jokes, wanted to stay up the latest, always proposed going to one more movie or seeing one more new place; he scorned inertia, was always on the move. He also, even then, loved to eat and had the body to prove it; but he put out as much energy as he took in.

Spencer was very friendly on the phone (I was nervous every time I called one of these men; I may not have been asking for a date, but I feared a comparable rejection) and again when he showed up at the seminary for his interview. He was so ebullient, in fact, so charged up and eager to get the next phrase out, that he rarely finished the previous one; my typist quite understandably garbled his transcription so badly that I had to go back and piece it together myself.

Spencer is a man who wants energy around him as well as within him; his desire for a personally satisfying priesthood has driven him to try to reshape at least part of the institutional church. He too is angry, he says, "at a lot of what goes on in the church now"; he is especially frustrated over the fact that the church is operating on "different levels" which don't intersect: "the old guard in Rome, various 'vice-presidents,' the bishops here in town, managers like us who are in the field doing the grunt work, and the few [lay] folks who get involved." On both the personal and the institutional level, Spencer has made it his goal "to integrate, to pull some pieces together" instead of drawing apart.

He is as interested in self-fulfillment as his classmates are and has attended a number of growth-centered workshops to that end. Yet he has discovered through his own painful experience that he cannot achieve what he values most in "my job, my ministry, and what I need personally" without trying to combine personal growth and institutional change.

Spencer insists that as a priest he needs "something more" than superficial camaraderie. Thus a stormy relationship several years ago with an assigned rectory mate, a relationship which involved deep temperamental differences akin to traditional gender distinctions, was particularly painful to him. It drove him to a series of therapy sessions in the desperate attempt to "make it work" and produced frustration and confusion when nothing helped. Ultimately, Spencer knew the pain of divorce—a pain rendered even more disturbing for him, I suspect, by our class's lingering conviction that commitment itself should be enough to make the rough ways smooth, that force of will and spirit should be sufficient to bring emotion into its proper, subsidiary place:

> The lowest [experience] was when there was another guy at the parish I worked at where nothing I would do was right. Nothing! I think I'm a pretty sanguine personality but I couldn't cope with that. I was more a people person than he was. He was more the type, if anything went wrong in this room he could take care of it. He had tools, it was one of the ways he worked out his life. Things got too tight, he'd go redo that lamp and all the wiring from here to that damn door. Then he worked on the thermostat, then he was on the roof doing something up there. We're in the city, I mean right in town, and he was screaming at the top of his voice from the top of the fucking building. I asked my-

self, What is going on?

So I checked up with one of the psychologists here in town and had six or eight sessions and worked things through. It was unbelievable shit that was going on. I just couldn't figure it out. I knew that he had had a history of stuff, and I'm not saying that I wasn't at fault in a lot of it. I thought I could deal with it, but I couldn't. It was a lot of hurt, and I guess the biggest part of the hurt, besides myself, was the parish community—sides being taken and all that kind of stuff. Holy shit. That was the lowest.

You don't have sexual involvement; you don't have that one-on-one. But it was the closest thing that I have personally experienced to a divorce situation. With just a whole fucking relationship part, trying to put some pieces in any kind of order. And nothing worked.

One unsatisfying relationship did not destroy Spencer's desire for intimacy, however; it was rather "a growing experience" which moved him to work even harder to achieve closeness. Hence he has involved himself for the last five years in an experimental team-pastor approach—a marriage of choice—in which he and two other priest friends (one of them a classmate), along with six lay women, collaborate in the running of three parishes.

Having "one team made up of nine people" makes possible administrative cooperation, shared financial responsibility, and a blurring of clergy/lay distinctions; it also allows the three priests to live in what Spencer calls a "formational community" characterized by frequent personal contact. Their dinners together are especially important; they see these as family time and are irritated at disruptions. "The other night," Spencer lamented, "we had just sat down to a little dinner, and shit, the phone rang about six times." Communal dinners also immerse them in many of the tradeoffs and ongoing negotiations of married life: "Okay, who's here on Monday and who's going to make dinner? You don't put the chicken in at ten to six when you're eating at six. . . . " The effort is worth it, Spencer feels, because "you have to have some community"; he also knows from his experience that "you are not necessarily going to get it" simply as a matter of course.

He and his colleagues aim partly to foster close relationships, partly to move beyond the solitary exercise of authority which many of my classmates have come to distrust. "I don't have this heavy drive to be the boss," Spencer says. Perhaps most significant, however, they hope "to make some significant changes in the way we run our church in Milwaukee." Thus the desire to satisfy these interlocking needs of personal fulfillment and institutional change—or, more to the point, the willingness to see them as interrelated in the first place—requires that they do not accept as inevitable the way the church is run now. Their desire for a less atomized, less lonely priesthood, in short, all but forces them to create a new model of how a parish might work, a model which would be "radically different from the way we've experienced church here in Milwaukee for at least the last hundred years."

Ironically, however, because this model is so different, many of the laity see it as an impersonal move away from them and a threat to their traditional definition of what a parish should be. The laity, Spencer admits, "want to know who the pastor is"; they feel abandoned because "they can't come over at 5 P.M. today and find somebody at home at each place." Furthermore, in two of the parishes, their sense of primacy is threatened: "I thought you guys were going to live at *our* rectory." In general, the laity fear that each parish—whose individual histories and identities were, Spencer admits, the backbone of the immigrant church for decades—may get swallowed up into a faceless conglomerate.

To Spencer, resistance to what he sees as an integrating move reveals that in this case too the priests and the laity are "institutionally at different levels"; he admits to "anger and frustration that we aren't somehow in sync." Ultimately, however, he is more worried about the tenuous institutional status of this experiment than he is about what he hopes will be the short-term resistance of his parishioners. For although the archdiocese has been supportive of the team concept so far, it has given Spencer no guarantee about later assignments. When one of the three priests moves elsewhere, he fears, the other two may be handed a replacement who says, "This is my turf, you son of a bitch; keep your hands off!"

So on the one hand, this experiment has been, in Spencer's words, "life-giving"; it renders the potentially lonely priesthood much more intimate and the bureaucratic church more flexible. It is not surprising that Spencer can say with conviction, "I've never been as happy as I am now." For men who consider "wholeness" one of their highest values, after all, energy directed toward integrating personal needs with institutional change is particularly satisfying. In any case, whatever the long-term prospects for the church, Spencer's reformist involvement works even from a personalist point of view, keeping his own energy affirmative rather than negative: "Who wants," he says, "to be an angry old man?"

On the other hand, paradigmatically for the more activist members of my class, the very engagement with reform which keeps alive Spencer's vision of a new church underscores and keeps always present to him his irritation at the persistence of the old church. He has not created a buffer zone; he cannot claim, as Father Eric does, that "they can't touch me." For Spencer is painfully aware that the fulfillment of his personal needs as well as his reformist hopes depends upon the uncertain cooperation of an institution whose impersonality and inflexibility drove him to action in the first place. His dissatisfaction with the church as it is drives him outward toward it rather than within in flight from it; for him, for activists in general, the paradoxical price of genuine happiness is persistent discontent.

I get a Christmas card from Spencer every year now, sometimes an Easter card as well. He addresses them to Ivona as well as to me, although he has never met her. I don't see this as an empty formality. He knows that she is emphatically part of my story, and his desire to keep in touch with me—to personalize as much of his world as possible—extends to her as well.

Alternative Structures: Model or Mistress?

As one of the bluntest critics of the institutional church in his class, Father Alex would seem to be a prime candidate for alienation. He openly and assertively resents the hierarchical church for dictating to priests instead of modeling collaborative behavior for them, for interfering with parish efforts instead of supporting them, for controlling priests through a paternalistic system of salary and residence which breeds dependence and inertia, for failing to offer acknowledgment and advancement to priests in proportion to their training and skill. "To me," he insists, "the priesthood is something that's personal"; hence his overriding frustration with what he sees as the church's pervasive insensitivity to the personal needs of priests.

Alex's gruff demeanor reflects this frustration. He is not, nor was he in the seminary, an outgoing or affable person; he was part of the same aggressively political group that Father Frank belonged to, and he could be brusque even then in his dismissal of the opposition. He agreed to talk with me, but his manner on the phone was curt, conveying none of the immediate warmth that characterized Spencer, none of Ralph's mildness. He met me at the door to his apartment as if I were a bill collector, smoked heavily during our conversation, and was evidently relieved when our taping session was over. He is respected by his classmates but categorized by some as a malcontent; if the number of times it was described to me is any indication, his public explosion over priestly salary policy at a diocesan-wide clergy meeting was already legend. Alex is bearish; he comes across as a force to be reckoned with, carefully.

And yet Alex did not stint with his time or energy—nor, ultimately, in his degree of openness—in discussing his priesthood with me. He eventually warmed to our conversation, breaking out into a wide grin a number of times as he described his pet projects both priestly and personal. After I turned the recorder off, he invited me back to dabble in his very extensive collection of cowboy movies; I think he meant it. He has an aggressive side, to be sure; but his aggression stems as much from earned outrage at specific issues as from inherent temperament. And more to the point, like Spencer, he seems less constrained by the institutional church and more excited by what he is doing than most of his classmates. He has at least as much positive energy as negative.

Alex makes a clear distinction between things he cannot change—the celibacy laws, for instance—and what he can; and his sense of what he can change is not limited to himself, although it starts there. What he cannot change, he doesn't fight—although he will complain. As a corollary, however, what he can fight, he does; and the fight keeps him going.

On the personal level, for instance, he is highly assertive in getting his needs met by the church. Incensed at his first pastor—he gave a talk at the parish school and the pastor immediately stood up and contradicted him—he demanded an immediate transfer, and got it. He has moved from parish work to teaching to educational administration, not by diocesan fiat but according to his own requests. So although he complains, as many other classmates do, of the lack of mobility within the priesthood, he has in fact created a considerable degree of it for himself—not upward mobility in terms of salary, but the kind of variety which at least short-circuits the accumulating frustrations of a single, long-term job. In effect, Alex has adapted to his own uses the contemporary, highly secular notion that he must take care of himself because no one is going to do it for him. "I'm part of the church," he acknowledges, "[but] I don't have to look to the church to make me who I am." Instead, he has "ended up taking control of my own life."

In general, then, Alex has traveled farther than most of his classmates from our generation's initial expectation that the church would be an all-provident parent, and so he is less vulnerable than those who still cling to her. Yet his efforts as principal of a Catholic grade school, like his determination to take disadvantaged children with him on his yearly trips to Disney World, make it clear that he is not content to live in self-actualized isolation. His administrative agenda is driven by a desire to personalize and democratize his corner of the church even though—or rather because—the larger church continues to act in an impersonal and authoritarian fashion.

Alex acknowledges that he is a "middle manager"; but because he identifies more with his clientele than with his own organization, he tries hard not to manage them in the way that the church manages him. His school, as he describes it, approaches children on their own level and regards their need for growth as central. He tries to lead the students gently in full knowledge that "it doesn't always go the way I plan. If I don't want the church to dictate to me who I am, I can't do that to anybody else either." In his weekly liturgy with the children, he is likely to ignore the assigned readings and allow them to establish their own theme—for instance, the notion that "I am special." He has question-and-answer sessions during the liturgy because "kids don't listen to homilies," and he uses their own recorded songs instead of prescribed, liturgical music: "I'm not going to not play a record with kids' music on it [just] so we can have the damn organ. That's not child-centered." Convinced that knowledge moves "from the known to the unknown"—an insight he traces back to Aquinas—he draws on the students' own experience whenever possible; he had recently explained the idea of Christ as the Good Shepherd in terms of their visit to a local farm. Overall, without skimping on the formal teaching of religion, he is much more concerned with "creating a Catholic community" in the school.

Similarly, in dealing with staff and parents, he tries to rely more on "person power" rather than "position power." Instead of dictating from the top, he fosters staff development, encourages collaboration, and tries to incorporate his teachers' input into his decisions. Whereas the seminary treated him, he feels, as "immature and noncreative," he tries to encourage imagination and initiative on the part of those with whom he works. To spark a staff discussion of student conflict—and to loosen up an inhibited teacher—he joined her in what turned out to be a raucous role playing of a student argument: "We just let it fly." To establish the "proper atmosphere" in the school, he decorates his office with clowns and begins the first day of teacher orientation in the fall by connecting a laugh machine to the P.A. system.

Alex's project has its underside, however, just as Spencer's does: his school embodies his sense of authentic Catholicism precisely to the extent to which it refuses to mirror the institutional qualities of the church to which it belongs. He can foster the church's ideals, but only by filtering out its typical practices. He is able to integrate his personalist theology and his exercise of power only by acting in ways the larger institution does not.

Thus his efforts and Spencer's not only remind them of the worst side of the church at every step; they also raise the difficult questions which reformist endeavors always raise. Do the appealing, alternate worlds which they have created function as an embryonic church within a church, a patch of yeast within the dough, and thus a source of hope for them and their institution? Or are both merely transitory enclaves, temporary buffer zones offering satisfaction to them and to a fortunate few laity but providing no ultimate defense against the more impersonal church awaiting all of them when they inevitably emerge—are forced to emerge—and look around them?

Or to put it differently, do the team parish and the collaborative school establish a genuinely different model of a priest's relationship to the church, a model which can reinvigorate both priest and institution? Do they offer hope of a redefined marriage to the larger church? Or do they function like a satisfying and stimulating mistress whose ability to gratify merely highlights and intensifies the deficiencies of a flawed but inescapable marriage?

These are, of course, long-term questions, often raised cynically to discourage the short run itself. What keeps long-term uncertainty from overwhelming Spencer and Alex, however, is that the effort itself gratifies their need for immediate personal fulfillment in the here and now. Their efforts suggest that the church's resistance to personalist psychologies may be misdirected; for ironically, the church's best chance for change may lie with just such men who do not think solely in long-range terms, men whose actions reach outward toward a future but whose motives originate in the immediate, highly personal, growth-centered question: Who wants to be an angry old man who never gave it his best shot?

Living with the Pain

Throughout these conversations, I was beset by metaphors. Herbert feels "out of shape" and isn't sure how to get back in; Frank cycles all over the country as if to counter the centripetal force of living at the center of the diocese; the most institutionally bound priest in our class walks with a markedly rigid gait. I noticed myself stumbling around a lot during this period—I blamed my rubber-soled Rockports—as if, indeed, I didn't know where I was going; my groping culminated in smashing my forehead into a glass door leading into the major seminary sacristy. And Father Brent, chronically and incurably ill with skin cancer, has learned, metaphorically as well as literally, to "live with his pain."

Brent always struck me as one of the most devout, aesthetically sensitive members of the class. I recall sitting in chapel once, watching him make his own private stations of the cross; I marveled at his evident but unstudied sense of rapture, a state I never reached. He loved Gregorian chant and church art; he seemed genuinely to enjoy praying, singing, attending mass. He is, by his own description, visual and tactile. His voice rose and fell in the manner of a stage actor when he described his first look at "those gawd-awful thin mattresses and those terrible water-stained curtains" in the minor seminary dormitory; I had no trouble believing what a shock to his sensibilities they were.

Brent is no mere aesthete, however; his voice and manner, even as he undergoes chemotherapy, are as energetic as they are refined. He not only likes direct contact—he *looks* at the person he is talking to, and he touched me on the shoulder several times to register our common ground—but feels strongly that the church should promote it. For he is a man of passionate convictions rather than a mere man of feeling; he seems moved viscerally by what bothers him in the church, and his emotions drive him to act. The office where we talked was half greenhouse, half art museum; but his efforts to counter institutional ugliness have by no means confined themselves to his immediate surroundings or to the realm of taste.

Although the phrase "convert from rigidity" applies to a number of the priests I interviewed, no one exemplifies that conversion more clearly than Brent, and no one has derived his focus more emphatically from that conversion than he. He now considers himself one of the least institutional, most liberal priests in the archdiocese, a view corroborated by his peers. He came to the seminary, however, as one of the most rule-bound members of the class. It was only after an anguished experience of personal revulsion toward seminary rigidity that he began to rethink his own docility and to reshape his sense of morality and spirituality.

Brent has spent much of his priestly life promoting collegiality between priest and laity, men and women in order to break down the traditional hierarchical distinctions that have characterized the institutional church; he is in fact a nationally recognized authority and activist in lay empowerment. He works extensively with parish councils to promote democratic processes; he supports the increased voice of women in the church and once wrote to Rome suggesting that a woman cardinal would be a good idea (he received a "polite" letter in response).

Brent feels that the "tension between spirit and law" characterizes his generation of priests, as it has characterized his own history; he is now convinced that spirit must be primary. He wants the church to rethink its priorities and procedures; in his view, the laity are more ready for this revision than the clergy. "The clergy need to be trained," he says. "The people need to be empowered."

In liturgical matters, for instance, he resists the "imposition of form on people who should be deciding for themselves how they're celebrating. The big criterion for me is, and I invite people to ask themselves, 'Does this energize us into really deeper charity, and if it doesn't, why are we doing it?' " More broadly, his concept of the will of God is not "abstract formulations" but an exploratory process of "looking for the ways in which you bring about the most goodness. Searching the word of God or the traditions or life."

He considers his mission not so much saving souls in the traditional sense but rather "healing and feeding" and promoting community. If established procedures have to be circumvented in the process, so be it. At this point in his life, "I don't do a lot of agonizing about 'Did I get the right permission?' I have the kind of personality that works with authority, but gets around it when he needs to. It's part of who I am."

But his reformist tendencies and his facility at slipping past formal roadblocks did not come easily for someone who entered the seminary at age fourteen in a stance of complete docility:

> I have a very different vision of church now than I had then. When I was a part of the seminary, my understanding was, "That [the rule] was the will of God." I didn't question it an awful lot. I was there with a different mindset, and so that particular discipline, as strange as it may be in retrospect, fit for me. I really felt that I was called to the priesthood. So whatever was part of it, I felt was right. I took it as part of the package. I was more of a judgmental person then. So that people who didn't, who weren't about to, accept this God-given way, that was their problem.

Eventually, Brent began to realize from studying church history that the people who accomplished significant things had been "open to the example of Jesus rather than to the structure." Nonetheless, it required a "traumatic opportunity," in his words, to bring about a radical, internal transformation in him. He sees it now as a "conversion experience" in which Monsignor Schneider, the major seminary rector, unwittingly forced him to see that the abstract mandates of obedience and discipline were not absolutes, that in certain circumstances, other human claims might take precedence—might, in fact, be more spiritual. Brent tells this story with great emotion:

> One of the pivotal experiences was while we were in the seminary, when my mother was so very, very sick and had cancer surgery. My father called, and Monsignor Schneider was very angry [we were not allowed to receive phone calls]. Before I had a chance to get to my father, he called again, and he wanted me to come home, because they had discovered that my mother had another kind of cancer and there was a very strong possibility that she would die. So I went to the rector and he said to me, "You know the rule: if your mother dies, you can go home."
>
> I came out of there, and I am telling you, Ray, to this day I can cry when I think about that. It was a painful experience—it's probably been one of the "Paul getting knocked off the horse" experiences for me. I really began to look at that and say, "This is not the will of God. This is not the will of God." It eventually became more and more a part of my being to begin to look at it a different way. But that was trauma, that was the catalyst for me.
>
> Schneider probably had no other choice. That was, I don't know—consistent to himself. So I don't know what that was for him. I just know what it was for me, and what it meant to me, and continues to mean to me—really, continues to mean to me. I feel it was a conversion experience. I really do. I just went, "God! You know, this can't be right!"
>
> When I went through it, it was terrible, but it has enabled me to have different kinds of appreciations. I don't know how I would ever have them any other way, or if they could come in other ways.

Six years ago, an encounter with the families of two men dying of AIDS gave Brent a chance to act on the "different appreciations" he had

developed, allowing him, in effect, to replay a version of his own experience with the seminary rector from the other end and to use his own
authority as a priest in a far different way than Monsignor Schneider
had used his. His story suggests how far he had traveled since that seminary trauma:

> I read in *Newsweek* magazine an article of a young man who had died
> of AIDS. He had written this letter about how lonely he was. I thought,
> God, this is awful. He died without his family; they didn't want to have
> anything to do with him. He just died without anyone, really, literally.
> I thought, what an awful thing.
>
> So I called St. Joseph's, because they had a hospice. I said, "Do you
> have anyone there whose family has deserted him?" And the nun said,
> "Well, we have two." I was really not ready for that. I said, "Could I do
> one?" Well, you know sisters, some of them still have that way of saying,
> "We have two." So, well, okay.
>
> Both of them were from out east originally, so their families weren't
> here. They were well enough to go home, but they needed people, so I
> used to go and bathe or get suppers and stuff like that for them. I saw
> them literally dying.
>
> I wanted first of all to see if I couldn't get them reconciled with their
> families. One of them, fortunately, was an immigrant family, and that
> was an easier one for me because it was my background. I went there,
> and they did not come because their pastor had told them that they
> shouldn't, that their son had lived a bad life and he was getting what
> God had said he deserved.
>
> And I said, "Well, I'm going to be really honest and very blunt, but
> that is really bullshit. I mean, this is a son who is dying." You knew
> that they wanted to be there. I said, "You have every right to be there,
> and you should be there." They did come. He died, but he died with
> them.
>
> With the other one I wasn't able to convince them. They were set, and
> they said that he had just brought this on himself.

If many of us left the seminary because of its rigidity, Brent's story
suggests a different response: he stood institutional rigidity on its head
and became an exceptionally undogmatic priest. The seminary's denial
of his human responses produced a priest willing to trust his own responses, a priest whose primary satisfaction now comes from "affirming people in their goodness" instead of laying down laws, in helping
people to "discover things about themselves that they didn't know."
Like Spencer and Alex, he has taken the church's worst tendencies and
used them to shape his own counterprogram: "You know, Catholics are
really good at guilt. And I think I'm really good at helping people get
over guilt" (*laughs*).

The characteristic price for this focus is that it keeps him acutely
aware of the church's inflexible positions. In his post-conversion stance,

however, he is able to be generous even toward the rigidity he now disdains. In his view, accepting the church's weaknesses is the necessary flip side of encouraging its growth. If he can look at himself and focus on his potential instead of his failings, he can do the same for the church:

> You constantly evaluate the accommodation that is part of it. When I look upon my relationship to the church, I just see fantastic potential, and I'm constantly seeing it come to life. I also know it's a human situation, and that there's a lot of crap in there. But I see that in myself too. I'm full of a lot of potential. Some of it is just marvelous and some of it is just crap. So that's the way I deal with it.

Seeing the institutional side of the church as a reflection of his own residual rigidity is perhaps the key to Brent's ability to remain a priest—and as far as I could see, an extraordinarily happy, unalienated priest; his was, I think, the most striking act of "integration" which I encountered in my conversations. Brent, more evidently than anyone else I talked with, refuses to demonize the institution, refuses to regard even the worst aspects of the church as completely "other." Just as he sees that he gravitated to a legalistic seminary out of his own legalism (don't most of us share traits with the institutions we seek out?), he stays with a flawed church partly because he knows he participates in at least some of its flaws. Thus to him, leaving the church would provide no easy solution; a genuine escape requires more than packing the bags.

Yet although he is still intertwined enough with the church not to leave it, he claims enough distance from it not to depend on church authorities for validation. He remains related to the church in fundamental ways, but not fused with it:

> I don't expect the church to be the experience of perfection. Recently we've gone through this restructuring in my current job. It doesn't necessarily mean that those of us who are here now will be in charge of the new structure. Well, some react by saying, "I must not have done my work right." I just don't believe that—I know I did my work right! It's been really good! I've had failures and I will continue to have failures, but by and large, I have had a lot of success and a lot of affirmation, so I don't look to authority to tell me I did a good job. I don't feel personally betrayed.

Still, it is not easy for Brent to accommodate some of the church's positions. When he cannot, the self-confidence and independence he has developed allow him simply to reaffirm the distinction between himself and the institutional church without changing his own convictions or behavior:

> I need sometimes to fortify myself in reflection to look at official church statements. I feel really good about some of the directions, and then [sometimes] I go, "Aw, it's bullshit." And I have to say, "So, looking at

that context, and looking at where I am, how do we reconcile the two, if we can?" If we can't, I will say that very honestly. I will say, "I have difficulty reconciling that at this point." So I have to continue to live with it.

*   *   *

If I had to choose a single phrase which captures the stance of those priests who most moved me in the course of these four years, it would be their complex willingness "to continue to live with it," however the "it" may vary in outline. I admired several of the former priests, to be sure; but they, like me, had refused to live with it. And by the end of this period, I realized that I had experienced often enough the underside of leaving things which were part of me and important to me not to want to repeat that choice, even though I still feel its lure.

But I did not come to this stance easily, nor did I come to it on my own; in the most basic ways, my classmates have helped me to shape my current—provisional, tentative—sense of an ending, or at least of a direction. For, like Brent, having learned the hard way to trust my own responses, I asked myself, when it finally came time to write, "Who genuinely impressed me the most—and why?" And I realized that it was those men who, in highly complex, reflective ways, despite their ambivalence and in full awareness of the costs and tradeoffs, have decided so far to stay with it and do something about it. And if I admired that in them, what did that leave me to do?

For them, I want to emphasize, living with it does not mean passive acquiescence to the inevitable; it is not an endorsement of the inherent value of suffering or a deferral of satisfaction to the afterlife; living with it is not reducible to endurance. Rather, priests such as Spencer, Alex, and Brent accept an imperfect relationship with the church because they still share a good deal with it on the level of ideals, if not on the level of current behavior and precept. They live with it because affiliation continues to make possible the activities they continue to value—and consequently they value the affiliation itself. They live with an internalized memory of the worst aspects of the church so as to prod themselves to counteraction. They live with it in the hope—though dimmer now, after twenty years of priesthood and the current, overwhelming regressions of the church—that in some way they can still change it, that ways to change it are still worth looking for. They not only live with it, they feel alive because of the ways they live with it.

The desire to participate in larger changes is rooted deeply enough in them, in many of us who identify with the 1960s, that, in conjunction with their traditional need to belong or affiliate, they cannot find contentment in total divorce from an institution which resists change but still offers an arena in which to seek it. Nor can they emulate the entrepreneurial (unmarried) independence of what they therefore see as the "me" generation, a version of which they detect and scorn in younger priests who want to use the church to advance themselves. My classmates and I are, I conclude, still fundamentally a married generation, however we redefine the relationship; in their ongoing emotional involvement with the severed priesthood or rejected church, the former priests I talked with confirm rather than undercut this conclusion. Hence the priests I came to admire live with "it" finally because they know that they will not escape it—or themselves—easily just by changing venues.

By "living with it" in all these ways, they turn the presence, not only around them but often *in them,* of what they feel to be an impersonal, potentially deadening church into something which, in the phrase Brent used to describe his still-vivid memory of his confrontation with the rector, "continues to mean to me—really, continues to mean to me."

I have been teaching African American literature for years, and now, in an entirely different context, I see more clearly than ever one of the reasons I am attracted to it. For the blues are arguably the artistic and emotional basis of most black writing; and the blues are characterized, as Ralph Ellison reminds us in *Shadow and Act,* not solely by the musician's desire for a protected space, a free zone in which to operate—although they can provide that at times—but by the bluesman's willingness to finger the pain of his worst experiences, to keep the pain alive because he needs it to spur his creativity.[6] I have been claiming for years that Ellison is right when, at the end of *Invisible Man,* his narrator says, "Who knows but that, on the lower frequencies, I speak for you?"[7] In many ways, the priests I ended up admiring most are the church's bluesmen, and they speak for many of us: their pain prods their best efforts, and their best efforts keep their pain alive.

9

A Sense of Story

*I*n some ways, this project has not moved my own story forward at all. Quite to the contrary, staying at the seminary on three different occasions, reconnecting with my classmates, and calling up from storage a vocabulary long dormant has done what I was afraid it would do: it has taken me back to my beginnings and reawakened in me some of the less attractive ways in which I was once Catholic.

Over the last few years, for instance, as I walk our family dog on his route of neighborhood lawns, I often find myself reactivating an old fantasy: I imagine that I have died and am facing St. Peter, gowned and bearded, holding a staff—the iconography of this scenario is as outdated as the theology behind it. He tells me that I cannot enter heaven until I count every blade of grass on earth, accurately. If I get it wrong—by one or one billion, it doesn't matter—I will have to begin all over. The world of lawns, golf courses, jungles, prairies, tundras, mountainsides, isolated patches in the midst of deserts, solitary blades poking through God knows where (that's the whole point), opens up its terrifying scope in front of me. I stoop over to begin: one, two, three . . .

I don't remember when I first began entertaining this grim vision, but I know that it was after I entered the seminary and had become exposed to a God who was interested in very fine distinctions, a God who expected His creatures to get things right. To satisfy this God, purgatory could not be something I would passively endure, roasting like a chestnut on an open fire for a few thousand years, but something which I would have to work my way out of; I would have to get something "right"—something very difficult—in order to be worthy to stare for eternity into the face of God, the perfect lover who was also, the fine print insisted, an assiduous accountant, the ultimate IRS man.

I know this scenario is absurd, a parody of judgment which enlightened levels of the church itself—my classmates, for instance—moved beyond long ago, after I was no longer around to register the change. Yet while walking my dog, I do not merely remember it; I enter it—not as a full-fledged believer, to be sure, but with enough energy that it frightens me in a way I have not felt in years. It gets me wondering, "What if . . . ?" How far have I come if I can still feel the force of such a medieval theology? I canceled my subscription years ago, but the issues have started to arrive again.

When I pull back in relief from such visions and consider what I have learned from Father Brent and other classmates, I realize that what I genuinely fear is not so much a rigid God but my own rigidity, a temperamental absolutism which I tried to flee by leaving the seminary, which drove me out of the church when it didn't measure up, out of one pretty good marriage in quest of an ideal marriage, then nearly out of another one as well when it too proved to be complex and human. My problem is not that I haven't gotten it right yet, but that I still insist on getting it right, just right.

To what extent have I deluded myself in the act of consoling myself, seeing the complex side of my partners—the church, my wife, the university—as the "other," hence the unknowable, the opaque, the villain, the not-me causing all of my troubles? I am left wondering to what extent this dichotomized vision of things has prodded me to rail at embodied, external sources of troubles which in fact originated—or at least had common ground—much closer to home. Granted that no partner is perfect, what are the relative advantages of scorn and alienation on the one hand and attempting to stay with it, to look at the long run, to redefine the relationship on the other? "Married couples come in," one of the priests said to me, "and they already have the divorce planned. You'd just like to tell them that if they would keep on making an effort and work through the rough spots, they might really end up with something very good." My classmates, married as they are to the church, are not, after all, totally lacking in insight into the complexities of central relationships.

They want the transcendent moments, to be sure, the moments of concentrated intensity imbued with meaning; if those moments were not available at all, many of them, they insist, would leave. But at the same time, they rely increasingly on the strength of an ongoing story, as when

Herbert is drawn to the long tradition of the church, or when Father Tod acknowledges, "Part of me is just beginning to say, 'So?' We're looking at thousands of years. So, there are difficulties." This is a recent, less eagerly articulated perspective for them, a hard-won, raspier, midlife voice rather than their passionate endorsement of the transcendent; but it has come to play an important role in their survival.

The church has a long history, they now acknowledge, full of failures, betrayals, outrages, to be sure; yet from time to time, at least, the church's spirituality breaks through again, as it did during the Vatican Council. At such moments, akin to bursts of passion in a longtime spouse, they see the church once again at her best, new again. The intensity of the satisfaction they feel at those times carries them through (or has carried most of them through, at least) the bad times, as now, under Pope John Paul II, and gives them hope that the plot will turn again.

It is in this context of the church's long, complex history and of their own extended engagement with it that they continue to find the church an intriguing partner, even in the bad times. Indifference, the conventional wisdom would have it, rather than hatred, is the opposite of love; and the priests I talked with are angry, but not bored, in their central relationship. Their marriage to the church has thrown them into an interesting story, and they haven't lost interest yet.

So if their moments of immediate satisfaction serve as an antidote to the downward pull of an institutional story that at a given moment seems to be going nowhere, their implicit sense of ongoing narrative also serves as an antidote to the downward pull of a depressing moment—or chapter. Those complementary perspectives—youth and midlife making a pact—are the closest thing to a formula matching satisfaction and survival that they have come up with.

My contact with them has fostered a similar perspective in me. Two years into this project, after I had done most of the interviews, Ivona took a scriptwriting course. In order to come to the States and be with me, she had buried her lifetime ambition to be a film director, and the frustration she felt at that loss played no small role in our tensions. Now, after the death of her mother, an intelligent woman who similarly had never found a professional outlet for her energy, Ivona began looking for a way to act on a version of her dream. In search of a plot to turn into a script, she read my transcripts, and they surprised her greatly, transforming her long-time atheist scorn for priests and all things Catholic into at first a sympathetic curiosity, then later a semi-messianic impulse to convey what she had learned to her own chosen audience in her own medium. Seeing her excitement, I saw a part of her that I had not seen for some time.

I became her cultural consultant as well as her editor as she wrote and rewrote several versions of a script that was initially inspired by my transcripts but quickly became her own. We have spent more time working on that script than on any other single shared enterprise (child-rearing aside) in the sixteen years she has been here. Working together has engendered a shared excitement—a shared transcendence—unlike anything we had known together for a long time. We haven't gotten it "fixed" or "right" once and for all (what would that be like?), but I've become less obsessed with that illusory goal, and we have both enjoyed again the movement that follows in the wake of intense effort and engagement. And a good, long-term story is hard to find; I don't want to abandon this one.

Meanwhile, my own rediscovered affinity with my priest classmates has also had the effect of forcing me to acknowledge that I still feel something akin to a priestly urge. I know that I still feel the impulse to save the world, although from what or for what is less certain. I know that I consider "meaning"—how to find or construct it, how to preserve it, what to do in its seeming absence—the central issue which unites students and teachers (and everyone else, for that matter), and that its deflection in the interests of getting on with business is perhaps the major source of discontent for those of us who have been getting on with it for quite some time.

So this project has also reminded me that, like most of the former seminarians I talked with—at least those who were in the seminary long enough for it to take effect—I have kept my connection to my beginnings, my old self, in a positive way as well. The problem for most of us is how to keep that connection alive in the actual, earthly institutions and businesses in which we now operate.

To be sure, most of us—priests, former priests, ex-seminarians—still long for a genuine community driven by ideals, for institutions which would provide both structure and the nurturing embrace, for institutions which would value in fact what they endorse in rhetoric. We feel the residual tug of an imagined Holy Mother, and our awareness that this desire is potentially regressive does not obliterate it.

Yet—this is what I try to accept—some of these institutions (it would be foolish to say "all") can more or less serve. They may not constitute the communities we still long for, they may not value sufficiently what my classmates and I value, and they may not be willing to acknowledge us, to affirm us sufficiently for what we do. Yet many of them—certainly the church and the university—have interesting histories, with occasional glory days that could come again, and those histories are worth engaging, feeling a part of. Moreover, they are our available mediums, and it is not clear that there are alternatives, if by that I mean an institution or channel free of its own institutionality.

That conviction—that "the grass is not greener on the other side of the fence, it just has different brown spots"—hardly constitutes a ringing endorsement or an achievement of peace; it simply suggests that we can, like Father Brent, learn to "live with it." Of course, my classmates remind me that living with it has to mean more than endurance. It means looking for outlets (however muted, secular, and uncertain) for our ineradicable messianic urges, for activities that matter—and to be willing to find some of them outside our institutions even while we stay affiliated.

In my case, that has meant, in the last few years, collaborating on a number of men's weekends, where the energy and openness of the participants have confirmed what my interviews suggested, that no one is without a complicated story and that nearly everyone benefits from telling it to people willing to listen. It has also meant becoming a speaker to business groups on midlife issues, and more recently on the role of stories in the creation and recovery of meaning.

This strategy of looking for less institutionalized outlets, however, far from freeing me, has immersed me more deeply in the basic paradoxes of institutional affiliation. First of all, as it does with the priests in my class, the satisfactions these enclave activities bring end up heightening my dissatisfaction with the institution's usual business. Furthermore, at least in the case of business groups, the mechanism that gives me a chance to talk in noninstitutional language to audiences surprisingly and intensely receptive to issues of meaning—precisely because their own institutions do not address those issues—is itself an institution, the Indiana University Executive Education Program.

Further still, at this point, I see no way to make these activities models of change instead of temporary alternate worlds. The problem with such gatherings—men's groups as well as business groups—is that their energy, like the energy engendered in the classroom, dissipates for lack (ironically, to say the least) of an institutional mooring or structure to keep it alive; they provide occasional transcendence but no narrative. Is it ever possible, my classmates and I wonder (we are surely not alone), to have them both?

Afterword

*O*ne of the driving forces behind this book has been my attempt to address the tension between academic writing and personal voice. Since that tension is shared by many in my profession, it is worthy of some comment here.

Six or seven years ago, I became convinced that I could not write another impersonal, magisterial sentence. I had come to feel that the omniscient voice of academic writing—like the omniscient voice of much nineteenth-century fiction—was a dishonest construct; after all, it is always the author whose ideas lie behind the mask of impersonal authority, so why not admit it and take the heat as well as the credit? I was equally uncomfortable with the rubric of "positionality," whereby contemporary academics label themselves in advance of their argument—"I acknowledge that I am a white, middle-class, heterosexual male"—to suggest that they are fully aware of their own biases before anyone else can attack them on those grounds. That strategy is far more protective than revealing; it aims to ward off vulnerability instead of accepting it as the price of the ticket.

I found myself drawn instead to Emerson's ideal of "man thinking," someone who brings everything in his experience to the questions he addresses and who acknowledges his engagement by speaking openly in his own voice; authority, Emerson realized, is inseparable from vulnerability. The fact that Emerson himself had trouble writing to his own standard—his life stays primarily in his journals, rarely moving directly into his essays—suggests what I can attest to firsthand, that this kind of writing is discomforting.

I could not avoid that discomfort, however, because I knew that I was a long way from detached; I would not have approached my classmates in the first place if I had thought that their stories had nothing to do with me. I also came to realize early on in the process that whatever insight into their lives this book would offer, it would offer because I had first been willing to tell them about my own life: they would not have told me the highly personal things that many of them revealed if I had merely crossed my knees and spent my time adjusting the cassette recorder. I would have felt fraudulent if I had exorcised my own problems from the text while exposing theirs.

I eventually came to realize that the connection between my classmates and myself reflected a larger, central tenet of the entire project: that all human beings are metaphors for one another, that to learn something about oneself is to learn something about others as well, and that to learn something about a seemingly "different" or "other" person or group, without presuming to know everything, is to learn something about the rest of us too. This view as well put me back in Emerson's camp, for Emerson had a writer's essential faith in the power of unexpected comparison to reveal truth—a faith that has served for centuries as the basis of literature.

It would not be worth the energy to assert these traditional claims if they were not under direct attack in the current cultural climate. Scholars as well as activists of various stripes now insist that "otherness" constitutes an all but unbridgeable gap between the observer and the observed, between the self and the world, between language and its seeming points of reference. In reaction against the smug confidence of privileged classes which presume too quickly to speak for others without recognizing their contours, they declare (I oversimplify only slightly) that no one can speak for or make useful statements about anyone else on the other side of the "difference" chasm. To the claim of Ellison's narrator in *Invisible Man* that on some level he speaks for the rest of us, they reply, no, not possible, and woe to him who tries.

By this logic—a political stance assuming an epistemological guise—men and women, gays and straights, blacks and whites, to name but the most obvious putative dichotomies, are assumed to be of such different orders with such different histories that it is impossible, i.e., impolitic, for members of one group (or rather constituency) to claim valid understanding of the other. The complaint is usually registered by a less powerful group in relation to the claims of a more powerful one, but the logic extends both ways. Any difference-bridging claim, the argument goes, constitutes appropriation, colonialism of the mind, the obliteration of diversity, cultural imperialism. Implicitly, this argument attacks the epistemological power of metaphor itself: for how can one side of any comparison open up an understanding of the other side if difference always overrides similarity?

Like so many other aspects of this book, the conviction that differences are not impassable has its roots in my own experience and con-

cerns. For I could never have begun teaching African American literature, nor could I have presumed to write about it, unless I believed that
a white American could come to an understanding, valid on some genuine level, of what African Americans have experienced. Now, in asserting a metaphoric connection between myself and priests, I was once
again discovering a bridgeable gap between me and a putative "other."

I did not start this project assuming that priests were like me, that
learning something about them could tell me something about myself.
Quite the contrary, I too assumed difference and hence first sought
out ex-seminarians as my likely analogues. Over a four-year period,
however, I came to conclude that priests—long considered the ultimate
"other" by believers and skeptics alike—are indeed a good deal like the
rest of us. Only after I came to that conclusion did I began using it as a
starting point to see how far it would take me.

It took me a long way. There are differences between priests and others, to be sure, and I have tried not to scant them here. But why emphasize what for too long has constituted our sole notion of priests, especially when that emphasis has blocked any attempt to find out what they
might in fact be like? The resistance to Andrew Greeley's novels, for instance, suggests not merely a literary judgment but a denial of Greeley's
basic premise of a priest's common humanity. As a culture, we tend to
acknowledge the humanity of priests only when it reflects our own best
side, ourselves stripped of our flaws or failings. We do not readily extend
recognition or acceptance to any complex, ambiguous form of behavior
in them or to any other trait facilely labeled "darker"—i.e., we imagine
them as free of those aspects of human nature from which we would
love to be free, and we get angry when they turn out not to be exempt.

The cultural assumption that priests are fundamentally "other" thus
damages us as much as it damages them; the basic difference we impute
to them does not serve to keep alive our idealism so much as it keeps
alive in us the illusory possibility of a superhuman immunity we can
continue passively to admire or long for. The otherness of the priest has
become a psychic utopia, a realm we can visit and admire that ends
up rendering us discontent with our own grubby terrain but no better
equipped or inclined to till it. It has been my intent to show as much of
their geography as I had access to, in the hopes of showing the considerable extent to which we all dwell in the same country.

Notes

Introduction

1. When relevant, I have tried to respect the distinction between priests in general and my particular priest classmates: members of a specific generation of priests located in one region of the U.S., all of them educated in one seminary with its own culture and history, functioning inside the Milwaukee archdiocese and influenced by the ethos established by its current leader, Archbishop Rembert Weakland. But if I tend to elide "my classmates" with "priests," I do so because, except in a few particulars—most noticeably their generational attitudes—I am convinced they are broadly representative of concerns permeating the American priesthood today.

See, for instance, the 1970 survey of the priesthood reported in Andrew M. Greeley, *The Catholic Priest in the United States: Sociological Investigations* (Washington, D.C.: United States Catholic Conference, 1972), which reveals a considerable discrepancy between official church teachings and the convictions of priests just at the time my classmates were ordained; that study also emphasizes the widespread discontent of associate pastors. See also *A Shepherd's Care: Reflections on the Changing Role of Pastor,* a study written collectively by the Bishops' Committee on Priestly Life and Ministry (Washington, D.C.: United States Catholic Conference, 1987), which touches on issues of collaboration and specialized ministry in the context of parishes altered dramatically by both Vatican II theology and changing demographics among the Catholic population. That same committee's 1988 summary study, "Reflections on the Morale of Priests," published in *Origins* (18, no. 31 [Jan. 12, 1989]: 497–505), points out widespread morale issues among American priests across the full range of age and region.

That all three of these studies were sponsored by the National Conference of Catholic Bishops suggests that the hierarchy are aware, at least on the level of sociology and statistics, of some of the central concerns which surface individually and personally among my classmates.

See also Dean R. Hoge, *The Future of Catholic Leadership: Responses to the Priest Shortage* (Kansas City: Sheed and Ward, 1987), and Richard Schoenherr, *The Catholic Priest in the United States: Demographic Investigations* (Madison: University of Wisconsin Press, 1989), both of which analyze the declining number of priests in the U.S. in light of issues which permeate my classmates' comments. Hoge's assertion, in particular, that the problems of the current priesthood are institutional at their source reflects my classmates' consistent, primary refrain.

Furthermore, Douglas T. Hall and Benjamin Schneider, *Organizational Climates and Careers: The Work Lives of Priests* (New York: Seminar Press, 1973), analyzes the uneasy fit between personal growth and institutional structures among priests of my classmates' generation. Their study suggests that to the extent that my classmates are of a particular generation, they reflect that generation well, far beyond the limits of a single midwestern diocese.

The parallels between what I suggest here and what sociologists have found are further evidence that there are deep, widely shared issues which dominate the contemporary American priesthood. What I hope to contribute here are not only some particular discoveries not mentioned in these studies but direct, personal insights into broad trends through the stories of my classmates and my own overall analytic narrative. I try to show how these issues have developed and how they fit together into something like a big picture.

2. The Haven of the Seminary

1. Although the twelve-year history of St. Francis Seminary which I sketch out in this chapter is derived primarily from the comments of my classmates and my own experience, the following sources helped me place these reflections in a larger context of seminary history both local and national: Rt. Rev. Monsignor Peter Leo Johnson, D.D., *Halcyon Days: Story of St. Francis Seminary, Milwaukee, 1856–1956* (Milwaukee: Bruce Publishing Co., 1956); Rev. Robert Massey, *St. Francis Seminary 1855–1981* (Milwaukee: Salesianum Alumni Association, 1981); the "St. Francis Seminary Self-Study" of 1962 and 1969; Joseph M. White, *The Diocesan Seminary in the United States: A History from the 1780s to the Present* (Notre Dame: University of Notre Dame Press, 1989). I am also indebted to Rev. Steven Avella, then assistant professor of church history at St. Francis Seminary and currently associate professor of history at Marquette University, for his extremely helpful comments on the history of the American Catholic Church, the Milwaukee archdiocese, and the seminary itself.

2. Pope Pius XI, "Ad Catholici Sacerdotii" (encyclical letter, Dec. 20, 1935); English translation: "The Catholic Priesthood," *Catholic Mind* 34 (Feb. 8, 1936): 41–79, n. 10.

3. *Catholic Encyclopedia* (New York: Robert Appleton Co., 1912), vol. 13, p. 694. The authors could be certain about the seminary's function because they were certain about the priest's function: "He teaches men what they ought to believe and what they ought to do." After Vatican II, both certainties became unmoored. The seeming timelessness of this period of American Catholicism is reflected in the fact that the 1912 encyclopedia remained definitive until the *New Catholic Encyclopedia* was published in 1967.

4. "The Catholic Priesthood," n. 35, quoted in the 1962 self-study.

5. William J. Kerby, *Prophets of the Better Hope* (Philadelphia: Dolphin Press, 1937), p. 19, quoted in White, *The Diocesan Seminary,* p. 339.

6. Cf. "Prologue: the Rise of Seminaries," pp. 1–23, in White, *The Diocesan Seminary.*

7. On July 3, 1907, the Holy Office published a list of sixty-five of Modernism's besetting errors; this was followed on September 8 by the publication of Pius X's encyclical, *Pascendi,* which, among other prescriptions, reasserted the centrality of Thomistic scholasticism in seminary study and the centrality of docility in seminarians themselves.

8. Massey, *St. Francis Seminary,* p. 54.

9. Tod Gitlin, *The Sixties: Years of Hope, Days of Rage* (New York: Bantam Books, 1987), p. 12. The first two sections of Gitlin's study, "Affluence and Undertow" and "The Movement," analyze the complex mix of continuity and repu-

diation which characterizes the relationship between two decades all too often depicted as totally opposed to one another. In that spirit, my references to the fifties and sixties should be taken as shorthand, not allegory.

Interestingly, Gitlin's world of radical SDS politics and the world of 1960s seminarians suggest significant areas of overlap amid their obvious differences. The insistence of 1960s radicals that they saw no older leaders worth following and that therefore they were inventing the world anew in splendid isolation from the past; their frequent gravitation to SDS and other such organizations in flight from dysfunctional homes and in quest of a "primitive fantasy of fusion with a symbolic, all-enfolding mother, the movement, the beloved community itself"; their hope that they would find in that community, as Kenneth Keniston put it, "the qualities of warmth, communion, acceptedness, dependence and intimacy which existed in childhood" (107); their vision of "a world divided between us and them"; their pervasive, enduring conviction—well after the sixties faded— that they were "different, special" (73) in their mission to change the world; their appropriation to their own world of the Beat Generation's insistence on "intensity for its own sake" (48); their "expressed solidarity with people who were systematically excluded" (27) from society's benefits—all these well-publicized aspects of 1960s radicals have, I will suggest in the course of this book, analogues in my generation of seminarians.

10. Cf. especially *Optatum Totius,* the council's decree on priestly formation; *Presbyterorum Ordinis,* its decree on the ministry and life of priests; and *Sacrosanctum Concilium,* the constitution on the sacred liturgy. The first two became primary documents in the St. Francis Seminary self-study of 1969.

11. Monsignor Schuit, quoted by Massey, *St. Francis Seminary,* p. 60.

12. White, *The Diocesan Seminary,* p. 412.

13. Erik H. Erikson, *Identity: Youth and Crisis* (New York: W. W. Norton and Co., 1968), p. 27.

5. The Personal Plight

1. My classmates' comments to this effect are corroborated by Thomas J. Reese, S.J., *Archbishop: Inside the Power Structure of the American Catholic Church* (San Francisco: Harper and Row, 1989), which details Pope John Paul II's successful efforts to create a more orthodox hierarchy in the U.S. and throughout the world. According to one unnamed church official involved in the process of selecting bishops, in the current pope's terms, orthodoxy is defined as loyalty to the pope, adherence to *Humanae Vitae,* the acceptance of priestly celibacy, and the rejection of women's ordination (35). The bishops appointed by John Paul II are older on the average than those appointed by Paul VI (45). Surveys now find that bishops as a whole are even more conservative in attitudes to religion and sexual morality than ordinary clergy over the age of fifty-five (35).

2. Eugene Kennedy, *Tomorrow's Catholics, Yesterday's Church: The Two Cultures of American Catholicism* (New York: Harper and Row, 1988), pp. 3–9 and passim.

3. Andrew M. Greeley with Mary Greeley Durkin, *How to Save the Catholic Church* (New York: Viking, 1984), p. 6.

4. Ibid.

5. In *Seasons of Grace: A History of the Catholic Archdiocese of Detroit* (Detroit: Wayne State University Press, 1990), the most recent extended study of a midwestern diocese, Leslie Tentler has shown in detail that between 1930 and 1940, for instance, assistants bristled at the eighteen-to-twenty-year waiting period preceding their assumption of power. She also shows, however, that Archbishop

Mooney, operating on the standard model of docility and on the realization that assistants had no rights whatsoever under canon law, made it perfectly clear that he expected priests "to get along if it is humanly possible" and above all "never let anything interfere with the work" (387). The political and social tensions of the 1960s exacerbated these longstanding stresses.

6. Hollywood, that supreme register of cultural assumptions, has often made the priest's mandatory silence the linchpin of its plots. Hitchcock's *I Confess* (1954), for instance, has its murderer confess his crime to a priest (Montgomery Clift) so that the priest, who then becomes a suspect in the case, will be unable to save himself by pointing the finger at the man he knows to be guilty. Of course, the criminal ultimately reveals himself, and the priest is saved without breaking the seal of confession; at that point the public, which had pilloried the priest, recognizes his reticence as the central mark of his heroism.

7. Cf. especially Murray Bowen, *Family Therapy in Clinical Practice* (Northvale, N.J.: J. Aronson, 1978); Michael G. Kerr and Murray Bowen, *Family Evaluation: An Approach Based on Bowen Theory* (New York: W. W. Norton, 1988); and Edwin H. Friedman, *Generation to Generation: Family Process in Church and Synagogue* (New York: Guilford Press, 1985). Friedman is especially useful because he extends family systems theory to religious systems.

8. In *Going My Way* (1945) and *The Bells of St. Mary's* (1946), Bing Crosby plays an utterly unflappable priest who breezes through a number of crises that bring other characters to near-despair; Crosby's reputation as a crooner dovetailed in these films with the concept of priest as pleasant smoothie who could dance his way effortlessly around any problem. A recent essay by novelist Mary Gordon, "Father Chuck: A Reading of *Going My Way* and *The Bells of St. Mary's*, or Why Priests Made Us Crazy," *South Atlantic Quarterly* 93, no. 3 (1994): 591–601, corroborates the centrality of these films in the imaginations—and expectations—of both priests and laity. She describes "Father Chuck" as the endless "meeter of needs who seems to need no comfort, to have no needs of his own" (600); she also paraphrases a Jesuit priest who told her that "he didn't think there was a priest in America who didn't have Father Chuck in the back of his mind as an ideal" (592).

9. In the Notre Dame Survey of Parishes, a study of 1,900 parishes throughout the country conducted from 1982 through 1984, for instance, parishioners overwhelmingly named sensitivity to the needs of others as the trait they most value in a pastor. Holiness, learning, good homilies, and effective organizing skill all came in far behind. According to Hoge (*The Future of Catholic Leadership*), this indicates that parishioners want "a pastor who understands them, who consults them as responsible contributors to parish life, and who respects them" (64). Hoge's own 1980 survey of 600 people led him to a similar conclusion, that "Catholic laity want personal and accessible priests" who "try to understand the problems in people's lives, and avoid aloofness." Everyone, he says, "appreciated priests who are human and approachable" (65).

10. Andrew M. Greeley, *The Catholic Myth: The Behavior and Beliefs of American Catholics* (New York: Charles Scribner's Sons, 1990), pp. 211–16.

11. Karen Horney, *Our Inner Conflicts: A Constructive Theory of Neurosis* (New York: W. W. Norton, 1945), p. 291.

12. Anthony Storr, *Solitude: A Return to the Self* (New York: Free Press, 1988). Storr in fact provides a psychological rationale for the behavior of men he himself describes as "celibate" (ix), although he uses the term broadly to encompass a wide range of unmarried or unlinked states both voluntary and enforced.

13. For an extended look at the process whereby American Protestant clergy

have elided theology and psychology, see E. Brooks Holifield, *A History of Pastoral Care in America: From Salvation to Self-Realization* (Nashville: Abingdon Press, 1983). According to Holifield, the Protestant clergy began to embrace—and wrestle with—this elision as far back as the late nineteenth century. My friend Richard Ruach, a former Methodist minister now a Unitarian minister, has alerted me to the ways in which the Catholic clergy seem to be moving again toward a more Protestant model—and toward the problems of that model. The sections on professionalism and money will elaborate this point.

14. Robert N. Bellah, Richard Madsen, William M. Sullivan, Ann Swindler, and Steven M. Tipton, *Habits of the Heart: Individualism and Commitment in American Life* (Berkeley: University of California Press, 1985).

6. Finding a Place in the World

1. Now that the college seminarians attend Marquette University, they are liable for standard Marquette fees and eligible for student loans; their earning power after ordination, however, leaves them less readily able to repay those loans than the average college graduate.

2. The 1990–91 *Clergy Manual* stipulates that "help-out compensation" for each weekday service—which includes mass, celebration of reconciliation, funeral vigils, etc.—is $15 or $10 plus stipend, in addition to $0.24 per mile travel expense; for weekend Eucharist, compensation is $25 or $20 plus stipend, in addition to $0.26 per mile travel expense.

3. The history of the benefice system sketched out here is drawn from Maurice Connor, *The Administrative Removal of Pastors* (Washington, D.C.: United States Catholic Conference, 1937); George Evans, "Stability in the Parochial Office in the United States of America," *The Jurist* 23 (1963): 227–37; Frederick Freking, *The Canonical Installation of Pastors* (Washington, D.C.: United States Catholic Conference, 1948); and "Limited Term of Office," a Milwaukee archdiocese document presented to the Priests Senate on September 27, 1974. Current financial data and the history of clerical salaries in the last twenty years are drawn from a variety of sources: the files of the Priests Senate throughout that period, especially the proceedings of the subcommittee on "Temporalities"; the archdiocesan *Clergy Manual* (1989–91); and the *Consultation on Priests' Compensation for the Archdiocese of Milwaukee* (1990), prepared by the National Association of Church Personnel Administrators. Diocesan officials were also cooperative in providing information.

4. The 1983 Revised Code of Canon Law, for instance, declared that pastors were now "removable" under certain circumstances and provided for an "objective" panel to be set up to handle lay complaints. Should a pastor be found guilty of certain defined offenses or failings, he can either be removed formally or allowed to remain pastor in name only.

5. For a description of arguments for and against open listing and of the ambivalence expressed by many priests toward it, see Thomas J. Reese, S. J., *Archbishop: Inside the Power Structure of the American Catholic Church* (San Francisco: Harper and Row, 1989), pp. 214–18.

6. Barbara Ehrenreich, *Fear of Falling: The Inner Life of the Middle Class* (New York: Pantheon Books, 1989), pp. 1–15 and passim.

7. See Holifield, *A History of Pastoral Care in America,* pp. 172–73. Holifield argues that at the turn of the century, at a time when ministers were already becoming convinced that "popular regard for the clergy had declined," progressive reformers began demanding increased competence from those who worked

in areas of social welfare. This demand put pressure on Protestant ministers to upgrade their own expertise; the result, he says, was "a rethinking of professional ministry—and of the cure of souls."

8. See Hoge, *The Future of Catholic Leadership*, pp. 86–206; Greeley, "Priests: Hints of the Transcendent?" in *The Catholic Myth*, pp. 199–225. Hoge cites eleven possible strategies; one of them, a limited term of service for priests, coincides in essentials with Greeley's favored approach, a "priest corps" of fixed, finite duration.

9. Donald Hambrick, Columbia University Business School, "Seasons of an Executive's Career," unpublished talk.

10. Daniel Levinson, *The Seasons of a Man's Life* (New York: Alfred A. Knopf, 1978), p. 199.

11. *In a Different Voice: Psychological Theory and Women's Development* (Cambridge, Mass.: Harvard University Press, 1982), Carol Gilligan's influential—and controversial—study of gender differences, provides a relevant perspective on my classmates' gender dilemmas. Drawing on Nancy Chodorow's "Family Structure and Feminine Personality," in M. Z. Rosaldo and L. Lamphere, eds., *Women, Culture and Society* (Stanford: Stanford University Press, 1974), Gilligan argues that women, still raised primarily by their mothers in their early years, tend to learn intimacy in the act of identifying with their mothers; they then learn the necessity of distance later in life, against the grain of their upbringing. Men, by contrast, learn distance early in their lives when they realize that to be male they must be different from their mothers, who are also—still—their primary early caretakers. Men then need to learn intimacy later, against their grain.

Gilligan's has been by no means the last word on this subject, and her own focus is on women. But her formulation offers some insight nonetheless into the confusions of a group of men—priests—raised (not from birth but extensively in the seminary) by a "Holy Mother" whose representatives are nonetheless males; who are asked (far more than most "workers") to *identify* with their organization-as-Holy-Mother, an organization/mother who/which precludes women and yet insists that the priest, as confessor, nurture (to accept the schematizing) the very female side that the church itself excludes—and which mandatory celibacy certainly seems to undervalue. The dilemma of the children Gilligan describes tends to work itself out (or not) in chronological fashion, with the felt need for intimacy (or distance) followed eventually by its learned opposite—or complement. My classmates, by contrast, were sent simultaneously confusing gender messages throughout their twelve-year training, and those messages continue.

12. The connections between authoritative preaching and maleness—and the drawbacks of that linkage—were acknowledged by Father Albert, for instance, who in other areas of his ministry values and promotes collaboration. Yet "it is very difficult," he says, "to preach by trying to arrive at a consensus. I have to preach as an authority figure." But because he sees the limits of his own (male) voice, he values the woman associate he hired a few years earlier (to the consternation of parish traditionalists) because "she preaches from a different perspective, less scholastic, more in line with current philosophies today, certainly more in touch with feelings than we were trained to be."

13. Levinson, *The Seasons of a Man's Life*, especially "The Masculine/Feminine Polarity," pp. 228–36.

14. Novelist John Irving recognized this—or else acted out of similar anxieties—in *The World According to Garp* (New York: E. P. Dutton, 1978). On the one hand, he turned Garp into a new man sensitive to his feelings and devoted to

his children to a degree uncommon in American literature; on the other hand, he was very careful to make him a wrestler first—just as Hemingway, decades earlier, had made the male protagonist of his short story "The Three-Day Blow" a hard-drinking, deeply involved baseball fan before he allowed him a rare (for Hemingway) moment of admission that he was upset that he had broken up with his woman friend. Irving also made sure that Roberta Muldoon, formerly Robert Muldoon, retained his/her instincts as a tight end while grafting on female sex organs and softer feelings; it is Roberta's aggressive strength that comes to the rescue of Jennie Garp, Garp's feminist mother, at a crucial moment in the story. Irving's new man is the old man plus refinements, not the old man minus his strengths.

Male writers are by no means the only ones who fear the danger to male characters of adding or acknowledging a vulnerable, feeling side unless the "strong" side is kept intact. In *The Golden Notebook* (New York: Simon and Schuster, 1962), Doris Lessing has Martha Quest—a protagonist self-consciously constructed as someone who moves through representative stages of twentieth-century experience—reject the overbearing and insensitive men in her life but at the same time ask, "Where are the real men?" when the nicer, alternative males leave her dissatisfied. And in *Life before Man* (New York: Simon and Schuster, 1980), Margaret Atwood's central character, Elizabeth, is sexually excited by Chris, the man who threatens her emotional immunity, rather than by her husband Nate, who is much kinder than Chris, loves his children, and has abandoned his fast-track job as a lawyer for a gentler, more androgynous—but less lucrative—job as toymaker. Atwood is no proponent of macho aggression; yet Elizabeth finds Chris emotionally and sexually "impressive," while Nate is someone "she married the way she put on a shoe"—and divorces just as easily. Nate, she admits, is "not necessary."

15. The subject has been much discussed in the media in the last decade. For the most extensive treatment, see James G. Wolf, ed., *Gay Priests* (San Francisco: Harper and Row, 1989). Wolf estimates that 48.5 percent of current priests and 55.1 percent of current seminarians are gay in orientation (p. 60). He also acknowledges that all such estimates are shaky; this is a loaded question for priests to respond to in the context of a disapproving church. He derived his own figures by asking 101 priests who had already identified themselves as gay in his survey what their guesses were concerning the sexual orientation of current seminarians and other priests. Of course his respondents could be projecting, he admits; on the other hand, they might be the most sensitive observers available in picking up clues.

16. Sam Keen, *Fire in the Belly: On Being a Man* (New York: Bantam Books, 1991). Instead of finding "maleness" inherently suspect, Keen consistently criticizes the socioeconomic systems which distort and limit the behavior of both men and women. It is power which tends to corrupt, he reminds us, not the gender of those who hold it. My classmates would seem to corroborate his claim that most men inside a hierarchical system feel much more powerless than those who are even more powerless realize—than women, that is, in the case of the church and many other systems.

17. Ehrenreich, *Fear of Falling*, pp. 78–82.

18. Robert Bly, *Iron John: A Book about Men* (Reading, Mass.: Addison-Wesley, 1990), p. 8.

19. See not only Bly and Keen, for instance, but also Robert Moore and Douglas Gillette, *King, Warrior, Magician, Lover: Rediscovering the Archetypes of the Mature Masculine* (San Francisco: HarperSanFrancisco, 1990). Moore has often lectured in tandem with Bly. And of course Levinson, an important source for much of

the more recent material on men though not himself an active force in the men's movement, is Jungian as well. Those predisposed to see men as predominantly (if not inherently) phallic/aggressive in inclination—hence embodiments of a reductive Freudian paradigm of maleness—should consider the predominance of Jungian theory, with its emphasis on male/female complementarity, among contemporary male spokesmen/mentors.

7. Divorced, Still Married

1. Judith S. Wallerstein, Ph.D., and Sandra Blakeslee, *Second Chances: Men, Women, and Children a Decade after Divorce* (New York: Ticknor and Fields, 1989), pp. 3–31 and passim. Wallerstein and Blakely have been criticized for not having a control group of long-term married couples—with children, since their main emphasis is on the effect of divorce on children—to compare with their divorced parents and children. For my purposes, the former priests and the ongoing priests provide contexts for one another.

8. A Livable Priesthood

1. For Freudian origins of this model, see, for instance, Sigmund Freud, *Civilization and Its Discontents,* ed. and trans. James Strachey (New York: W. W. Norton and Co., 1962), p. 25: "The most interesting methods of averting suffering are those which seek to influence our own organism. In the last analysis, all suffering is nothing else than sensation; it only exists in so far as we feel it, and we only feel it in consequence of certain ways in which our organism is regulated." The notion that the self is the site where personal satisfaction originates is, of course, central to Freudian analysis and permeates Freud's work. But Freud's comment immediately before this, in which he speaks approvingly of "becoming a member of the human community" so that "one is working with all for the good of all" (pp. 24–25), is one of several glances he gives to the more outward orientation which family systems therapists such as Bowen and Friedman now combine with a continuing emphasis on starting with the self.

2. Donald Goergen, O.P., *The Sexual Celibate* (New York: The Seabury Press, 1974).

3. Eugene C. Kennedy and Victor J. Heckler, *The Catholic Priest in the United States: Psychological Investigations* (Washington, D.C.: United States Catholic Conference, 1972), pp. 3–16, 79–106.

4. Levinson, *The Seasons of a Man's Life,* pp. 218–21.

5. Ibid., pp. 245–51.

6. Ralph Ellison, "Richard Wright's Blues," in *Shadow and Act* (New York: Random House, 1964), p. 78.

7. Ralph Ellison, *Invisible Man* (New York: Random House, 1952), p. 439.

RAYMOND HEDIN spent his high-school and college years at St. Francis Seminary in Milwaukee, studied theology for a year at Catholic University, and then left the seminary in 1966. After receiving an M.A. in English from the University of Wisconsin, he taught for two years at Norfolk State College in the late 1960s in a federal program for black colleges. He received his Ph.D. in American Literature from the University of Virginia in 1974. Since then, he has taught American Literature, Afro-American Studies, and American Studies at Indiana University in Bloomington, where he lives with his wife and two children.

Hedin has published a number of essays on teaching as well as articles on African American literature. He has taught at Warsaw University in Poland and in five Indiana prisons; he now lectures regularly to business and alumni groups on the role of stories in shaping culture and in making sense of human experience. His return to the seminary in 1985 for a class reunion served as the inspiration for this book.